LESSONS
OF THE
RAINFOREST

LESSONS
OF THE
RAINFOREST

edited by
SUZANNE HEAD
and
ROBERT HEINZMAN

SIERRA CLUB BOOKS • SAN FRANCISCO

The Sierra Club, founded in 1892 by John Muir, has devoted itself to the study and protection of the earth's scenic and ecological resources—mountains, wetlands, woodlands, wild shores and rivers, deserts and plains. The publishing program of the Sierra Club offers books to the public as a nonprofit educational service in the hope that they may enlarge the public's understanding of the Club's basic concerns. The point of view expressed in each book, however, does not necessarily represent that of the Club. The Sierra Club has some sixty chapters coast to coast, in Canada, Hawaii, and Alaska. For information about how you may participate in its programs to preserve wilderness and the quality of life, please address inquiries to Sierra Club, 730 Polk Street, San Francisco, CA 94109.

Permission to quote extracts from the following sources is gratefully acknowledged:

Words written by Bruce Cockburn. From the song "If a Tree Falls" © 1988 Golden Mountain Music Corp. Used by permission. All rights reserved.

Words by Edward Abbey, *Hayduke Lives! A Sequel to the Monkey Wrench Gang.* New York: Little, Brown & Co., 1989). Copyright © 1989 by Edward Abbey. Reprinted by permission.

Cover image: Jesse Allen, "Moa" (detail), etching and aquatint, 20″ × 24″, 1988. © and used with the kind permission of Jesse Allen and Vorpal Gallery, New York City.

The giant moa began its evolutionary journey in the ostrich family of Gondwanaland, the enormous land mass from which the continents of the Southern Hemisphere originated. After New Zealand split off, the moa continued its journey there, free from mammalian competitors and predators—until the first humans appeared. When humans arrived hundreds of years ago, they found one of the largest birds in the world, a delicious flightless creature without defenses. It wasn't long before this primordial king was dispatched, leaving only bones for the human imagination.

LIBRARY OF CONGRESS CATALOGING IN PUBLICATION DATA

Lessons of the rainforest / edited by Suzanne Head and Robert Heinzman.
    p.   cm.
    ISBN 0-87156-678-8   0-87156-682-6 (pbk.)
    1. Rain forest ecology.   2. Rain forests.   3. Man—Influence on nature.
I. Head, Suzanne.   II. Heinzman, Robert.
QH541.5.R27L47   1990
333.75—dc20   89-27661
                                                              CIP

Cover/Jacket design by Bonnie Smetts
Book design by Wilsted & Taylor
Composition by Wilsted & Taylor
Production by Felicity Gorden
Printed in the United States of America
10 9 8 7 6 5 4 3 2 1

Dedicated with love

for the Earth

CONTENTS

ACKNOWLEDGMENTS

For any book that is the collaboration of so many authors (24!), the editors owe a debt of gratitude to all. But in this case we feel especially grateful to all the authors: each and every one contributed generously and patiently to the synergy of this volume. *Lessons of the Rainforest* would not have emerged at all without the nurturing friendship of John P. Milton and Robert Grantham. Nancy A Smith was also integral to this project, far beyond her roles as critic and typist, for which we thank her. Ruth Franklin's copy editing was trenchant, creative, and liberating just at a time when we needed it. Jesse Allen and the Vorpal Gallery very generously contributed the image for the cover, which we think conveys the aliveness of tropical Nature in a uniquely fitting way. Thanks, too, to Bruce Cockburn for his contribution and inspiration. And to Danny Moses, who guided this endeavor—our first in book publishing—with loving kindness and a deft and gentle hand, we are deeply grateful. To all these friends and many more we wish to express our heart-felt appreciation for helping us to bring the lessons of the rainforest to life.

VISIONS
OF THE
RAINFOREST

ROBERT HEINZMAN

•

~~~~~~

Vision One. The bus pulls away in a burst of exploding cylinders that push black diesel smoke into the afternoon sky. The smoke rises with a thick red dust, churned from the exposed earth of yet another new road cut into the forest. Tropical heat burns the air. Dust settles. Green vegetation along the road turns powdery red. The hurriedly constructed shacks—housing landless newcomers drawn to a region with few people, pushed from a region with too many—are showered with another layer of the dry, red mist. Cooling sweat trickles through the dust caked on a woman's neck. On her head she balances a basket full of tortillas to sell to hungry bus passengers. The road has brought all these things: the dust, the shacks, the settlers. Next to the road, beyond the dust, is a field; fire-blackened tree trunks lie in a mosaic on the red earth. A white, wide-brimmed hat affords shade for a man preparing his newly cleared land for a planting of corn and beans—and security and hope. Beyond him, in the distance, a wall of green forest seems to quiver in the heat above the open land, defying the expanding agricultural fields—if only until the next year. Above, the sun is a dull red-orange fire, filtered by the smoke of 6,000 patches of burning forest. In the dry season, the Earth awaits rain.

Vision Two. A satellite passes over the agricultural frontier of a tropical region; a shutter opens and an image of a road and the deforested land it bisects enters a technological matrix of digitizers, electromagnetic waves, radars, and computers. Eventually transposed as a two-dimensional image onto the emulsion of a photograph, the image reappears in a lab on Earth. As a transparency, it is projected onto a large, pale-grey screen in an air-conditioned auditorium, where neatly dressed people, eager to record the image in their own way, write in notebooks. A speaker interprets the image of the road and the path of disturbed vegetation for miles on either side. The buses, the settlers, and the dust are not within resolution. The smoke, thousands of tiny, frozen plumes, makes the image hazy—as if the landscape seeks to obscure itself and resist interpretation. "Satellite imagery," states the lecturer, "suggests . . . extensive deforestation . . . many complex reasons . . . scientific implications of this are uncertain."

Vision Three. The manager of a Danish-design furniture store is preparing for a big day. Frightfully busy, he thinks, but delightfully profitable. From the back of the store, he notices a group of young people walk in. He takes them for college students—not the usual customers for expensive furniture made of tropical woods. Maybe they have wealthy parents. Suddenly, one of the students produces a piece of green paper, and begins to read. Her voice is forceful, demanding. "Tropical deforestation," the baffled manager hears, and then, "indigenous people," and "species extinction." Customers listen as the young woman describes the destruction intrinsic to making the elegant furniture that fills the store. Her T-shirt reads, "The Rainforest. It is us; we are it. Let's save what remains." A mechanical scream from the front of the store draws the attention of the customers to a wild-eyed activist brandishing a roaring chainsaw, harmless without its chain, but clear in its meaning. He proceeds to mime the slaughter of the forest. Students representing the howler monkey, the toucan, and the mahogany tree all fall amidst the furniture. It is a die-in. "We will not leave until the destruction of tropical rainforests stops," says the woman to the manager. The manager wonders, "Should I call the police?"

Vision Four. The old ones teach an ancient lesson: The forest is the giver of all things. They teach as they were taught by those who came before them. The lesson reminds the People to walk barefoot and sit upon moist earth and know a mothering power. It reminds them why and how the forest rises from the Earth, trees in every direction, a greenness broken only by great rivers, slow waters that flow to where they will again fall from the sky. The lesson is told through stories about the ancestors and their lives in the forest. The People know the stories are true. The stories are recreated each day with each fruit from the forest, with each sacred medicine from the forest, with each brilliant flickering of the firebug. The forest is all life.

These are just four of the many visions of Earth's remaining tropical rainforests that this book attempts to weave into a common vision, a vision unified by concern and a desire for change. Each of the many contributors to this collection examines the complex issues surrounding tropical deforestation, each offers facts and well-argued opinion, and each advocates new strategies for slowing the pace of destruction.

Part one introduces tropical Nature and our relationships to it, including the global connections. Part two examines the history of tropical rainforest exploitation and presents an overview of each of the rainforested regions. Part three outlines the principal forces of deforestation. Part four offers solutions, ideas for reforming both forest uses and the institutions that promote these uses. The final section, part five, encourages us as individuals to participate in the movement to stop tropical rainforest destruction.

There are many visions other than those in this book, and all are collectively brought to bear on rainforests by the global movements of people, things, ideas, and ideologies. All told, not only have humans destroyed a great deal of life, but also whole ecosystems from which more life could evolve. What remains of the rainforests is quite imperiled: as we work together to safeguard life on Earth we would do well to consider the many visions that determine their fate.

Some people have a human-centered vision. They speak of the complete conversion of rainforests as "alternative land use." The partial depletion of forests—selective cutting of lucrative tree species is the most common example—is seen not as forest destruction, but instead as a resource use that leaves many options for future human use. Other people embrace an Earth-centered view that sees *any* transgression upon pristine old-growth forests as a violation of a sacred trust. They see the many levels of forest disturbance not in shades of grey but only as black destruction.

Such are the visions of scientists, policy makers, or activists. Other visions reflect the experience of forest dwellers, who see the forest as part of themselves. These run counter to the visions of large and ever-increasing, ever-encroaching populations, mostly poor, who see the forest as an obstacle that must be cut and burned to make way for food crops. Finally, there are the visions of those who see the forest as a capital asset, to be managed by multimillion-dollar bank loans for huge development projects or converted into agricultural exports for foreign currency.

Some people use numbers to reconcile the differences between these visions, but the numbers say different things to different people. It is likely that ideology, more than acreage, frames the visions of those who tell us how much, how fast, and how to think.

For example, two popular estimates place the rate of destruction at either 76,000 or nearly 100,000 square kilometers per year. Such differences reflect different data but also different accounting criteria. One person's deforested landscape may be another person's natural resource that has been properly managed; fewer trees, or remnants of once mighty forests, may still be called forests. Nuances aside, each year about 1 percent of the remaining 9 million square kilometers of rainforest is completely cleared—razed to the ground by machetes, chainsaws, and fire. Each year, another 1 percent is either utilized or deforested, either sustainably or destructively, depending on whom you talk to.[1]

At this pace, some people argue, rainforests—and well over half of the genetically distinct life on Earth—will be eliminated by the middle of the next century. Others are more, or less, pessimistic. That many people attempt to predict the future is not surprising. Controlling the fate of these forests is a preoccupation of both those who would save them and those who would profit from their "conversion." But nobody knows the future. All that is certain now is that already half of the rainforests are gone, eliminated principally through economic manipulations and the pressures of burgeoning populations in the second half of the twentieth century.

BEYOND DEBATE

The range of numbers and visions cannot obscure the fact that tropical rainforest destruction is fast eroding the integrity of life processes and menacing the ecology of the Earth, including ourselves. Nowhere is life more abundant, and nowhere is more life threatened. We have a serious problem, one that is likely to persist and, unless we act, become much worse.

Unfortunately, powerful forces inhibit the search for solutions. These forces are inherent in poverty and overpopulation, and in the economic inequities between people and countries, international debt included. These forces work together to diminish human welfare, abetted by unprecedented levels of consumption in the United States and other wealthy countries.

A common worldview links these forces. Given humanity's negative impact upon the Earth's ecology, we can justly term this worldview predatory. We are, after all, very successful predators; yet, disastrously, the entire Earth has become our prey. We stalk her resources, devour them, and move on—a strategy that has gotten us this far. But where are we? Some assert that we are at the pinnacle of civilization, but we would do well to heed those who sense that to destroy the rainforest is to eliminate life.

All of the contributors to this collection share an awareness of the ecological irrationality of our way of life. Out of their concern, and the concern of countless others, a new worldview may be evolving—

or perhaps a suppressed worldview is regaining strength—to counter the unprecedented destruction. New symbols and new ways of communicating signal this change, and three of these appear in this book.

The first is *Earth*—capitalized. The conventional usage is earth, which in this book is reserved for soil. By convention, we capitalize Mars, Venus, all the rest of the planets, and all other proper nouns, but not our own planet. However, we can no longer afford to think of the "earth as quarry." The Earth is our only home.

Likewise, Nature signifies all that we view as not human or human made. Given the second-class status to which it has been relegated for the last few hundred years (or, perhaps, thousands), we wish to reinstate Nature to first class, where it belongs: Nature, again, is capitalized. This is less of a departure from convention than capitalizing Earth, and may seem like a trivial step back to a 19th-century usage. But the symbols we use, the conventions that guide our collective actions, even the jokes we make, express our worldview. The Earth and Nature give us everything. It would not be unreasonable to show some respect.

The third symbol of the emerging worldview in this book is *rainforest*. Technically, we should say *rain forest*. One word as an adjective, two words as a noun: "The rainforest people live in the rain forest." Yet technically, what is often referred to is not rain forest, but rather, one of the many other tropical forested ecosystems. Many popular maps, for example, indicate that the forests of northern Guatemala, the last great forests of northern Central America, are rain forests. Technically, these forests are not rain but seasonal tropical. What's an editor to do?

One thing does unify these regions: the political ecology. Expanding agricultural frontiers, development and debt, overpopulation, poverty, and inequitable land tenure, economies dependent on raw material exports, high biodiversity, ecological limitations to many forms of agriculture—these and many similarities exist independent of ecological classification. And labeling these interregional similarities and connections is part of the new worldview that leads away from life's destruction.

The movement to protect these forests focuses upon many forested habitats, most of them subtropical to tropical closed-canopy, broadleafed, semideciduous or evergreen, seasonal wet/dry or moist (rain) forest; all of them more wet than dry. All of these habitats are imperiled. In this book we cluster these habitats, many of them rain forest, under a political and ecological term: rainforest. Besides, it saves space, which saves paper, which saves trees.

That a new, life-protecting worldview is emerging is obvious. People everywhere are moving from concern to action; this book is rich with examples. Of course, greater efforts must come. But before we can design solutions, we need to achieve a global perspective that identifies the forces that bear down upon the tropical rainforests. What follows are components of an emerging worldview, most of them taken from the essays that follow, that no one with vision can overlook.[2]

1. *The rainforests are fragile, nonrenewable resources. Once large areas are cut and the land used, the forests are gone. Something will grow back, but it will be a remnant of what once covered the land. Because rainforests are remarkably dense with life's diversity, they cannot be—and currently are not being—manipulated for high economic productivity without the loss of species.*

2. *The rainforests are poorly understood by the Western world. Scientists are just beginning to extensively catalogue their complexity. But centralized planners, as well as those who implement centralized planning, so far have not exhibited much appreciation for this complexity.*

3. *The forests are home to indigenous peoples and other forest dwellers. After centuries of abuse, the erosion of these cultures continues. This also means the loss of intimate knowledge of rainforest ecology.*

4. *Human welfare and forest conservation are inextricably linked. As long as forests are conserved, their inherent fertility and biodiversity may benefit rural people and the entire Earth. On the other hand, as long as rural people are motivated to clear forests for survival, forests will be cleared.*

5. *Tropical rainforest development is plagued with problems. One important problem stems from the predominance of infertile soils. An obvious mismatch occurs when forests are cleared to permit agriculture and cattle ranching. Too often the end result is social chaos and ecological desolation. Another problem is that since most rainforests occur in countries with large and rapidly growing rural populations, many people are* pulled *to the forest by opportunities to gain land for growing food. At the same time, they are* pushed *into forested regions by economic inequities: by limited access to productive land— most of which is controlled by a few people—and to resources to make the available land productive.*

6. *Rainforests occur primarily in countries with developing economies. These economies can be characterized by two factors: instability and a dependence on—or at least a proclivity for—agricultural and timber exports. Tied to the vicissitudes of international markets and financial arrangements, these instabilities translate into short-term forest use and, consequently, abuse.*

7. *There are many alternatives to forest clearing. Protection is the most obvious alternative. But long-term solutions must also address population growth and its partner, poverty. Family planning, basic health services, and literacy campaigns— efforts that empower rural people, particularly women— provide opportunities to improve human welfare and reduce population growth. Other alternatives include increased access to resources (like fertilizers) that rehabilitate the fertility of disturbed lands; crop systems that mimic forest diversity and structure, such as agroforestry and agroecosystems; and the*

sustainable extraction of many diverse and economically valuable forest products.

8. *Tropical deforestation is a global problem requiring global solutions. The blame for cutting the rainforest often falls upon the Third World, though many destructive forces originate in the First World. We in the First World share the blame. And we share the repercussions. Therefore, we share the responsibility for developing solutions. Fundamentally, change will not happen unless we make it happen.*

9. *The rainforest issue is a hologram that presents an urgent and powerful challenge to the dominant worldview. Each piece of the complex puzzle of rainforest destruction reveals the entire pattern of the current world situation—what it is and what it could be. Thus, each facet of the rainforest crisis, discussed in the following chapters, contributes to the new, larger worldview that we must grow into—if we are to survive the planetary crises that the old worldview has created. With the new worldview we are empowered to act.*

10. *Future generations will find it incomprehensible if we do not act. At current levels of destruction, we—particularly in the United States, with all of our great wealth and opportunity—may be the last generation on Earth with the capacity to stop the widespread destruction of these great forests.*

LESSONS OF THE RAINFOREST

In the late 20th century we are faced with two conflicting options: we can either protect the Earth's remaining tropical rainforests or continue to destroy them. We still have a choice. But if we delay, our inaction authorizes the forces of destruction to continue. We cannot expect somebody else to solve the problem. Each of us has to act. This is the first lesson.

Another lesson has to do with our personal connection to the destruction: the state of the Earth reflects the dominant state of mind of her people. The rainforests have indeed been mismanaged, but this only reflects the mismanagement of ourselves. It is our fragmented vision that has fragmented the rainforests—for example, by separating our civilization's economy from our planet's fertility.

A third lesson quickly follows: we have somehow managed to become quite arrogant. Could it be that humans are really more "intelligent" than the cumulative "intelligence" of 3.5 billion years of evolution? The answer depends upon each individual's vision. One person, contemplating a modern skyline, may offer a resounding Yes. Another person, being more humble, aware of how much we do not yet know, or perhaps a bit in awe of the simple miracle of being alive, may respond No. Either way, Yes or No, we have but one Earth. "Intelligence" based upon numbers, data, theories, models, uses, abuses, or classifications has not led us to protect the rainforests, the richest of all life systems.

The final lesson is the most obvious. As the prophet Isaiah reminds us, "All flesh is grass." Our life processes are linked to those of the rainforests by the simplest things: air, water, food, and medicine. We also are linked spiritually (or psychologically, if you will), each in our own way, each according to our own vision, to all life. In either case, whether for physical or spiritual reasons, saving the rainforests and their people will save a part of ourselves.

PART ONE

THE
TROPICS

•

*"I never beheld so fair a thing:
trees beautiful and green,
and different from ours,
with flowers and fruits each
according to their kind,
many birds and little birds
which sing very sweetly."*

CHRISTOPHER COLUMBUS

•

1

TROPICAL FORESTS AND LIFE ON EARTH

NORMAN MYERS

•

I stood in the midst of an Indonesian rainforest. It struck me as the most impressive patch of tropical forest I had experienced during my 20 years of exploring these exuberant expressions of Nature. True, I did not meet an orangutan. The orangutan is an unusually cautious creature, and an orangutan or two may well have viewed me without my setting eyes on a single one. I did not mind that I missed seeing these charismatic creatures. What I did see in the forest—almost entirely plants and insects—made it an occasion to remember.

Indonesia's rainforests are striking because of their extraordinary grandeur and stature. A typical tree soars 50 meters into the sky, higher than the Statue of Liberty. Certain of them weigh as much as 45 metric tons, and a few twice as much or more. When you are in an area with millions of such trees, you become aware that you are in a forest of a different sort. As I flew back a few days later to Singapore, and as the plane droned across one stretch of towering forest after another, I reflected that this forest is as different from a forest in my native Britain as is a St. Bernard dog from a common pooch. Whereas a temperate-zone forest generally represents a few sprouts, so to speak, of timber sticking up above the ground, a tropical forest amounts to a veritable dynamo for generating wood. Forest ecologists have found that the amount of "woody biomass" in an Indonesian forest can reach as much as 700 metric tons per hectare[1] (about 2.5 acres or the size of a football field), or five times as much as in a conifer forest of New England.

But these statistics, as is often the way with statistics, tell only a fraction of the story. What matters more to the workings of a tropical forest is the variety of parts that make up the whole. In the richest temperate forests, such as those along the Atlantic coastline of the United States, we do not generally find more than about 10 species of trees and woody plants in a typical acre. But a tropical forest can feature well over 100 woody plants, counting bushes and shrubs as well. As for nonwoody plants, there are thousands to be seen during a single afternoon's walk in a tropical forest. Especially numerous are climbing plants, making for a sort of forest piled upon forest.

There are plenty of animals, too. Butterflies abound, birds flit through every stratum of the forest, small creatures rustle around in the undergrowth. Watch carefully, and you will surely count dozens of animals in a single day, many more than in a forest outside the moist tropics. Until quite recently, scientists reckoned that all tropical forests contained several million animal species, at least half of all species on Earth—and in a mere one-fifteenth of Earth's land surface.

Yet, it turns out that even these riches of animal life are only a small part of what actually exists there. Now that scientists are exploring the "last great biological frontier" of the forest canopy, they are finding exceptional concentrations of species. There could be as many as 30 million and conceivably a full 50 million insects alone in this newly unfolding world of life somewhere between the soil and the sky (for comparison, there are only about 30,000 insect species in the whole of the United States).[2] This means the forests could well contain many times more species than the rest of the planet put together. But we do not know for sure. Our minimum certain estimates for now are no more than 5 million species. What is yet to be learned will far exceed all that we know.

This curious situation raises some basic questions about our life-rich Earth. Doesn't it speak volumes, that we don't know *within an order of magnitude* the number of unique life forms that inhabit our tropical forests? In other spheres of modern science we do things more precisely: we can determine the distance from a given point on the Earth's surface to a given point on the moon's surface at a given moment in time to within a quarter of an inch. Yet when it comes to figuring the number of life forms that share our planet—the sole cosmic body, so far as we are aware, to support life of any kind—we are absurdly ignorant.

FORESTS DISAPPEARING—SPECIES TOO

What we do know is that tropical forests are disappearing. As the forests disappear, so too do their species. If present exploitation patterns persist—and indeed they are likely to accelerate—there could be little left of these forests by the end of the century, except for four large remnants: one in the Zaire basin, another in the western half of Brazilian Amazonia, a third in the Guyana countries of northern South America, and a fourth in New Guinea. Worse still, even these four extensive areas may not survive more than a further few decades into the next century. The result will be the extinction of millions of species of animals and plants.

Already we are losing several species a day in these forests. Eventually the toll will surely represent a greater setback in the abundance and variety of life forms on Earth than any since the mass extinction at the time of the dinosaurs' demise 65 million years ago. Other types of environmental degradation such as pollution and desertification are intrinsically reversible—albeit at much cost to us—but extinction of species is another matter. Once gone, a species is gone for good—and all too often, that will be bad for us, and even worse for our children; for we enjoy hundreds of products that owe their origin to genetic materials from tropical forests. Tropical forests amount to much more than living space for tigers, chimpanzees, gorgeous butterflies, and a host of ornamental plants such as orchids. They contribute to our daily lives in ways we are not always aware of. So important are these products that we should take a quick look at them.

Our wake-up cup of coffee comes to us by courtesy of a bush in Ethiopia's forests. Being the ancestral source of all coffee plantations throughout the tropics, this wild bush continues to supply germplasm materials to boost coffee productivity and to resist diseases. Without these genetic contributions from Ethiopia's forests—which are 90 percent gone—we could soon be facing the two-dollar cup of coffee.

By the time we have finished breakfast, we are likely to have enjoyed a wide range of foods, notably fruits, that owe their existence in one way or another to tropical forests and their genetic materials. And so it goes throughout the day, right up the late-night cup of hot chocolate, which originally derives from the cocoa tree native to western Amazonia and the Pacific coast of Ecuador. In the latter country, a particular variety of cocoa, with better taste and other virtues than almost all other gene pools of wild cocoa, has been reduced to just a few survivors in the 1.7 square kilometer biological reserve at Rio Palenque.

In addition to coffee and cocoa, tropical forests offer genetic improvement of several major crops, such as corn, rice, and bananas. The greatest corn-growing country is the United States, which not only supplies its own citizens with a staple food but also helps to feed many millions in other parts of the world. In 1970 the U.S. corn crop was hit by a blight that destroyed half the crop in many areas. The costs amounted to $2 billion in one year: costs not only to corn growers but to corn consumers, meaning everyone who enjoys a morning bowl of cornflakes and an evening packet of popcorn, and, via other corn products, soft drinks, beer, and bourbon, plus (since corn is a major grain-feed) a beef steak, pork cutlet, or an omelet. The crisis was remedied through interbreeding an immune form of corn that originally derived from the ancestral home of corn, Mexico.

This is only a small sample of ways that tropical forests contribute to existing foods and beverages. How about entirely new foods? As agriculturalists investigate more of the abundant stocks of foods to be found in tropical forests, we can look forward to an ever-greater selection on our meal tables. In New Guinea alone, over 250 kinds of trees bear edible fruit. Only 100 or so of these are consumed locally, only a couple of dozen reach the marketplaces of Southeast Asia, and a mere 2 or 3 reach the supermarkets of the wider world beyond. There is plenty of scope, then, for agronomists to develop entirely new, nutritious, and tastier forms of food.

Even more significant are pharmaceutical drugs. When we visit our neighborhood druggist, there is roughly one chance in five that our purchase owes its manufacture, whether directly or indirectly, to raw materials from tropical forest plants. The product might be an analgesic, an antibiotic, a tranquilizer, a steroidal compound, or cough drops. Other plants supply an assortment of birth-control materials that are more effective and safer than the famous "pill"—and could soon meet the needs of men as well as women. The commercial value of these end-products now amounts, worldwide, to some $16 billion a year.[3]

As for industrial products, we can list aftershave lotions, deodorants, lipsticks, perfumes, phonograph records, and squash racquets, all of which are likely to contain some form of a tropical-forest material. The thick soles of jogging shoes are held together with a uniquely resilient adhesive from a tropical forest tree.

And this is just for starters. Agronomists, pharmacologists, and industrial researchers have taken a cursory look at barely one in 10 of the 125,000 known plant species in the tropical forests, and a close look at only one in 100. Thus, there is tremendous scope for the future—provided the pharmacologist and industrial chemist can get to the forests ahead of the sawman and the bulldozer driver.

CLIMATIC CONSEQUENCES OF DEFORESTATION

It is increasingly conjectured by climatologists that as the "green band" around the equator becomes transformed into a bald ring, there will be an increase in the "shininess," or reflectivity, of the Earth's surface. This so-called "albedo effect" could eventually influence convection currents, wind patterns, and rainfall regimes throughout the tropical-forest zone—and even in areas in the subtropics, and conceivably further afield. Changes in rainfall in once-forested regions are increasingly acknowledged by local people. The Panama Canal watershed has been losing its forest cover throughout this century—and during the same period there has been a marked decline in rainfall. Parallel processes have been noted in southwestern Côte d'Ivoire, montane areas of Tanzania, several parts of India, northwestern peninsular Malaysia, and a number of localities in the Philippines. Although the mechanism is not yet established, there is now too much evidence accumulating for us to ignore this potent linkage—even though it has been dismissed by many foresters for many decades.

True, the albedo phenomenon is still speculative. More conclusively known is the climatic disruption that has begun to ensue through the build-up of carbon dioxide in the global atmosphere.[4] Today some five billion tons of carbon are injected into the skies each year through the burning of fossil fuels, together with around two billion tons of carbon from the burning of tropical forests at the hands of large-scale cattle ranchers and small-scale cultivators. There looks to be a steady increase in the burning of tropical forests as the present 200 million slash-and-burn farmers swell in numbers with every passing year. The upshot is the well-known greenhouse effect, which is projected to cause climatic regimes and vegetation zones to move outward from the equator. Our sun-worshipping descendants may approve the prospect, but the grain growers across North America would be devastated. Indeed the great grain belt could soon start to become unbuckled, as the United States experiences warmer temperatures and decreased rainfall.

In these several ways, then, the future of the American corn farmer is tied in with the future of Amazonia and Borneo. Let's remember this the next time we sit down to a breakfast bowl of cornflakes, or enjoy a bowl of popcorn with the evening television show.

Interestingly enough, tropical forests could supply a further linkage to the greenhouse effect. A tree is half carbon; a tree plantation soaks up a sizable amount of carbon dioxide from the global atmosphere. Were we to plant enough trees, we could do much to stem and eventually even contain the greenhouse effect. Of course trees can be planted anywhere, but there is no environment so good for growing trees in a hurry as the humid tropics, with their year-round warmth and moisture. By comparison with temperate-zone trees, tropical trees sprout like mushrooms. Were we to plant three million square kilometers of tree plantations on already deforested lands (eight million square kilometers of former forests have already been eliminated), we could soak up the three billion metric tons of net annual build-up of carbon dioxide in our skies. Cost: $120 billion. This might sound like a huge sum, but not if the tree-planting effort were spread over ten years. Let's bear in mind, moreover, that in just the United States, a single greenhouse-effect cost, that of protecting coastal settlements against sea-level rise, would amount to at least $120 billion.

Of course there may be still other ways in which tropical forests contribute to climatic stability. Given the complexities of the interactions, how can we be sure we are even asking the right questions? As James Lovelock, originator of the Gaia Hypothesis (asserting that the planetary ecosystem acts as a living organism), points out, we are, so far as forest geophysiology is concerned, very much in the natural-history phase of information gathering: systematized analysis of a comprehensive sort, even in preliminary form, remains way beyond us.[5]

Let us note, moreover, a parallel linkage between tropical forests and environmental services. When forests are felled in upland watersheds, the "sponge effect" of tree cover is lost. Result: massive floods during the rainy season. In the Ganges Valley of India, struck each monsoon season by massive flooding in the wake of deforestation in the Himalayan foothills, damages to crops, buildings, and other property (apart from the loss of thousands of human lives) is now estimated at an average of $1 billion a year.

TREES VERSUS TANKS

There are still further broad-scope linkages between our own fortunes and those of tropical forests. Consider the security implications of deforestation in Ethiopia, for example. The country's highlands used to feature much forest cover, which, as we have seen, has
declined today by nine-tenths. As a result, there has been much soil
erosion in the fertile highlands that have traditionally supported the
bulk of the country's populace. This environmental impoverishment, compounded by population growth, meant too little food for
too many people. This led to food riots in cities, and in turn to the
overthrow of the former Emperor Haile Selassie.

More recently, there has been a large-scale "spillover" of peasantry
from the denuded highlands to Ethiopia's lowlands. In the mid-
1970's this migratory surge was directed notably toward the Ogaden,
a zone of long-standing conflict with the neighboring country of So-
malia. As a result, the Ogaden War erupted in the late 1970's. If this
had been a local punch-up between two of the most backward countries on Earth, that would have been regrettable enough. But because the Horn of Africa is adjacent to the strategic oil-tanker lanes
from the Persian Gulf, the superpowers intervened, pouring in $2
billion worth of weaponry and other forms of military support. If a
small part of the military dollars eventually expended had been assigned during the 1960's—a mere $50 million a year, according to
the United Nations—to reforestation of the Ethiopian highlands,
among other kinds of environmental rehabilitation, the migration
of peasantry could have been largely stemmed and the conflict
avoided.[6]

In short, we can perceive an emergent relationship between tropical deforestation and our back-home security. For sure, the links
cannot be readily demonstrated in strict cause-and-effect terms.
Nonetheless they exist, and they will become increasingly significant
as deforestation becomes more widespread. Recall that the country
in Central America where forests are largely a matter of history, and
where soil erosion is hence worse than in any other part of the re-

gion, is El Salvador, where economic stagnation, social disorders, political upheaval, and military confrontations have been more pervasive than in any other country. Much the same applies in Haiti. The ties between forestry and security have been well summed up by a former deputy director of the United Nations Environment Programme, Peter S. Thacher: "Trees now or tanks later." Where U.S. political and economic security are perceived to be at stake, the U.S. military budget—and tanks—are inevitably involved.

These, then, are some of the connections between the way tropical forests are disappearing and the way people in the United States are thinking. Each of us could well learn more about the complex relationships that characterize the "economic ecosystems" of the international marketplace. It is difficult to see these relationships in principle, let alone to track them down in practice. If we wish to develop the ability to "think ecosystems," however, we can take a lesson from the forests' wildlife communities as exemplified by the durian story.

THE DURIAN STORY

The durian is a fruit from Southeast Asia, now reaching luxury food shops in the United States by cargo jet. It has a strong and distinctive taste, and the same goes for its smell—akin to a mixture of the best strawberries and rancid garlic. Connoisseurs believe there are few better fruits anywhere, even though the act of consuming a durian can be compared, because of the odor, to eating a superlative dessert in a run-down public toilet. The durian crop in Southeast Asia is worth $100 million a year to local economies.

The famous, or infamous, smell of the fruit plays a key part in its tree's life cycle. Like virtually all trees of tropical forests, the durian occurs only sparsely at best. Yet no matter how isolated it may be, the powerful smell attracts animals that disperse the seeds. Moreover, the durian, together with a good number of other tropical forest trees, is pollinated by a single species of bat, which uses the tree as one important source of nectar. Like many other bat species, this one spends a large part of its daily round roosting; vast numbers occupy caves in the environs of Kuala Lumpur, about 40 kilometers from coastal mangrove swamps that harbor a particular flower that is the predominant food of the bat.

The swamps are being reclaimed for building land, which reduces a major source of food for the bats. In addition, peninsular Malaysia, like most other parts of the Third World, has developed a hearty appetite for concrete, with the result that the bat's caves have been steadily exploited for their limestone. In the wake of these two assaults upon its life-support systems, the bat's populations have declined, with an economic backlash that affects large numbers of local people who trade in the durian fruit, and the even larger numbers of people around the world who enjoy a mealtime delicacy.

This is just one example of ecological linkages within a tropical forest community. Many fruit-eating bats are similarly important to the "food webs" of tropical forests. Bats pollinate hundreds of tropical trees and shrubs, and they thereby foster the prosperity, and often the very survival, of plants that contribute to our meal tables—including guavas, bananas, and breadfruits—and plants for which we have found other uses, such as the kapok tree, the chicle tree (a source of chewing gum), the rubber tree, and many timber trees.

EVERYTHING IS CONNECTED

Such, then, is the exceptional intricacy of a tropical forest's fabric of life, where a key factor lies with interdependency. So perhaps the main benefit we may ultimately derive from tropical forests is the insight into the other, more integrative nature of North American society—a society that extends way beyond Maine and California. Through consumerist lifestyles, and specifically through marketplace demands for unrealistically cheap supplies of hamburger beef, hardwood timber, and other tropical forest products, we threaten the survival of tropical forests. Conversely, the continuing decline of tropical forests will eventually levy a heavy price on our temperate-zone lifestyles, through the loss of many potential sources of new foods, drugs, industrial raw materials, even sources of energy. Thus do the linkages between ourselves and those distant tropical forests exemplify the first rule of ecology: everything is connected to everything else.

All these things I pondered as I ended my Borneo walkabout. I was feeling as I generally do after such sojourns in tropical forests. My day of field research had not been another day of work for me. Rather it had been a day of recreation, in the sense of re-creation. Something of the forest around me served to stretch something inside me. It made my faculties operate with a sharpness that I do not generally sense; a host of additional nerve endings came alive. I felt as if my whole being were standing on tiptoe. I would not be the same again—thank goodness. I would look at things differently, and not just the natural world, but cities, newspapers, friends, and unknown faces. I had grown a little, and what better place to do so than that luxuriant community where the growing of life forms, evermore growing, is the essence of it all.

What a place to be! And what a time to be alive, to explore the most remarkable manifestation of Nature ever to appear on the face of the planet—and to be engaged in the most important conservation effort underway on Planet Earth today, the campaign to save these forests. During the past few years, even as the problems have been growing steadily worse, those same years have seen a regular sunburst of interest on the part of both the general public and political leaders. In 1985 there was only one Rainforest Action Group in the United States; today there are more than one hundred. There are myriad bills on Capitol Hill in Washington, D.C. The United Nations, the World Bank, and numerous conservation bodies have joined together in a Tropical Forest Action Plan, with an annual budget set at $1.3 billion. In 1985, all development-agency funding for tropical forests was less than $500 million, and today it is more than $1 billion. Furthermore, the emphasis is on *protection* forestry (safeguarding forests, and planting more trees) rather than production forestry (chopping trees down).

Several countries, notably the Philippines, Thailand, and India, have declared their deforestation a "national emergency." Citizen activists are becoming so numerous in tropical-forest countries that grass-roots organizations are blossoming on every side. The Indonesian Environmental Forum wields such political clout that it even has access to the ear of President Suharto; in India there have been remarkable breakthroughs via the Chipko movement and the Silent Valley campaign. In Kenya the Green Belt movement has planted more trees in one year than the government achieved in the previous ten years, and there has been a similar quantum advance in tree planting in Colombia. Although these good-news items are still only bright stars in an otherwise dark sky, we seem to have made light-years of advances in just the last few years.

After poking away at the problem for 20 years, I sometimes feel that the problem has simply grown too big; that it will get on top of us before we get on top of it. But in light of the extraordinary interest now demonstrated by political leaders, and the exceptional enthusiasm manifested by public opinion, I feel more heartened than I could have imagined just a few years back. What a splendid campaign to be involved in; what a marvelous opportunity to take part in the great battle to save tropical rainforests, *everybody's* forests.

2

TROPICAL BIOLOGY

A Science
on the Sidelines

DONALD R. PERRY

•

Smooth, glassy water flowed over the basalt precipice and plunged
into a black lagoon. This exhilarating spectacle was made all the
more so for me because I was hanging in space at the brink of the 30-
meter waterfall. I was test-driving a new vehicle, the Automated Web
for Canopy Exploration (AWCE), for studying the tops of tropical
trees.[1]

The vehicle gave the sensation of being a bird or of riding in the
gondola of a hot-air balloon. I gripped the steel cage of AWCE
tightly as it swung gently to and fro and was startled by the shrill
screeching of white-collared swifts. Miraculously, their vocalizations
could be heard above the cataract's roar. To my surprise, they ap-
proached the falls and disappeared into an air pocket behind the
water.

An ornithologist with an interest in swifts would find AWCE in-
valuable for studying this bird's behavior, as would any investigator
wishing access to the aerial world of tropical rainforest treetops, a region that holds the most complex communities of life on the planet.[2]

Unlike temperate forests, tropical rainforests contain lush communities of life that inhabit the limbs and trunks of tall trees. From

the ground, one's view of these communities is obstructed by multiple layers of leaves. The lowest portion of this aerial zone, known as the canopy, arbitrarily begins at about 10 meters above ground and extends upward through successive tiers of leaves to heights that can exceed 60 meters, which is about the height of a 20-story building. Numerous species thrive in the canopy's airy, three-dimensional spaces, and many of these seldom or never visit the forest floor.

LIFE IN THE FOREST

Tropical rainforests are found within the tropics of Cancer and Capricorn in a belt that girdles the Earth between 23½ degrees north and 23½ south of the equator. That belt crosses through the heart of South America, Africa, northern Australia, Malaysia, Indonesia, and the Philippines, to name a few.

Tropical rainforests flourish only in those regions where the average monthly temperature remains close to 80 degrees Fahrenheit throughout the year. True to their name, these forests receive ample amounts of rain: three to six meters annually. Sun, rain, and humidity combine to make a natural "hothouse" for nurturing a diversity of life.

When entering the shadowy interior of a mature rainforest, it is difficult not to be overwhelmed by its vast botanical wealth. Everywhere one looks there are plants: hundreds of tree species, hundreds of species of bushes and smaller plants, and dozens of species of large and small vines. Among these are dwarf and stunted trees, such as mature waist-high palms, or skinny trees two meters tall that may be 50 years old. The latter are waiting for a flood of growth-stimulating light from a new opening in the forest roof. These diminutive trees seem like tiny weeds at the feet of the forest's giants, the emergent trees. Emergents stand out above the forest canopy, and they may exceed 60 meters in height.

While wandering through a forest and enjoying its exotic birds, animals, flowers, and plants, one begins to sense many well-kept secrets. The eye catches a vine—perhaps a monkey ladder, or a *Mon-*

stera—and follows it upward through successive forest layers. Each level harbors a story. Finally the vine disappears above a screen of leaves into the hidden kingdom of the forest's roof. Here and there, windows through the screen allow a glimpse of the lofty realm. How amazing it is to see that dozens and dozens of floral species struggle to stake a claim in the most precarious gardens ever brought forth by Nature.

Towering limbs might seem an unlikely place to find communities of life, but there are powerful biological reasons for living in the canopy. Sunlight and ample rain, distributed more or less evenly throughout the year, charge the canopy with thriving life. Just below the forest's topmost layer of leaves, light intensity is reduced by 75 percent, but at the forest floor only 1 percent of the energy remains.[3] No wonder thousands of plants have adapted to life on high limbs.

The whole forest seems involved in a free-for-all, a race to reach the sun's light. Numerous plants like the balsa wood tree are adapted for rapid growth in light gaps formed by huge fallen trees. In contrast, many tree species must begin their development in the low light of mature forest. The Brazil nut tree, for example, discussed in chapter four, often has large seeds that store abundant energy. This allows the seedling to establish itself under shady conditions where sunlight is a weak energy source.

Even after trees have gained a position at the forest's roof, the competition continues. Adjacent tree crowns are in a constant struggle to overtop one another. The contest for light at the roof is joined by other plants adept at "crawling" over the upstretched limbs of their hosts. Vines and lianas scale tall trunks and ensnare treetops in a leafy web that steals the host tree's energy.

One aggressive group of light thieves are a type of hemiepiphyte whose seeds begin life when they are dropped on tree limbs. Known as stranglers, these trees send roots to the ground that multiply and eventually encase the host's trunk. After the host tree succumbs, its trunk decomposes, leaving a hollow within the insidious guest's trunk. This vacancy will become the home of bats, mammals, scorpions, and dozens of other animals that seek shelter during the jungle day; the forest ecosystem thrives on the continual process of death and renewal.

A group of plants somewhat less burdensome to trees are epiphytes. These plants have small seeds that are carried to tree limbs by birds and other animals, or by the wind. They simply reside as piggyback plants that are nonparasitic. Epiphytes are the most numerous plants in the forest. They include algae, mosses, fungus, ferns, liverworts, lichens, and flowering plants. Flowering epiphytes include certain varieties known to horticulturists as "air plants." Among them are anthuriums, orchids, cactus, bromeliads, and gesneriads.

On some limbs epiphytes grow so thick that they form miniature forests. The ropelike roots of these plants often intertwine with those of other plants, tying them tenaciously to their perilous perches. These roots can become so dense they form a spongy mattress that collects detritus, such as fallen leaves, fruits, and flowers. Humus, a form of organic soil, soon develops and fills the spaces in the tangle of clutching roots. Thus, a new habitat is created. It is capable of holding rainwater, as well as housing numerous animal species. The host trees themselves may sprout roots from their limbs to tap the nutrients locked in this aerial soil.[4]

Sheltered among epiphytes one can find birds, rodents, snakes, frogs, termites, ants, beetles, cockroaches, pill bugs, dragonflies, spiders, ants, and grasshoppers—a nearly complete terrestrial community that seems to have been elevated into the treetops.[5] Even earthworms and salamanders can be found on tree limbs between 15 and 45 meters high.

The canopy contains most forest biomass and it is the farmland where nearly all food for the entire community is grown. Thousands of species of plants flood the environment with new leaves, flowers, nectar, seeds, spores, and fruit. This feeds arboreal animals such as sloths, monkeys, kinkajous, and parrots; and it feeds ground-zone animals such as wild pigs, deer, rabbits, rodents, cats, frogs, and snakes. In river and swamp areas, the canopy is a source of food for frugivorous fish. By consuming fruit, all of these animals may be important dispersers of plant seeds, which in turn helps to maintain the forest community.

It has often been said that tropical rainforests are the richest ecosystems on Earth, but just how rich is only beginning to be appreciated. Terry Erwin, of the Smithsonian Institution, has investigated canopy communities and produced some amazing estimates for the number of Earth's insect species. Extrapolations from his quantitative collections suggest that between 10 million and 30 million *yet-to-be-discovered* insect species live in canopy trees.[6] Presently, fewer than 2 million plant and animal species have been described by science.[7] The rainforest contains up to 95 percent of the planet's species, two-thirds of which are in the canopy, but it remains a virtually unstudied ecosystem.

If Erwin's figures are anywhere near correct, and I believe they are, then rainforests and their canopies emerge as an incomparable factory of evolutionary invention. Looking into the past, it would appear that flight in birds, pterodactyls, and bats more than likely evolved in tropical rainforest canopies, but from a human perspective they are even more important. Less than two million years ago our australopithecine ancestors probably spent considerable time living in tropical treetops. Before that, our ancestors probably spent 60 million continuous years evolving in an arboreal environment. Tropical treetops were the womb and nursery of humankind. This arboreal phase, critical to our evolution, has left an indelible stamp on both our body design and the workings of the human mind. It comes as no surprise to me that we have a deep aesthetic love of forests; in our desire to preserve them, we are also preserving something of ourselves.[8]

STUDYING THE AERIAL KINGDOM

For over a century, tropical biologists have recognized the importance of the canopy, but due to its inaccessibility, most canopy research has been carried out from the ground. Although Marston Bates, Elliot McClure, Andrew Mitchell, Peter Ashton, the adventurer William Beebe, and a handful of others have endeavored to study the treetops—with varying degrees of success—precious little attention is being given to this arboreal habitat.

To say that the canopy remains inaccessible does not adequately explain the barriers to treetop exploration. Large jungle trees are forbidding. Trunks rise like gigantic columns to the forest roof, their lowest limbs often 25 meters or more above ground. Add to this a menagerie of scorpions, centipedes, ants, wasps, bees, and potentially deadly tree-climbing vipers, and it is easy to understand why treetops have remained unexplored. Few scientists care to risk their lives climbing, with or without ropes.

To aid tropical biologists in their study of the canopy, I have been developing new methods of access. AWCE is the first vehicle for canopy exploration. This vehicle can carry two people and their equipment from ground level to above the treetops over a long transect of pristine rainforest. AWCE was designed and fabricated by John Williams, an engineer from California. With the help of a construction team, we installed the system in November and December of 1987.

AWCE is located at Finca Rara Avis, a private forest reserve in Costa Rica, in the foothills of the Caribbean slope rainforest. One attractive feature of the site is its elevation, 300 meters, which places it between highland and lowland research sites. Just as life changes from the forest floor to the canopy, higher elevation reduces average temperatures and increases rainfall. This produces a cooler climate that promotes the evolution of species unlike those living at higher or lower elevations. This intermediate level possesses rare species, still unknown, that will undoubtedly lead to fascinating and productive scientific discoveries.

AWCE is a tramlike cage that rides a 244-meter-long stainless steel cable that spans a narrow valley. The cage also can travel up or down at any point along the cable through a distance of 46 meters. The cage's position is determined by radio control.

Let's now return to the waterfall where this story opened, and ride on AWCE through the surrounding forest community. Here we will be able to explore the natural history of a vine whose tendrils are biological threads that unite North and Central American forests in a common and interdependent ecosystem.

Pressing "up" on the radio-control joystick causes the steel-frame platform to rise like an elevator. On our left is the brink of the cataract and on our right dangle 30 meters of vines. Even though they are small and spindly, these vines are not immune to epiphytic growth. Mosses, anthuriums, lichens, and small orchids cling to their surfaces.

A meter or two higher a new world comes into view. We see the blossoms of a vine. It is being visited by several species of butterfly, flying jewels of the forest's roof. Butterflies, along with numerous other pollinators such as hummingbirds, bats, bees, moths, and flies, are essential to the regenerative processes of tropical rainforests. With very few exceptions, no tropical forest plant uses wind to disperse pollen; all rely on animals. Wind pollination requires dense populations of a given plant species, the antithesis of the high species diversity and low population densities typical of rainforest flora.

Higher still we find a tree-climbing tarantula. Numerous kinds of spiders live in trees, each having its own means of catching prey. Some weave orbs; others, like the ctenoids, or wandering spiders, have 10-centimeter leg spans that enable them to leap after large insects or even small lizards. Spiders, of many species, are the most frequently encountered predators in the forest.

Hanging under a nearby leaf is a katydid. Its forewings fold above its abdomen, creating the appearance of a single large green leaf. Many insects are a favorite food of forest animals, and so must protect themselves with cryptic coloration. This means their color is identical to that of the plants on which they are frequently found: usually green or brown. As browsers of tree leaves, they are called primary consumers. Higher up in the food chain they become nourishment for birds, snakes, and frogs, which are thus secondary consumers.

Soon we rise from the waterfall's mists into the canopy's lush greenery. At the top, near the support cable, I press the stick to the left and our platform lurches into motion, carrying us out over a precipitous cliff into an exotic world where Central American forest meets tropical sky. AWCE is hanging in the middle of a canopy amphitheater where hectares of life can be seen. Here, inspiring beauty can overwhelm the scientific mind. Rising mist catches shafts of sunlight that slip through the branches of ridge-top trees. *Morpho* butterflies, their metallic wings flashing iridescent blue, dance through the arc of a rainbow on their flight up the canyon.

This beauty is seldom noticed by the farmers who till the soil. To them, the undulating carpet of dense forest represents a livelihood: land for raising crops and pasture for grazing cattle. When they see the forest's botanical exuberance, it implies fertile productive soil; however, what they are seeing is a nutrient mirage. Tropical soil tends to be poor. Most nutrients are not in the ground; they are locked in the living biomass. Once the forest is cut and burned, nearly constant rainfall quickly leaches nutrients from the soil, after which they are washed to the sea. Within a few years the land becomes barren, devoid of nutrients, and is abandoned, but only after irreparable damage has been done.

I push the joystick to the right, back toward the cliff. We come to a stop in a tree overhanging the lagoon. A vine weaves through its branches. Here and there, the vine displays long flower spikes that emblazon the tree with brilliant red ornaments. It is a species of *Norantea*, a member of the family Marcgraviaceae. *Norantea's* flower structure is so unique it may become a new chapter in books on pollination ecology.

BIRD FEET LINK THE HEMISPHERES

Norantea sessilis blooms during our late winter months. The vine can easily be found by using field glasses, as it is usually wrapped around the tops of canopy trees. It is a favorite gathering spot for several species of birds, ranging in size from large, gaudy oropendolas to tiny, emerald honey creepers and migrant warblers. But watching bird activities from the ground does not reveal the truly interesting aspects of the plant's pollination system.

In February of 1986 I climbed into the crown of a *Ceiba pentandra* and made observations of the vine's reproductive system.[9] Groups of unique ladle-shaped nectaries on each spike of flowers produce great volumes of nectar each day. Most of the nectar is produced during the early morning hours, and on some occasions large beads of nectar nearly overflow the cups. When birds land on inflorescences during these times, they cause a sweet rain to fall on the forest floor.

When a bird lands, the plant seizes the opportunity to paste pollen on the bird's feet. Most pollen is like sticky dust that when dry will fall free of smooth active surfaces. Bird feet are thus not generally considered ideal sites for carrying pollen. Gary Stiles, a tropical pollination biologist, examined *Norantea's* pollen under a microscope and found it to be different from most. It was embedded in a thick, transparent glue. The substance would stick to any smooth surface, including bird feet.

From the perspective of the *Norantea*, great physical abuse is delivered when bird feet tightly grip the flower spike. Not surprisingly, *N. sessilis* has adapted to the abuse. The vine's small female flower parts are broad conical mounds, and unlike most flowers, they can withstand incredible shearing and compressive forces while remaining viable.

The natural history of *N. sessilis* is intimately linked to annual events in North America. I took Gary Stiles on a climbing trip to see the vine and he immediately discovered exciting information about the visitors to *Norantea*. Its unique flowers attract many species of North America's migratory birds: Tennessee, Chestnut Sided, Bay Breasted, Yellow, and Prothonotary Warblers, and Northern (Baltimore) Orioles. A flock of colorful tropical birds also visit the vine. These observations added support to Gary's view that Central American canopies may be a primary habitat for North America's migratory species, although he sees those birds as tropical species that fly North.

As new information is unveiled by tropical research, it becomes clear that we live in a world ecosystem in which rainforests play an important role. The destruction of rainforest means not merely the loss of a beautiful ecosystem: it creates an ecological short-circuit that will disturb the balance of life around the globe. How this might come about is the subject of other chapters, and nothing is more frightening than the bleak prospects they paint for Earth's future. We can be certain that as tropical forests are destroyed, a multitude of species perishes forever; a year may soon come when our beautiful migrant birds fail to announce the coming of spring.

TROPICAL BIOLOGY:
LOOKING TO THE TWENTY-FIRST CENTURY

For decades tropical biologists have been standing on the sidelines as other scientific fields gained powerful tools for exploring inaccessible subjects. Marine biologists obtained ships and deep-diving submersibles for exploring the ocean's depths. Physicists spent billions of dollars on sophisticated equipment to study subatomic particles, and astronomers spent huge sums in their search for life in the universe.

Tropical biologists are dubious about research priorities that bet heavily on long-shot gambles and invest virtually nothing on sure winners. Our pursuit of knowledge seems infected with an exaggerated case of greener grass elsewhere. As we lean against the fence, squinting to find a single blade of grass in the cosmos, Earth's pastures are wilting.

Cynicism, however, does not advance science. What does advance science is the bold and persistent pursuit of new frontiers. In our quest for knowledge about the natural universe, however, tropical biologists have been handicapped.

Tropical biology is an orphan science that has inherited the ancient tools of a long-gone ancestor. Not unlike Galileo, we collect data with field glasses, a pencil, and a notebook. A romantic calling, to be sure, but effective it is not. With our research subjects disappearing at an alarming rate, tropical biology cannot afford to continue these sleepy ways.

With growing human population pressures, even rainforest reserves will come under attack if they are not demonstrating a positive economic value. We cannot expect Third World governments to maintain their conservation efforts if scientists are not diligently investigating the forest's potential. Therefore, to preserve the rainforest, scientists must uncover its hidden wealth.

Tropical biology must move as quickly as possible into a productive technological era, but for this we need new tools as sophisticated as those of other sciences. One such tool I am proposing is a device called the Robot Observation-Access Module (ROAM). It will travel from ground level to above the trees over an area exceeding 80 hectares.

ROAM will hang from cables over a broad valley. The system will have a robot arm for collecting canopy plants and insects; also video cameras and other specialized instrumentation that will allow it to observe the nest sites of rare birds, experiment with exotic plants in their natural habitats, and take physiological measurements. Infrared lights will enable ROAM to explore the forest at night, when approximately 80 percent of all activity takes place.

The motors adjusting ROAM will be computer controlled from a ground station that will house an assortment of electronic equipment for recording and analyzing data. The system will make a precise digital, three-dimensional map of the entire study area. With a single command, ROAM could revisit any position. This system would permit a phenomenal range of scientific research at no personal risk to the researchers. At this time, however, ROAM's future, like that of the rainforest, is uncertain.

I could summarize the importance of tropical rainforests and how their unique forms of life unite the planet in a single ecological web. And I could remind you that in a few short years, a century of work by dedicated but underequipped tropical biologists may become the obituary of the rainforest. I could urge you to help fight the battle that lies ahead, but instead, I'll conclude with a story.

With great expectations we look forward to the moment when our calendar turns to the 21st century, now only a decade away. But I fear that turning point may be like the one when my senescent VW bus was approaching the 150,000-mile mark. I filled it to capacity with good friends and went for a ride. When the odometer turned over, there was an outburst of cheers that drowned out the car's desperate groans. As I coaxed my old friend home, I knew she had carried a burden too great. After the turn of the odometer, that old VW just wasn't the same.

As the wheels of time carry our overburdened planet into the next millennium, no doubt you and I will celebrate the event with the rest of humanity. But when we wake up the next day, will we be wondering what will carry us through the next hundred years?

PART TWO

BIOREGIONAL HISTORY

•

*"What the people of the city do not realize
is that the roots of all living things are
interconnected. When a mighty tree is felled,
a star falls from the sky. Before one
chops down a mahogany, one should ask
permission of the guardian of the stars."*
CHAN K'IN
LACANDON MAYAN PATRIARCH

•

3

FIVE HUNDRED YEARS OF TROPICAL FOREST EXPLOITATION

RICHARD P. TUCKER

•

~~~~~~

• *Exploitation* is a richly ambiguous word. Now that we know that what remains of the tropical rainforest must be preserved, when we speak of exploitation we mean destruction. But until recently, the word was used with pride by those who harvested tropical wealth. Even those who had no thought for regeneration of what was cut or cleared saw themselves as pruning Nature's excessive abundance and meeting humanity's growing needs. Today we might be more explicitly ambiguous and speak of "sustainable exploitation," but that sounds too harsh.

This chapter explores that ambiguity, tracing the history of the Western world's exploitation of tropical forests. It surveys only two facets of that history: plantation agriculture and tropical logging.[1] Other forces have also been at work in recent years, but these two are the oldest and most deeply rooted in the Western world's attempts to conquer the rainforest.

EXPORT CROPS: DISPLACING THE RAINFOREST

Europe and its children, the white-skinned cultures of the temperate zone, began to confront the tropical world more than five hundred years ago, driven by a craving for profits. Commercial capitalism spread worldwide from northwestern Europe, promoted by gunboats and colonial bureaucrats. For centuries, Southeast Asians had been gathering spices, aromatic woods, and other rainforest products in a complex and profitable regionwide trade. But this level of extraction had remained largely within the productive capacity of the natural forest. Even for European markets, for 300 years more, pepper and spices could be extracted without crippling the forest ecosystem. The colonial trade expanded and redirected the flow of an ancient system, but it did not destroy its biological base. In equatorial Africa's rainforest belt the experience was similar: the only forest products exported before the late 19th century were small amounts of hardwood timber for Europe's furniture makers, and oil palm nuts harvested in the deltas of the Niger and Congo rivers.

The tropical forests of the Americas had a different fate during those first 300 years of European penetration. Though less domesticated than Southeast Asia in 1500, some New World forests were entirely eliminated by plantation agriculture before the French Revolution transformed Europe's colonial regimes. The agent was sugar, the first widespread tropical monocrop. Europe's appetite for sugar had long exceeded the honey supplies of its own forests and fields, so Europe turned to importing sugar from Arab sources. The Portuguese, taking control of coastal Brazil after 1530, leveled a long forest belt, replacing it with sugar plantations. Sugar requires highly intensive labor, but indigenous tropical populations never willingly submitted. So Portugal and its rivals enslaved Africans to do the work. Colonial commercial capitalism thus disrupted both natural ecosystems and the cultures traditionally adapted to them on two continents.

By 1600 Dutch entrepreneurs took sugar production techniques from Brazil to their Caribbean islands. Island ecosystems are more fragile than continental systems. Consequently, sugar radically impoverished the vegetation of major Caribbean islands during the 1600's and 1700's.[2] English planters in Barbados and other islands first cleared the lowlands for canefields and then, more gradually, the hill woodlands for the estates' fuelwood. France did the same in Haiti, permanently impoverishing the island's resource base. Spain followed suit in Cuba, where in the 1700's the rich lowland soils of the Matanzas plains were cleared of both mahogany forest and old grasslands.

The export crop yielded greater money returns to the planters than would growing food for the laborers, so for survival the slaves became dependent on grain imported from Spain, Mexico, and colonial North America. From the time of the U.S. War of Independence, French Haiti ate grain from Louisiana, and Cuban workers consumed wheat from the Atlantic seaboard colonies. Caribbean ecological stress thus was linked to the prosperity of farmers on the northern colonial frontier.

Sugar production replaced entire forests; the other early-modern rainforest export from the Americas, hardwood timber, selectively removed certain tree species from standing forests. In the 1500's red dye woods were cut to supply Europe's cloth industry; Brazilwood came from the same coasts as Portugal's sugar plantations, and logwood from the coastal lowlands of Central America. By the early 18th century, as Europe's supplies of hardwoods for furniture and housing construction dwindled, mahogany from the Caribbean Basin filled Europe's workshops. Some was exported from Cuba, but the greatest source was the Central American mainland, where the Spanish overlords failed to prevent British pirates from penetrating the coastal rivers with their axes. These were the "Baymen," loggers who took pride in the dangers and difficulties of struggling with the forest. As a traveler in the mid-1700's described their work:

During the wet season, the land where the logwood grows is so overflowed, that [we] step from [our] beds into water perhaps two feet deep, and continue standing in the wet all day, till [we] go to bed again; but nevertheless account it the best season in the year for doing a good day's labour in. . . . When a tree is so thick that after it is logged, it remains still too great a burthen for one man, we blow it up with gunpowder.[3]

In limited areas near rivers and coastlines, the dominant hardwoods were reduced to old, injured, or juvenile specimens, with diminished capacity to produce seed. Farther inland, as in similar settings in Africa and Southeast Asia, the forest remained largely untouched by alien intrusions until more powerful transport and sawmilling systems appeared in the late 1800's.

THE MODERN EXPANSION OF
TROPICAL PLANTATION CROPS

When the Bastille fell in Paris in 1789, the power structure of Europe changed in ways that ultimately transformed the tropics as well. Political and military struggle consumed all of Europe until 1815. When it was over, four colonial empires—Portugal, Spain, France, and the Netherlands—were crippled. For nearly a century thereafter, the British Empire shaped natural resource exploitation throughout the tropical world. The militarization of Europe, culminating in World War I, began to break Britain's power, enabling the United States to supplant Europe for a half-century in Latin America and parts of tropical Asia.

In 1815 the tropical forest zones of three continents were still largely intact except for the imposition of sugarfields on river-basin peasant cultures and widely dispersed hill tribes.[4] But during Queen Victoria's long reign British industry produced the iron and steel, and London's banks provided the speculative funds, to clear forests for commercial agriculture on all continents. Until the last years of the century this did not penetrate true rainforest on a large scale, but it transformed temperate and subtropical zones, setting the stage for an escalating challenge to the rainforest as the century ended.

Railroads and roads, harbor installations, and then ironclad steamships dramatically reduced the costs and time for transporting the world's primary resources to Europe. The British, and then their European rivals, carved great territories from the tropics, both to protect their strategic flanks against each other and to extract wealth from tropical terrains. But the military and bureaucratic costs of empire were high; this translated into pressure to expand cash crop production for tax benefits. Moreover, 19th-century Europe was obsessed with a vision of expanding production as the key to universal human progress and happiness. The result was a potent mixture of visionary hope for the human species and ruthless exploitation of "backward" peoples and "unproductive" lands.

The colonial powers supported the new capitalist agriculture by transforming the legal status of Nature, making forest clearing more efficient than ever before. Premodern governments both in Europe and elsewhere had traditionally encouraged the clearing of the forest, since that resource had been virtually unlimited, and tilled land had been scarce. But on the colonial frontier, European law defined land largely in terms of private ownership of tilled land and government ownership of forest and grassland. This gave colonialism new tools for forcing back the boundaries of the forest. In the course of the 19th century, European property law was imposed throughout independent Latin America as well as the colonized regions of Africa and Asia, sweeping away the communal rights of forest and grasslands Indians.

Hand in hand with European legal principles, European consumer tastes—both at home and in the tropics—posed a long-term threat to tropical ecosystems. The newly independent elites of Spanish America after 1825 were determined to match European affluence in their own homes. As daughters and sons of the continent they shared Europe's new confidence in capitalist and industrial values and its contempt for Indian cultures' ways on the land. Since finance capital was available only in a metropolis like London, the new regimes looked to the land for profit-generating exports to Europe, to repay loans which they had no other way of financing. The forest was their collateral.

Latin America's export strategy centered on coffee, which swept forest from subtropical areas of Brazil, Colombia, and Central America from the 1830's onward. By 1900 the fragile subtropical hills of Brazil's São Paulo state dominated world coffee production, and most of their produce was shipped to markets in the United States. Coffee bushes required well-drained soils, and planters believed that "virgin" soils were necessary for competitive production. By the 1860's, great tracts of the São Paulo hills were denuded and eroded.[5] Yet the frontier of unclaimed forest land was seemingly limitless, so there was no economic incentive for more sustainable cultivation methods until very recently. Brazil's frontier was advancing toward Amazonia.

In the moist-forest region of West Africa, British investors promoted cacao plantations rather than coffee. From the 1800's onward wide stretches of lowland forests of the Gold Coast and western Nigeria were transformed into plantations of cacao, a perennial tree crop but nevertheless a monocrop that eliminated biodiversity.

With corporate sugar investments in the Caribbean and the Pacific, the American economy entered tropical agriculture on a large scale. Beginning in the 1880's, major investors from Boston and New York built giant processing factories so expensive that most Spanish producers could no longer compete. The American political takeover of Cuba followed in 1898, in part to protect those investments.

The refiners had no interest in intensifying production in the canefields; the centrals fed on a rapidly expanding acreage under production. The sugar frontier advanced steadily eastward after 1900, spearheaded by new American-built railroads that linked Havana with hillier, less fertile Camaguey and the Sierra Madre of remote Oriente Province. In the marginal lands between the estates, displaced peasants felled the last of central Cuba's mahogany forests. By the 1930's, when investors centered in New York began divesting their ownership shares in Cuban sugar centrals, the transformation of Cuba into an export monocrop landscape was nearly complete. Even Fidel Castro's revolutionary regime after 1959 was unable to diversify Cuban agriculture; sugar's stability as a cropping system helped assure that more varied vegetation does not return to the island.

Parallel to the Cuban adventure, American sugar barons began transforming islands in the Pacific into sugar plantations. By the 1870's Yankee planters were taking control of the Hawaiian Islands, and then on to the Spanish-ruled Philippines, where they began clearing tropical forests. The large island of Negros came to be a vast sugar estate controlled jointly by American and Filipino landlords, and profits rolled in from sales to the United States. The forests of Negros are now long gone, and in the present global sugar depression the farm workers of Negros are impoverished.

Tropical fruit plantations followed sugar as the conquerors of the lowland moist forests. Today's multinational tropical fruit companies began with United Fruit and Standard Fruit, the two Yankee firms which Central American regimes at the turn of this century invited to domesticate their formidable Caribbean lowlands. The Costa Rican government put the machinery of rainforest exploitation in place when it invited Minor Keith to build a railroad across its rainforest belt and gave him potential banana lands in partial payment. Keith saw the conquest and domestication of tropical Nature as one of the great challenges to human ingenuity and an expression of Anglo-Saxon superiority. This was more than insatiable economic greed; it was also a romantic adventure. As the first historian of the United Fruit Company described its early successes in 1914:

> It is a splendid victory over Nature, the stern but fair giantess who enforces the decree that the soil of this earth shall yield its treasures only to those who battle with her, but who smilingly submits to the ardent and intelligent trespasser on her domains.[6]

For the region's governments the issue was as much strategic and cultural as it was romantic or commercial. These Hispanic regimes had never been able to subdue the Indian cultures of the lowland forest. But their dominance could be consolidated with railroads. The Nicaraguan banana concessions, for example, simply ignored the traditional rights of the Miskito and other Caribbean-coast cultures. The Indians' rearguard struggle for survival had begun.

By 1920 Yankee entrepreneurs controlled hundreds of thousands of acres of rainforest, much of it never before altered by human interference. Only a small portion of the companies' land was levelled and replaced by rows of fruit trees, but by planting monocrops the banana companies invited a massive counterattack from Nature. By the early 1920's the Gros Michel banana became the host for two epidemic diseases, Panama Disease and Sigatoka, which crippled every tree in a plantation. The only alternative to collapse was to move the plantations every ten years or so to lands that had never been cleared. By the 1930's, tracts of what had been Caribbean coastal rainforest were virtually deserted, and the companies set up a second generation of clearances on the narrow Pacific lowlands.

Even after World War II new plantations continued to replace primary lowland forest, but now the reasons were largely political. By the 1950's, tropical governments and multinational corporations were competing for control over natural resource systems. The multinationals' trump card was their capacity to move investments from an uncooperative country to one that was more eager to advance its agricultural frontier. Ecuador was the prime example. In cooperation with the Quito government, the banana tycoons cleared large areas of the Pacific coastal lowlands after 1945. By the 1950's Ecuador was one of the world's major banana exporters, and its previously rich forest belt was in rapid decline.

The fruit companies in the 1950's also moved to diversify their marketable commodities and exploit a wider range of tropical lands. Corporate mergers with sugar and pineapple growers in the Pacific resulted.[7] A commercial steamroller was accelerating, and by then consumers throughout the urban world were happy with the greater variety in their diets. In the rural tropics, though, subsistence foods were often relegated to marginal production, along with the people who grew them.

EXPLOITING THE RAINFOREST FOR TIMBER

As tropical forests have receded, forest managers have become more central in manipulating forest ecosystems. Since its inception more than a century ago, the profession of tropical forestry has both served the industrial revolution and attempted to curb its recklessness. In the tropical timber industry, as in agriculture, there was a massive acceleration after 1950. For centuries prior to that, the only international markets were for a few species of hardwoods, which were selectively cut, leaving the forest damaged but basically intact. Yet the patterns of financing, felling, and marketing were established during that era.

During the 19th century the demand for timber escalated globally. Clearing and burning forest for crops entailed a huge loss of timber potential, inviting more efficient management. Organized forestry was already an old tradition in Germany and France, as it was in Japan as well.[8] In Britain it lagged behind, but the British Empire's forestry service, established first in India in the 1850's, soon took the lead in both expanding production and studying how to sustain the forest cover in tropical and subtropical regions.

The Napoleonic Wars were the first example of military demands in the industrial world dictating the exploitation of the tropical world's natural resources. The British Navy had long since depleted the mature oak forests of England to build the ships on which Queen Elizabeth I established her naval supremacy. New England and maritime Canada then provided oak for hulls and white pine for masts until the American colonies broke away in the 1780's. British shipwrights were then forced into an unknown world of tropical timbers. After searching coastal Brazil and West Africa, they finally seized upon Malabar teak from southwestern India, which resisted saltwater parasites exceptionally well. This made additional teak forests a major prize in Britain's later conquest of Burma and the revival of the Dutch empire in Java.

Malabar teak had been exported to markets around the Indian Ocean for several centuries, but the British Admiralty introduced a new scale of exploitation. Quickly depleting natural stands, they launched the Nilambur teak plantation, which remains today one of the most successful of all tropical hardwood plantations. Harvested on regular rotations, it is highly productive, but at a price: the elimination of almost all other flora and fauna in a mature stand.

The Caribbean Basin sustained the first severe depletion of a tropical hardwood: mahogany. By the late 1800's so much mahogany had been shipped to markets in Europe and the United States that those forests were largely stripped of their easily accessible trees. Dealers in specialty woods at European dockyards such as London, Rotterdam, and Hamburg began turning their search to West Africa. Several African hardwood species, especially okoume, came into large-scale use among European cabinetmakers at a time when colonial forest services were being transplanted from India to equatorial Africa to assist but also regulate the loggers. As this century began, the terms of a gamble were emerging: would orderly exploitation of additional rainforest species guarantee that forest products could compete successfully with agriculture as a sustainable use of land, or would the increasing scale and profitability of tropical logging make timber concessions an irresistible prize for the politically and commercially ruthless?

American colonial forestry in the Philippines took the lead in urging technical modernization as the key to sustained yield in the rainforest. George Ahern, first director of the Bureau of Forestry there, presided over passage of a forest law in 1904 that gave the bureau power to issue timber concessions on whatever scale and duration were appropriate for a lumberman's resources. Using his close connections at fledgling forestry schools on the U.S. mainland, Ahern recruited energetic young foresters to plan lumber modernization for the islands. Moreover, he convinced W. P. Clark, a leading Seattle lumberman, to ship a copy of the most advanced lumber mill in the Pacific Northwest to the Philippines. Clark organized Insular Lumber Company there, which became the islands' leading firm; among other projects it cleared forest for sugarfields on Negros.

Large areas of the Philippines, as well as other Southeast Asian countries, were covered by a rainforest dominated by several hardwood species of the Dipterocarp genus. Dipterocarps had been prized for centuries throughout the western Pacific as elegant furniture and housing timbers; Chinese traders controlled marketing through their regionwide networks. These timbers became known as Philippine mahogany on American markets, where Clark introduced them profitably as a substitute for the declining stocks of Central American mahogany.

But more important economically than American markets for the colonial foresters was the fact that the islands became a consistent importer of building timber. Manila and the smaller Philippine ports were being built of redwood and Douglas fir. If modern forestry could turn the island colony into a major exporter of dipterocarps to eager markets throughout the western Pacific, it would make a major contribution to the colony's prosperity as well as to American timber exporters and consumers. This goal was achieved in the early 1920's, and the Philippine Islands for 40 years thereafter were tropical Asia's greatest exporter of rainforest timbers. Metropolitan countries were helping to accelerate the timber consumption of the Third World itself.

The decade of the 1920's saw an acceleration of the scale of technology and investment in tropical logging. Foresters on all three tropical continents worked in timber physics laboratories to devise new commercial uses for both familiar species and others unknown in metropolitan markets. Equally important, World War I's urgent demands on timber resources had brought motor vehicles into colonial forests for the first time. In the 1920's many tracts were penetrated by bulldozers and gas-powered logging trucks, which were able to provide far more timber. Now it made economic sense to introduce advanced sawmills that could mill a wider variety of species and with a higher degree of efficiency than ever before.

Moreover, Japan entered tropical timber operations in the late 1920's. Japanese traders had been settling on Taiwan and in coastal towns of Southeast Asia since 1900. One of those frontier towns was Davao, on the southeast coast of Mindanao, where the Philippines' richest untapped rainforest lay. When Japan's industrial economy boomed in the 1920's, the great corporate houses began to import timber from around the Pacific basin, a foretaste of Japan's emergence as the world's largest tropical forest products importer in the 1960's.

Few tropical forests were totally cleared before 1929, except for those which foresters and agricultural planners agreed could be transformed into sustainable farming belts. Moreover, tropical silvicultural experiments had not yet clearly shown the grave difficulty of reforesting the fragile, nutrient-poor soils of the rainforest, and ecologists' warnings of the danger of irreversible damage were still to come.

The African rainforest and its people suffered some of the worst effects of colonial rapacity in the areas of French and Belgian control. Both countries, short on trained administrators, adopted an extreme version of the concessions system. Paris and Brussels granted private development companies virtual sovereignty over entire rainforest regions, and the concessionaires forced many forest villages to deliver wood and other forest products to riverine ports for export. The system was violent and primitive, postponing the advent of modernized resource exploitation until recently in Gabon and Zaire. As a result, those governments now have little capacity to control the European timber firms' movements on the most important new frontier of rainforest logging.

During the 1930's the tropical timber trade suffered the same decline as trade in other tropical agricultural products. But World War II brought unprecedented demands on timber resources. Housing and urban construction were devastated everywhere the armies moved. In the aftermath arose an international effort to harness the world's forest resources for rebuilding shattered economies in Europe and Asia. The new United Nations included global forestry as one wing of its operations, under the Food and Agriculture Organization. In the early postwar years its overriding priority was to expand tropical forest production so as to achieve worldwide "Freedom from Want." FAO foresters were convinced that a new political determination and scientific management could overcome the economic and ecological distress of the Third World.

Under FAO auspices, in the 1950's professional forestry emerged throughout Latin America, where previously it had existed only as laws and plans on paper. British and French foresters in tropical Africa trained local workers to begin replacing them, as Europeans and Americans were doing in Southeast Asia. For 20 years and more their overriding goal had been increased timber production. As one of the foremost of them, Gerardo Budowski, observed in retrospect in 1970:

"I believed, like everyone else—in fact I may even say today that I was 'obsessed'—that the greatest potential of my country was in those vast areas of 'virgin forests' . . . that were sparsely settled and just awaited the drive of ambitious government planners to be opened to civilization."[9]

But technical excellence in timber production, and a fuller understanding of the intricate web of rainforest ecology, were not adequate tools for enlightened rainforest management. They had to be backed by political controls on hit-and-run logging. This task fell to the new regimes throughout the tropics, and the consequences were often discouraging. Forest leases and concessions were being handed out to politicians and military officers at a dizzying rate. Possessing the tools of modern logging, the new owners were clearcutting entire forests for global markets, and little sustained management was possible under financially strapped bureaus of forestry. If such irresponsibility was what made the Philippines Asia's greatest timber exporter, it could not last long. By the late 1960's Philippine exports were in permanent decline, and even Filipino firms were investing abroad—in Indonesia and elsewhere.

Malaysian and Indonesian exports had rapidly overtaken Philippine production by the late 1960's.[10] Japanese and Singapore Chinese investors led the new round of exploitation, with European, U.S., New Zealand, and Australian firms participating too. The days of select logging were over, but the era of clear-cutting had arrived, with large-scale, multipurpose processing plants specializing in pulp and paper.

The pulpwood processing industry had begun in the tropics on an experimental scale in the 1920's, led by Scandinavia's centuries-long experience with soft-conifer exports. But clear-cutting in the rainforest accelerated only during and after the 1950's. Unprocessed logs constituted most of the timber exports from tropical countries at first. But by the 1960's, tropical governments began insisting that the logs be processed before export—despite the resulting industrial pollution—so that the sellers could retain more of the ultimate value of the timber resource. A precarious symbiosis developed between host bureaucracies and foreign concessionaires. The timber industry of Sarawak, a Malaysian state in Borneo, now provides the second highest source of income for its government, and fortunes for some of its top officials. But even today that industry is largely financed by Japanese interests.[11]

In the course of these years clear-cutting has left broad rainforest tracts devoid of tree cover, to be massively eroded or covered with low-value grasses. No indigenous culture of the forest could survive in this transformed habitat: entire systems of knowledge of rainforest ecology began to vanish along with the ecosystem itself.

In the wake of the loggers, the forest peoples began to defend themselves. The history of tropical deforestation is paralleled by a history of their self-defense, but until recently the outside world knew little of that tragic story. In India, villagers began protesting against the incursions of logging contractors and Forest Departments in the earliest years of this century; the well-known Chipko movement today is the latest expression of the movement.[12] In recent years forest communities throughout the tropics, facing cultural collapse, have launched a series of resistance movements. Today the Penan of Sarawak, the Kayapo of southern Amazonia, and many other rainforest peoples struggle to defend some remnant of their ancient habitat and traditional wisdom against the hostility of their own ethnically alien national governments. Western imperialism's techniques have been adopted by many a local regime, and the imperial foolishness of powerful humans has subdued, domesticated, and oversimplified tropical Nature.

4

RAINFORESTED REGIONS OF LATIN AMERICA

GHILLEAN T. PRANCE

•

The tropical rainforests of the Americas are located in five main regions: Mexico and Central America (Mesoamerica), Pacific Coastal Colombia and Ecuador, the Caribbean Islands, the Guianas and Amazonia, and the Atlantic Coastal region of Brazil. The forests in these five areas are similar to each other in the many aspects that define rainforests, but numerous regional differences also exist due to history, topography, geology, and climate. For example, some common rainforest plant species occur throughout the region. Other species are restricted to one, or even a small part of one, of the five regions.

Central American rainforests are located from Mexico south to Panama in the wetter lowland areas, which tend to occur more on the Atlantic side of the various countries. Rainforest is the natural cover for part of each of the Central American republics; however, it has been greatly reduced, and completely eliminated from El Salvador and much of Honduras. The rainforest of the Osa peninsula in Costa Rica, now protected in a forest reserve, is particularly important since it contains the northernmost distributions of many South American rainforest species. The southernmost country of this region, Panama, is still well endowed with rainforest, especially in the province of Darién.

Caribbean rainforest occurs, or formerly occurred, scattered throughout this archipelago in areas where rainfall is high enough to sustain it. This is mainly in areas where the presence of mountains increases rainfall, such as the northern part of eastern Cuba, eastern Hispaniola in the area of Sierra de Bahoruco, northeastern Puerto Rico around the Luquillo mountains, and small patches in some of the Lesser Antilles.

Pacific Coastal South America, commonly known as the Chocó, extends from the Panama border south to northern Ecuador, and it all lies to the west of the Andes. It is the wettest region in the world and an important center of rainforest endemism—that is, it contains many species that are found nowhere else. In terms of overall rainforest diversity, this narrow strip of forest, which runs between the western slopes of the Andes and the Pacific Ocean, is one of the most important in the world. But the Ecuadorean part is almost entirely destroyed, apart from the tiny Río Palenque reserve; and the Colombian part is severely threatened by logging.

Amazonia and the Guianas contain the largest contiguous rainforest in the world. It includes part of the territory of eight countries: Bolivia, Brazil, Colombia, French Guiana, Guyana, Peru, Suriname, and Venezuela; and covers an area of approximately seven million square kilometers. The region with the highest known rainforest diversity occurs in Amazonian Peru at Yanomono, with 300 species of trees recorded from a single hectare.[1]

Although rainforest is the predominant forest cover in the region, it is by no means the only type of vegetation. The region is covered by a mosaic of rainforest, floodplain forest, savanna, and white sand formations; and there are great variations within the Amazonian rainforests themselves due to local variations in climate, soil, and topography.

Atlantic Coastal Brazil is a narrow rainforest belt, 120 to 160 kilometers wide, that formerly stretched along the coast of Brazil from Rio Grande do Norte south to Rio Grande do Sul; only about 4 percent remains. This area has a high degree of plant endemism, which makes the forest destruction all the more tragic. For example, 53.5

percent of the woody forest species are endemic to that region.[2] These forests also harbor many interesting and important species of animals such as the woolly spider monkey, the lion tamarins, and an endemic sloth—each of which is almost extinct.

BIOGEOGRAPHICAL HISTORY

Many popular and scientific publications have referred to the stability of Latin American rainforests over time. But recent evidence indicates that this region has been anything but stable over the last hundred thousand years. There have been many fluctuations in vegetation cover; areas where the natural vegetation seems always to have been rainforest have not necessarily always been forested. Changes in vegetation in tropical regions have corresponded to the natural cycles of glaciation in the temperate regions. With each ice age a cooler and drier climate in the tropics has favored savanna and other, more arid vegetation types. The rainforests were pushed into smaller regions where the climate was still humid enough to support them. Each region that remained forested through these climatic transitions is called a refugium.

These refugia are thought to have been the evolutionary nurseries of the rainforests. In them, species became isolated and concentrated; and faster-breeding organisms quickly evolved into new species—one cause of the incredible diversity of life in contemporary rainforests. Refugia theory, the idea that patches of forest become isolated and grow back together over time, also helps to explain why certain species are found only in specific areas and nowhere else.[3] Because of their diversity, these refugia are now an important focus for conservation efforts.

By studying changes in forest cover we can learn much about the make-up and evolution of the rainforest. In the past, the forest was reduced in area by natural causes and recuperated naturally to again cover large areas as climate changed. Although the rainforest does express recuperative power when given the right conditions, the current spread of human-induced deforestation is much more rapid than was gradual climate-induced change. Because of this heightened pace of deforestation, many more species are becoming extinct. Information about rainforest recuperation and coalescence is vital for contemporary management and conservation. This information helps to unravel the complexities of species diversity and gives us tools for preventing extinction, revealing the ecological patterns of deforestation, increasing the benefits of forests that must be used, and regenerating forests on once-forested lands. All this knowledge can help us to minimize forest destruction.

THE FOREST

The Latin American rainforest is an awesome place. Its tall trees produce a dense overhead canopy that keeps all but a tiny fraction of sunlight from reaching the forest floor. This semidarkness is filled with thousands of different species of trees, many with strangely shaped trunks, no two alike. Any visitor to the Latin American rainforest has been spellbound by the haunting sound of the howler monkey echoing for kilometers over the forest. How many times have I been attacked by the spider monkey as it either tries to throw tree branches or urinate on the human invader of its territory—presenting a fascinating experience for a naturalist but an easy target for the hunter.

These are the forests that house the capybara, the world's largest rodent; the tapir; and the jaguar. My favorite of all animals is the giant otter. How privileged I feel to have been in a canoe on the Uraricoera River in Roraima territory, Brazil, and on the Rio Negro of Mato Grosso, surrounded by a group of these curious beasts popping out of the water and barking right beside the canoe. Again, alas, an easy target for the marksman. This animal has provided me with more pleasure than any other I have met, yet it is now confined to only a few of the least disturbed areas of forest where hunters have not eliminated it.

The plants are equally intriguing, varying from enormous buttressed trees—such as the giant angelim in the legume family, whose trunk frequently attains three meters in diameter—to small flowers growing inconspicuously among the litter layer of the forest floor. Bizarrely contorted vines are abundant, and varied in shape and form—and fascinating also for their diverse chemical potency, which has been put to many uses by the Indians. It is from vines that curare, the arrow poison and the muscle-relaxing drug, is extracted; *timbo*, used for poisoning fishes, contains the insecticide rotenone and comes from the *Lonchocarpus* vine; and the stems of the caapi vine are the basis for the hallucinogenic beverage ayahuasca.

The animals and plants of the Latin American rainforests are legion. This diversity is linked together in a large web of food chains, defense mechanisms against predators, pollination and dispersal interactions, and links between fungi and tree roots that are essential for the rapid recycling of nutrients. The study of one organism in the forest soon leads to the others with which it interacts.

For example, I have studied many aspects of the *castanha-de-galinha*, a common tree in the forests of Brazil around Manaus. The flowers open at night and are born on long peduncles that hang below the branches. This makes them easily accessible to the nocturnal bats that visit the flowers to feed on the abundance of nectar that they produce. The bats brush against the mass of pollen-filled stamens and are dusted with pollen. As they fly from tree to tree each night, they cause pollination by transporting the pollen from one tree to another. After pollination the fruit gradually matures. The egg-shaped fruit falls to the forest floor, where it is collected up by agoutis. These rodents scatter-hoard fruit and nuts the way a squirrel does in the temperate region. Some of their caches are forgotten, and so dispersal of the seed from the mother tree takes place. On the underside of the leaves and the outside of the sepals are small nectaries that secrete sugar. Ants drink this nectar and when other insects land on the leaves or flower-buds they are driven off by the aggressive ants that are fed by the plants. In return for nectar the tree has an army of small protectors. The wood of the *castanha-de-galinha* is very hard. This is because it is full of small silica or sand grains. This serves as good protection against the hordes of wood-boring insects that are to be found in the tropical rainforest. This single species of tree links together a species of bat, the agouti, and ant into the web of interactions that make up the Amazon rainforest.

INDIGENOUS POPULATIONS

No account of the Latin American rainforests would be complete without reference to the indigenous peoples who were originally to be found in all the major regions of rainforest, varying from Maya people in Mexico and Guatemala, through the Kuna of the isthmus of Panama, to the numerous groups of forest Indians in Brazil. The surprising and most significant fact in the history of these people is that, although in pre-Columbian times there was an extremely large human population, *the rainforests were largely intact.* Early accounts of exploration in Amazonia describe large quantities of what are now rare animals, such as turtles, manatees, piraracu fish, and jaguar; yet they also describe large groups of Indians such as the Omagua and the Tapajós, which would indicate a population density that far exceeded later populations.[4]

Since the sighting of the first Carib Indians by Columbus, the native populations of the Americas have had their rights severely abused, whether in the North or the South. What we have left today are the scattered remnants of some 500 distinct rainforest groups. Many of the original ethnic groups have disappeared along with an enormous body of cultural information about living in the rainforest. Recently anthropologists, ethnologists, biologists, and ethnobotanists have been conducting many studies on the remaining Indians. These have concentrated more on their ecology, agriculture, and management practices. The further we study these peoples, the more we begin to respect their wisdom and their knowledge of the forest.

A study of quantitative ethnobotany of four groups of Indians showed the extent to which the Indians use rainforest trees. The Chácobo of Bolivia have uses for 78.7 percent of the tree species in a sample hectare, or 92 percent of the individual trees. The Panare Indians of Venezuela use 48.6 percent of the species on a sample hectare. The Ka'apor Indians of Brazil use 78.6 percent, and the Tembé 61.3 percent.[5] The difference between the Indians and contemporary settlers in the Amazon is that the Indians live with and use the forest diversity, whereas the settler wants to cut the forest down and replace it with monoculture. Indigenous systems of cultivation make use of diversity rather than monoculture and rely more on woody perennials than on short-lived herbaceous crops. Both these management practices are far more suitable for the fragile soils of Amazonia than are monocultures of grass for cattle pasture or of *Gmelina* for timber plantations.

HISTORICAL SETTLEMENT

The destruction of the Latin American rainforests began with the arrival of Europeans in the New World. Early destruction focused more on the indigenous inhabitants than on the forest, and so the great Aztec and Inca civilizations soon fell to the conquistadors. The Caribs, who knew so much about the Caribbean forest, were some of the first people to be eliminated because of the utility of their island territory for such crops as sugar cane.

Each rainforest region has its own history of genocide and slavery as the thirst for land, gold, and territory became the dominant motive of countries and individuals. For example, in Amazonia, after the initial battle for territory between the Indians and the Spanish and Portuguese colonizers, the worst atrocities were committed in the wake of the discovery of the rubber vulcanization process.

Some of the most lucrative Amazonian rainforest species were brought near to extinction in those early days, long before any "red books" of threatened and endangered species were known. In the rainforests of eastern Brazil, a tree called pau-brasil yielded a purple dye that became a much-sought-after item of commerce for European fashion. This tree also gave its name to what is now the largest country in Latin America. Pau-brasil is scarcely known in the wild today because it was mined out of the forests for its dye and for wood used in constructing musical instruments. The story is the same for several other species.

When the rubber boom ended with the establishment of lower-cost rubber tree plantations in tropical Asia, the destruction caused by the hunger for rubber continued on Henry Ford's million-acre plantation, Fordlandia in the Rio Tapajós region of Brazil. This was the first of many attempts to introduce large-scale monoculture plantations into Amazonia. Needless to say, like many plantations, it was a failure. Fordlandia failed because of two ecological factors: the use of a floodplain forest species on the upland terra firma, and a leaf rust fungus disease that attacked the leaves. Like most species, the rubber tree is adapted to a certain niche within the complexity of habitats in Amazonia, and becomes vulnerable when moved to the habitat of the plantation.

In Central America, especially in Guatemala, Honduras, and Nicaragua, the early part of the century saw large areas of species-rich rainforest turned into banana plantations. In the banana republics created by the United Fruit Company the land tenure policies are responsible for much of the tension in regional politics today, which in turn leads to further destruction as landless peasants are pushed into the rainforest.

RECENT SETTLEMENT

Although the early settlement of the tropical American rainforests had a devastating effect on indigenous cultures and on the vast body of their ecological wisdom, it did not have an extensive effect on the forest cover of the region. The last two decades have changed the whole picture and led us to the current and well-justified concern for the Latin American rainforests.

The causes of the current wave of destruction are many but they have been associated largely with two factors: increased population growth and therefore increased pressure on the land, and readily available international capital from the developed countries in the form of loans and investments. These two factors have been closely linked in some of the vast settlement programs, such as Polono-roeste, in Rondônia, funded by international capital. A few of the most important examples of forest destruction, especially in Amazonia, will illustrate the seriousness of the crisis.

Amazonian forest destruction really began in earnest in 1971, with the commencement of the Transamazon Highway in Brazil. President Médici visited the drought-stricken northwest of Brazil in March 1971 and was appalled by what he saw. His solution to the plight of the northwesterners was a highway linking that region to the rest of Amazonia. This was accompanied by an ambitious colonization plan to resettle the drought-stricken people in the lush, always humid Amazon rainforest. By July 1971, legislation for the road was passed by Congress, and by October the bulldozers were rolling. The first settlers soon began to migrate into the region, and farms, towns, and villages sprung up along the eastern part of the highway near Altamira. The settlers were given land, a house, and agricultural advice—most of it to do with planting upland rice. The first rice harvests fared poorly and showed what ecologists had long said: that this was an inappropriate use of the soil. The news got back to the northwest that Amazonia was not the paradise it was expected to be, and the migration slowed down.

By the time the next president, Ernesto Geisel, assumed power, it was obvious that the trans-Amazon settlement program was not a success. He blamed this on the quality of the settlers and their lack of capital, and thus the small size of the farms. So his policy was to encourage large investors to open up huge tracts of land for cattle ranches by introducing favorable tax incentives and the availability of loans through a rural credit program. Companies could invest profits from the south of Brazil in ranches rather than pay income tax. The late 1970's was a time of vast destruction of forests as industries from the south of Brazil and abroad all invested in cattle. Today there is much abandoned cattle pasture and much poor-quality pasture supporting less than one cow per hectare. The investors have lost little because profits have been made on tax incentives and speculation in land prices. However, as of 1983 the tax incentives and loans are no longer available for new cattle projects because of the failure of this scheme.[6]

In 1968 billionaire Daniel Ludwig thought that he had the answer to a predicted shortage of the world supply of paper. His solution was a reputedly fast-growing tree in the teak family called *Gmelina arborea*. From the Brazilian government he bought a tract of land on the Jarí River that was almost the size of Connecticut, and began to plant *gmelina*. The trees did not grow as fast as expected, because by clearing the forest with bulldozers he removed all the nutrients, which were in the forest, not in the soil. He replaced bulldozers with work-gangs to fell trees with axes and plant *gmelina* among the debris. This worked in some areas but not in others. It was then found that the Jarí property was on two major soil types, clay and sand. The *gmelina* grew well in clay soils but not in sand, so he had to import the slower growing Caribbean pine for sandy soils. In 1984 he finally sold the project to a consortium of Brazilian companies at a financial loss of $600 million. This is another example of vast deforestation for a poorly researched and economically unsound project.[7] Finally, in October 1988, President Sarney, in his first environmental speech, promised to end all tax incentives in Amazonia and take many other measures to protect the forest.

However, hydroelectric dams are another major threat to the Amazon rainforest still occupying the planning boards. The giant Tucurí Dam on the Tocantins River is now functioning and providing electric power for the city of Belém, the Carajás iron mine, aluminum refineries, and the new railroad to São Luís. That dam was probably a regional necessity. On the other hand, the Balbina Dam north of Manaus is a complete ecological disaster that should never have been built. It floods a larger area of rainforest than Tucurí and has the potential to produce only one-tenth of the energy. Balbina is flooding the territory of the Waimari-Atroari Indians, a center of rainforest species endemism. The lake depth in many places is only three meters. Balbina was partially funded by the World Bank, and Brazil has a whole series of yet other dams planned for Amazonia that it hopes to fund with international loans. This is a case for concerted, logical activism by all people concerned about rainforest destruction.

The state of Rondônia, in the west of Brazilian Amazonia where it borders Bolivia, is the site of another World Bank–financed fiasco called Polonoroeste. The bank funded the paving of a road across Rondônia and the construction of many lateral feeder roads. As a result, the forests of Rondônia have disappeared at an alarming rate. In August 1987 a satellite passed over a small band in the south of Rondônia, north of Mato Grosso and south of Pará states. The images clearly show a huge smoke cloud over the region and 6,803 individual sources of fire. These were 6,803 fires large enough to be seen burning an estimated 12,000 square kilometers of forest.[8] Recently it was noted that there was a marked reduction in the ozone layer of the atmosphere shortly after those fires. It is the first time that rainforest destruction has been connected to ozone depletion, a loss that affects every citizen on this planet.

There now remains only about 3.5 percent of the rainforest of Atlantic Coastal Brazil, due to devastation by farming, colonization, and especially by sugar cane and cocoa plantations to satisfy the world demand for chocolate. Because the area was home to an extremely high percentage of endemic species, many extinctions have already occurred in eastern Brazil.

The Panama Canal is threatened by rainforest destruction in two ways. Deforestation on the isthmus has reduced rainfall so that there is not enough water to replace what is lost as ships pass through the canal. Also, deforestation has caused soil erosion that is silting the canal so that the deeper-draft ships will have difficulty passing through.

This catalog of Latin American rainforest destruction could be vastly extended, but the above is surely enough to demonstrate the gravity of the problem of rainforest destruction from Mexico to Brazil. Population growth, poor distribution of land, debt, and greed have led to unprecedented levels of destruction. It is a crisis that demands our response.

THE LESSONS

Rather than dwell on the unfortunate past, let us ask what lessons can be learned from the world's most species-diverse forest and its terrifying history of the wholesale destruction of life. The most important lesson is the interdependence of all living creatures. The global ecosystem is now threatened because of the extent of deforestation in Latin America. The impact of the fires is now so great as to affect the ozone layer of the upper atmosphere and world climate patterns. Regional systems of interaction are being broken down. Trees are no longer being pollinated properly because their animal pollinators are being eliminated or replaced by introduced organisms. One example is the Africanized honeybee, which has outcompeted many of the natural pollinators from South America. To maintain a future for the human race, the other creatures upon which we depend must be preserved and defended.

Our future depends on diversity. Latin American rainforests, with up to 300 species of trees per hectare, epitomize diversity. Many of these species may yield useful drugs and other products of economic potential, but we must not look on the forests merely as sources of future economic gain. They are sustainers of life on Earth, the organisms that regulate the balance of gases in our atmosphere to maintain human and all other forms of life.

The history of the Latin American rainforest demonstrates the failures of our current economic systems. Human greed, excessively luxurious lifestyles, and fixation on short-term profit have been the moving forces in our society, and this has been accompanied by a loss of spiritual values. Nature is rebelling and telling us that we cannot continue this process indefinitely. We would do well to go back and look at the concepts of those who have lived closer to Nature. American Indian culture, for instance, is based on consideration for the needs of the seventh unborn generation. How differently we would manage the rainforests of Latin America if we were thinking of our great-great-great-great-great-grandchildren rather than short-term personal profit or the reaction of current shareholders. Our society would do well to regain the art of sharing, and of caring for the sacredness of all forms of life.

The lesson from the Latin American rainforest is loud and clear: one organism has dominated, to the exclusion and at the expense of all others upon which it depends. This could bring about the destruction of all organisms—of life on Earth—through the breakdown of interdependent chains of interactions, through the excessive use of natural resources, and through the inability to control population growth. The study of the wonders of rainforest biology helps us to gain a renewed respect for all life, which must in turn lead to reforms that will ensure the sustainability of life on our planet. If we have learned anything from the rainforest, it is that we are responsible for using this knowledge to rescue our world from impending disaster.

5

ASIA'S FORESTS, ASIA'S CULTURES

J. BANDYOPADHYAY

AND

VANDANA SHIVA

•

~~~~~~

For the cultures of Asia, the forest has always been a teacher, and the message of the forest has been the message of interconnectedness and diversity, renewability and sustainability, integrity and pluralism.

India, the largest country in tropical Asia, and the cradle of many cultures of the region, has taken pride in calling herself a "forest civilization," an *aranya samskriti*, even in contemporary times. India's wisdom has been drawn from the forest. Her ancient texts are called *aranyaka's* (forest texts) because they were written by sages living in communion with the forest. India's challenge to colonialism was empowered by a revitalization of the concept of the forest as teacher, a model for humane society. Gandhi, the political activist, J. C. Bose, the scientist, and Tagore, the artist, communicated in different ways the message of the forest as the language of liberation. During the struggle for India's independence, Tagore wrote an essay called

66

"Tapovan" (the sacred forest), in which he contrasted the culture of the modern West, modeled on the industrial city, with the culture of India, modeled on the forest. He wrote:

Contemporary western civilization is built of brick, iron and wood. It is rooted in the city. But Indian civilization has been distinctive in locating the source of regeneration, material and intellectual, in the forest, not in the city. India's best ideas have come where man was in communion with the trees and rivers and lakes, away from the crowds. The peace of the forest has helped the intellectual evolution of man. The culture of the forest has fueled the culture of Indian society. The culture that has arisen from the forest has been influenced by the diverse processes from species to species, from season to season, in sight and sound and smell. The unifying principle of life in diversity, of democratic pluralism, thus became the principle of the Indian civilization.[1]

The cultural lessons that Asian societies draw from the forest apply at two levels: the relationship between society and Nature on the one hand, and between people within society on the other. Societies modeled on the forest are based on the lessons of diversity and democratic pluralism. Just as the tropical forest is rich in diversity and has a niche for every life form, including the smallest and apparently insignificant ones, society based on diversity allows the preservation of diverse life both in the forest and in society. Asian societies still close to the forest are thus able to be culturally plural societies.

The second lesson is one of renewability and sustainability. It is based on the recognition that sustenance comes from the forest, not the factory, and that sustainable reproduction of the society can only be based on the maintenance of diversity in the forest, which contributes to human needs in diverse ways: agriculture, animal husbandry, water and irrigation, housing, and health care.

The forest as the source also means that forests and trees must be treated as sacred. The sacred is inviolable: its integrity cannot be violated. If Asian civilizations have survived over centuries it is because they learned to be like the forest, sustaining both the forest and culture through time. Sacred groves such as the *aurans* of Rajasthan, the *Devaranyas* of the western ghats in India, and the ancestral sites of all forest peoples have been Asia's mechanisms for perennial maintenance of the perennial forest. But when this sacredness is violated, and society is separated from the forest, renewability, sustainability, and diversity are lost.

This is everywhere evident as Asia's forests are everywhere being violated. From the monsoon-drenched southwest coast of India and southern Sri Lanka, east through Thailand, Malaysia, and the many large islands of Indonesia, north through the Philippines and south through New Guinea, accelerating rates of deforestation are threatening the ecological equilibrium of the region and the cultures of her forest people. Even the rainforest of Australia's Queensland Peninsula, now three-fourths reduced, has not been spared.

COLONIZATION AND "SCIENTIFIC FORESTRY"

When the West colonized Asia, it colonized the forests, but with the ideas of Nature and culture derived from the model of the industrial factory. The forest was no longer viewed as having intrinsic value; its value was defined solely in terms of commercially exploitable timber. Having depleted their forests at home, European countries started the destruction of Asia's forests.

British military needs for Indian teak led to a proclamation in the late 18th century that wrested the right to teak trees from the local government and vested it in the East India Company. It was only after more than half a century of uncontrolled exploitation of forests by British commercial interests that controls were introduced. In 1865 the Supreme Legislative Council passed the first Indian Forest Act, which authorized the government to appropriate forests from the local people and manage them as profitable, reserved forests.

The introduction of this legislation marks the beginning of what state and industrial interests have called "scientific management," which for indigenous peoples initiated the destruction of forests and the erosion of people's rights to use of the forest. "Scientific forestry" was the false application of narrow commercial interests that reduced the value of diverse forest life to the value of a few commercially valuable species. Scientific forestry's reduction of the forests violated both the integrity of the forests and the integrity of forest cultures. People who needed the food, fiber, and shelter of the forest's diversity saw their culture erode as forest productivity was transformed to meet commercial markets.

Extinction is implicit in scientific forestry's conception of the forest, which is defined as "normal" according to the objective of "managing" it to maximize production of marketable timber. Since the natural tropical forest is rich in biodiversity, including the diversity of nonmarketable species, scientific forestry declares the natural forest to be "abnormal."

According to R. S. Troup, a leading forester in the 1920's, "The attainment of the normal forest from the abnormal condition of our existing natural forests, involves a certain temporary sacrifice. Generally speaking, the more rapid the change to the normal state, the greater the sacrifice. . . . The question of minimizing the sacrifice involved in introducing order out of chaos is one which is likely to exercise our minds considerably in connection with forest management."[2]

The natural forest is thus seen as "chaos." The man-made forest is "order." "Scientific" management, therefore, has a clear anti-Nature bias, and a bias toward industrial and commercial objectives for which the natural forest must be sacrificed. Diversity thus gives way to uniformity of even-aged, single-species stands, and this uniformity is the ideal of the "normal" forest toward which all silvicultural systems aim.

In biological terms, tropical forests are the most productive systems on our planet. The quantities of wood average about 300 tons per hectare, compared with about 150 tons per hectare in temperate forests. However, in commercial forestry the overall productivity is not important, nor are the functions of tropical forests in the survival of tropical peoples. Forest value is based upon the volume of industrially useful species that can be profitably marketed; productivity is measured in terms of industrial and commercial biomass alone. The rest of the forest is waste or—as Bethel, an international forestry consultant, states, referring to the large biomass typical of the forests of the humid tropics—"weeds."[3]

The industrial-materials viewpoint of capitalistic forestry converts biodiversity into money and destroys the rest as "weeds" and waste. This "waste," however, is the wealth of biomass that maintains Nature's water and nutrient cycles and satisfies the needs for food, fuel, fodder, fertilizer, fiber, and medicine of the agricultural communities. Increased commercial productivity destroys Nature's productivity and the local economies that depend upon Nature.

THE NONSUSTAINABILITY OF SCIENTIFIC MANAGEMENT

Scientific management, in the form of plantations and select logging, is meant to generate "sustained yields." However, this approach destroys the conditions of renewability within tropical forest ecosystems, and is therefore ecologically nonsustainable.

In commercial forestry, "sustainability" refers to supply to the market, not to the regenerative capacity of an ecosystem to sustain biodiversity, hydrological and climatic stability, and local economies. Sustained-yield management aims to produce "the best financial results, or greatest volume, or the most suitable class of produce."[4] "Sustained yield" assumes that natural forests are not "normal." When "normalcy" is dictated by the market demands, and nonmarketable "abnormal" biodiversity is destroyed, the natural forest becomes a nonrenewable, nonsustainable resource.

Forest uniformity is demanded by centralized markets, centralized industry, and centralized thinking. However, uniformity acts against Nature's design. The transformation of mixed natural forests into monocultures allows direct exposure of the ground to tropical sun and rain. Forest soils are baked dry in the heat and washed away in the rain. And when the canopy is even partially destroyed, humidity also is lost. This is what happened in Kalimantan, Indonesia, where partial logging and the conversion of forests into plantations of eucalyptus and acacia dried out the forests. Consequently, immense forest fires—unprecedented in this rainy region—consumed 3.5 million hectares, an area 56 times the size of Singapore.[5]

In tropical forests, selective felling of commercial species produces only small yields—perhaps only 5 to 25 cubic meters per hectare—whereas clear-felling might produce as much as 450 cubic meters per hectare. But both forms of cutting are nonsustainable. An example of the nonsustainability of selective fellings is the experience of PICOP, a joint venture set up in 1952 between the American firm International Paper Company, the world's largest paper producer, and the Andre Soriano Corporation in the Philippines. PICOP takes only about 10 percent of the total volume of wood, roughly 30 cubic meters per hectare of virgin forest. But the company's measurements of annual growth show that the second rotation will yield only 15 cubic meters per hectare of useful wood, half as much as the first cut and not enough to keep the company's sawmills functioning at a profitable level. PICOP's plantations have also failed. The corporation had to replant 12,000 hectares of a variety of eucalyptus from Papua New Guinea that was attacked by pests. Pine plantations of 10,000 hectares have also failed. At $1,000 per hectare, that was a $10 million mistake.[6]

Angel Alcala, professor of biology at Silliman University in the Philippines, observes that selective logging is good in theory, but does not really work: "With selective logging, you are supposed to take only a few trees and leave the rest to grow, so you can return later and take some more, without destroying the forest. This is supposed to be a sustainable system. But here, although they use the phrase selective logging, there is only one harvest, a big one. After that no more."[7]

One study found that 14 percent of a logging area is cleared for roads and another 27 percent for hauling logs to the roads. Thus more than 40 percent of a forest can be stripped of protective vegetation and rendered highly vulnerable to erosion, which can be as high as 60 percent.[8]

Dipterocarp forests average 145 valuable trees per hectare. For every 10 that are deliberately felled, 13 more are broken or damaged. Once a tree is damaged, its defenses against insects, fungus, and other pests are impaired. In one Malaysian dipterocarp forest, where only 10 percent of the trees were harvested, 55 percent were destroyed or severely damaged. Only 33 percent were unharmed. In Indonesia, according to the manager of Georgia-Pacific, loggers damage or destroy more than three times the number of trees that they deliberately harvest. According to the 1978 UNESCO report on tropical forest ecosystems, "True selective felling is impracticable regardless of the structure, composition and dynamism of the original stands."[9]

The annual commercial production per hectare of tropical broad-leaved closed forests is one-fifth that of temperate broad-leaved forests, for the high diversity of tropical forest ecosystems leads to low populations of commercial species. In contrast, temperate forests are poor in species biologically, but rich in commercially valuable species. Further, the already simple structure of temperate forests has been further simplified by artificial regeneration and plantations. Although simplification may be a viable management strategy in temperate forests, it destroys both the genetic wealth of tropical forests and their biospheric functions. When genetic variability, species diversity, water balance, and biogeochemical cycles are severely reduced, tropical forests lose their regenerative capacity.

If sustained yields were conceived in terms of species richness and diversity and biospheric and climatic functions—instead of board-feet, a temperate-zone commercial concept—then the forests would not lose their regenerative capacity. But, as it is, scientific forest management destroys the regenerative capacity and renewability of tropical forest ecosystems by converting biodiversity into the uniformity of the assembly line. Instead of modeling human uses of the forest on Nature, the forest is modeled on the factory. "Scientific management," as it has been practiced for over a century, is simply a system of tropical deforestation.

Asia's forests have been most attractive to loggers because they are the richest in commercially valuable dipterocarps. Twelve genera and 470 species of the Dipterocarpaceae family occur in the forests of tropical Asia.[10] In the past, Thailand used to be a timber exporter, but now has become a timber importer.[11] Thailand's forest area has fallen from 53 percent in 1961 to 29 percent in 1985. Almost all 11,000 islands of the Philippines used to be covered with rainforests. Large areas were lost earlier to commercial agriculture and plantations as part of colonial policy. Logging has destroyed what remained. The ratio of forests to total land area in the Philippines fell from 60 percent in 1960 to 27 percent in 1985. India is losing 155,000 hectares of forest annually. Deforestation in Asia is taking place at the rate of 2 million hectares a year. Given this trend, the closed forests of tropical Asia will decrease from 306 million hectares in 1980 to 266 million hectares in the year 2000.[12]

Reforestation projects planned and financed by international agencies and national bureaucracies have failed to reverse deforestation trends because these projects are not based on the lessons of the rainforest. Most plantation schemes have been dominated by large-scale monocultures of exotic industrial species like eucalyptus. This approach violates the principle of diversity and fails to contribute to the ecological regeneration of degraded ecosystems.[13] In India and Thailand, peasant communities have staged protests against large-scale eucalyptus planting because these plantations fail to satisfy local food and fodder needs, and accelerate soil erosion while polluting water.[14]

But from the scientific forestry viewpoint, these tropical peoples are as dispensable as the tropical forests. In place of cultural and biological pluralism, the factory model produces nonsustainable monocultures in society as well as Nature. There is no place for the small, no role for the insignificant. Diversity is weeded out, and uniform monocultures of plants and people are managed externally. Those who do not fit into the uniformity are declared unfit. Symbiosis gives way to competition, domination, and dispensability. There is no survival possible for the forest or its people when they become fodder for industry.

The survival of tropical forests depends on the survival of human societies modeled on the forest. These lessons for survival do not come from the texts of "scientific forestry." They are innate in the lives and beliefs of the forest peoples of the world.

There are in Asia today two paradigms of forestry, one life-enhancing, the other life-destroying. The life-enhancing paradigm emerges from the forest and forest communities, the life-destroying one from the factory and the market. The life-enhancing paradigm supports a sustainable forest that renews food and water systems. *Renewability is the primary management objective.* The maximizing of short-term profits through commercial extraction is the primary management objective of the life-destroying paradigm. Since maximizing profits depends upon destruction of renewability, the two paradigms are cognitively and ecologically incompatible. Today in the forests of Asia these two paradigms are struggling against each other.

FOREST STRUGGLES IN ASIA

The Penan of Borneo are one of the last hunting and gathering tribes left in the Earth's tropical forests. For centuries, the Penan have lived in and with Borneo's forests—in Sarawak in Malaysia and in Kalimantan in Indonesia. Wild sago (*u'ud*) has been their staple food, along with fish and game. Everything they need comes from the forest.

Today, their survival is threatened because the forests that give them life, which are also the dwelling-place of their gods and ancestors, are also sources of commercial tropical timber and foreign exchange. Loggers from across the world have been attracted to the dipterocarps of these Asian forests: the red merantis, Shorea, and the yellow and white *Anisotera*. Eighty percent of the tropical hardwoods traded globally come from the forests of Malaysia and Indonesia.

Timber is a major source of revenue for Malaysia. In 1960 timber exports from Peninsular Malaysia brought in $55 million. By 1982 this had risen to $1,013 million. Sarawak alone earned $1,093 million by exporting logs in 1983.[15] Indonesia invited foreign companies to "develop" forest resources in 1963. In 1967 the actual logging operations were started, and in less than two decades, 521 logging companies held forest concessions (Hak Pengusaha Hutan) in Sumatra, Kalimantan, Sulawesi, Irian Jaya, Maluku, East and West Nusa Tenggara.

In March 1987, the Penan, along with the Melabit and Kayan, decided to fight back—peacefully. They formed human barricades across the logging tracks in a bid to stop the destruction of their forested homelands by timber companies. By June 1987 they had set up 12 blockade sites along a 150-kilometer stretch of Sarawak's timber-rich northern districts of Limbang and Baram. As they proclaimed:

This is the land of our forefathers, and their forefathers before them. If we don't do something to protect the little that is left, there will be nothing for our children. Our forests are mowed down, the hills are leveled, the sacred graves of our ancestors have been desecrated, our waters and streams are contaminated, our plant life is destroyed, and the forest animals are killed or have run away. What else can we do now but to make our protests heard, so that something can be done to help us?

AVEK MATAI AME MANEU MAPAT (Until we die we will block this road.)

Like the Penan of Sarawak, peasant women in the Garhwal Himalaya have been blocking logging operations for two decades, embracing trees to protect them from being felled. The famous "Chipko" movement, which derives its name from this act of embrace, is both an expression of protest against destruction and an expression of oneness and harmony with the forest.[16] For the women, the forest is the basis of life, not a timber mine.

The most dramatic expression of the clash between destructive forestry and a life-conserving ecological view of Earth took place in 1977, when Bachni Devi of Advani, in Garhwal Himalaya, led resistance against her own husband, who had a local contract to fell the forest. The forest officials came by to bully and threaten the women and the Chipko activists. They found the women holding up lit lanterns in broad daylight. Puzzled, the forester asked why they had come with lanterns. And the women replied, "to teach you forestry, to show you the light."

The forester said, "You foolish women, how can you who stop the timber felling know the value of the forest? Do you know what forests bear? They produce revenues, profit, resin, and timber."

And the women immediately sang back in a chorus,

> What do the forests bear?
> Soil, water, and pure air,
> Soil, water, and pure air,
> These are the basis of sustenance.

The Advani *satyagraha* (fight for truth) created new directions for Chipko. The movement's philosophy and politics now evolved to reflect the needs and knowledge of women. Peasant women openly challenged the commercial forestry system on the one hand, and also the local men who had been transmogrified by that system— cognitively, economically, and politically. The slogan created at Advani has become the the scientific and philosophical message of the movement and has laid the foundations of an alternative forestry science, feminist and ecological in nature.

These foundations shift the ground from reductionistic perceptions of the forest to a more holistic perspective. The forest provides sustenance, and its conservation as a life-support system is the objective of the Chipko movement. The protection of the forest's ecological productivity implies the protection of women's work in food production and their productivity in sustenance. This challenges the concept of foresters (largely male, Western trained) as forest experts, since women, through their daily interaction with the living forest, know far more about the diversity of life in the forest than does the profit-minded forester who relates to only a few species of dead wood. The Chipko movement makes visible Nature's work in the forest and women's work in managing the forest. It challenges the concept of "yield" as measured in commercial products and replaces it with biological yields: the diversity of life and the water wealth produced by the forest. It challenges the concepts of "productivity" and "productive work" as measured through destruction, and shifts attention to the invisible work of women and Nature in maintaining and conserving the forest as an ecosystem, which, through its renewal, supports human needs and human life.

The quiet actions of protest of the Penan in Sarawak and the hill-women of Garhwal to prevent deforestation are echoing the message of the liberation of life from the culture of death, decay, and destruction. They are challenging the linear view of history, which sees the diverse forest cultures of Asia as relics of the past, relics that must be destroyed for progress to occur. The meaning of progress here implies the universal spread of the monoculture of Western industrial society. These forest cultures are showing that such a model of progress—so-called "development"—is ecologically counterproductive and ethically undesirable. It is unworkable as a universal prescription because its adoption by a privileged minority involves the annihilation of the world's ecosystems and cultures. "Development" proceeds from the industrial worldview that tropical forests or tropical forest cultures are merely objects of consumption, to be used and disposed. This logic of disposability and dispensability of tropical Nature and tropical peoples stands in opposition to the logic of renewability, diversity, and democratic pluralism that the tropical forest has bequeathed to Asian cultures.

Indigenous communities in Asia's tropical forests have inhabited and used the forest sustainably over centuries in the knowledge that the survival of the forest is the condition for their survival. For these cultures, all life, both human and nonhuman, is in symbiosis. Human society is not predatory but in rhythm with the forest.

6

NO CONDITION PERMANENT

The Rainforests of Africa

JULIAN GERSTIN

•

~~~~~~

The supposedly inimical jungles of the Dark Continent have for thousands of years been places where people have lived and flourished. From the coast of Sierra Leone to the interior of Zaire 4,800 kilometers distant, Africans have farmed the thin soils of the forest, gathered and hunted among its looming trees, and found cause for celebration in the most daunting circumstances.

The Pygmies of the Ituri region in Zaire, perhaps the most ancient of the world's surviving forest-dwellers, worship the forest as a protector and the source of life. Their music celebrates this relationship. With its bright, swooping melodies tangling in several registers, its cross-rhythms bursting from drums and handclaps, it suggests the dense interwoven harmony of the forest itself.

In West Africa, rainforest agriculture has for centuries supported sub-Saharan Africa's densest populations. Several ancient West African cities became the seats of powerful kingdoms: Benin, Kumasi, Wadai, Oyo, Ile-Ife. Sacred groves and hunting reserves dot even the deepest forest. The orisha (deities) of the Yoruba of Nigeria represent natural forces personified, and human characteristics magnified in Nature. The beautiful forest river Oshun is sacred to the goddess of the same name, deity of fresh water and gold, beauty, and fertility. Osain, the god of leaves, herbs, natural medicines, and the hunt, is represented as a still pool of water among the trees. Ochossi, god of the forest itself, is a spirit "who passes along the ways, leaving no footprints." All forest-goers should tread so lightly.

But the recent history of Africa's rainforests has been largely one of exploitation and destruction. Since 1850, when the era of direct colonial rule began, the continent's rainforests have been reduced by 20 percent. Nearly one-half of this destruction has occurred just since World War II.[1] At this rate, by the year 2000, little of the forest may remain.

WHERE THE WILD THINGS ARE

The African rainforest has two major sectors. The West African portion, known as the Guinean forest, once stretched from Senegal through Nigeria along the coast of the Atlantic and the Bight of Benin, and inland 320 to 450 kilometers to the northern savannas. This forest has been devastated. Gambia, Senegal, Togo, and Benin have been virtually denuded. Guinea, Sierra Leone, Liberia, Côte d'Ivoire, Ghana, and Nigeria retain sizable portions of forest, but the rates of deforestation in Côte d'Ivoire and Nigeria are among the world's highest.

The Central African forest covers the basin of the Congo (now the Zaire) River. This forest, the Zairean, is much larger than the Guinean; it comprises 18 percent of the world's rainforest and is second only to the Amazon rainforest in size. Zaire alone accounts for 10 percent of the world total.[2] Cameroon, Gabon, Central African Republic, and the Congo Republic also contain large forest tracts, and scattered bits remain in Equatorial Guinea, Sudan, Angola, Rwanda, Burundi, Uganda, and Kenya.

Much of the island of Madagascar was once covered with rainforest, but this is rapidly disappearing. Isolated from the mainland for 100 million years, the island has an incidence of endemic species that is one of the highest on Earth. Almost all of its forest birds and mammals (notably, the remarkable lemurs) are unique, as are nearly 75 percent of its plants.

In 1987, the World Resources Institute reported the closed forests of the Guinean and Zairean regions as covering, respectively, 172,670 and 1,705,420 square kilometers, a total of 1,878,090.[3] This report also estimates 103,000 square kilometers of rainforest in Madagascar. Norman Myers, in his book *The Primary Source*, estimates somewhat less: a total of 1,800,000 square kilometers of rainforest for all Africa, including 24,000 in Madagascar.[4] Of the WRI total for the mainland, Zaire accounts for 56.3 percent, Gabon 11.4 percent, Congo 10.9 percent, and Cameroon 9.5 percent. Nigeria has 3.2 percent, and the other nations even less.

HOW THE LAND IS USED

An estimated 70 percent of all Africans are subsistence farmers, and clearing for small farms—followed by degradation and erosion of the soil—accounts for about 70 percent of the continent's annual rainforest loss.[5] Most of the remaining loss is from commercial logging. It is important to put these factors into context. In particular, it is important that subsistence farmers not bear all the blame. Rather, they should be seen as among the many victims of endemic poverty that grips Africa and prevents it from flourishing.

Centuries of economic exploitation have left African nations dependent on the developed countries and international moneylenders of the Northern Hemisphere. Debt-servicing requirements, particularly crushing since the global rise in interest rates that began in the late 1970's, drive African nations to emphasize exports and quick profits over internal development (industry, transport, education, and social programs). This forces them to lay waste their own natural resources, or to allow foreign corporations in for the plunder. For example, commercial logging in Africa is controlled largely from abroad, as detailed below. In this light, excessive logging and agricultural overuse must both be seen as responses to the demands of global economic inequity and of survival—responses good for the short term only.

We note that Africa's situation differs somewhat from that of South and Central America, where cattle grazing, hydroelectric projects, and mining also play major roles in deforestation. These factors, along with clearing for plantations and the expansion of towns, do contribute to Africa's deforestation, but not substantially. Similarly, firewood collecting—often cited as a major cause in discussions of deforestation—is actually more of a problem in arid regions, where trees are already scarce and their loss keenly felt. In Africa, firewood collecting poses a major problem only in the dry savanna belt. The expansion of the Sahara southward is also confined to the savanna, as the rainforest's dense stands of trees naturally resist the desert's spread.

TRADITIONAL AGRICULTURE

The great majority of African farmers practice shifting cultivation, also known as slash-and-burn. Where population densities are low and access to land equitable, shifting cultivation can be an ecologically viable adaptation to the rainforest. As already noted, the Guinean rainforest region has long supported sub-Saharan Africa's densest population. But shifting cultivation requires extensive reserves of land set aside for fallow: up to 20 years may be required to restore the fertility of rainforest soils. As forest plots produce for only two or three years, the farmer will shift several times before returning to a fallow plot.

When such reserves are not available, farmers must either change to continuous cultivation on fixed sites, or must cut down more forest sooner. During the population explosion in Europe in the late Middle Ages, farmers developed methods of rotating crops, rather than fields, and entered into permanent cultivation. In Africa, cutting down forest has been the norm.

In Africa's traditional subsistence economy, much of the best land was reserved for farming. Such land tended to be surrounded by forest, which could recolonize the small fallow plots relatively easily. But in contemporary Africa, logging concessions, plantations, industries, and the physical expansion of towns have begun to preempt this territory. The expanding market economy has created an increasing pressure to sell land, most of which, traditionally, was held communally and was not alienable.

These forces are pushing small-scale farmers from prime farmlands, from plots surrounded by forest to plots adjoining other plots or the forest's edge. Such lands are drier and more exposed, and farming them is more damaging. In this light, some authors distinguish between traditional "shifting cultivation" and contemporary "shifted cultivators." Shifting cultivation does little permanent harm to the forest; shifted cultivators are a more serious problem.

Accelerating this situation is the rapid growth of population in West and Central Africa. In much of the Third World, food production per capita has increased over the past decade, but Africa's has decreased. The nations of the Guinean rainforest have among the world's highest population growth rates, averaging above 3 percent annually. These nations' combined population in 1987 was 146 million, and by 2020 it is expected to have swollen to 369.5 million. The five major nations of the Zairean rainforest had a combined population in 1987 of 48.1 million, which will increase by 2020 to 119.3 million.[6] But the epidemic spread in Central Africa of gonorrhea (which, untreated, as is frequently the case in this area, can cause sterility) and AIDS (the world's highest per capita incidence is in this region) may temper these figures.

It is important to understand that, despite the problems of "shifted cultivators" and population growth, most of West and Central Africa's subsistence farmers still have access to land. Much of the land in West and Central Africa was traditionally and still is held communally, by kinship groups and villages. These groups allot portions to their members according to need. The severe inequities of land ownership typical of other parts of the Third World do not as yet exist. As Herbert Kwesi Acquay, a Ghanaian environmental scientist and activist, told me, "It is not like South America, where you have a lot of landless people." Acquay estimates that, in Ghana, kin groups still hold title to more land than all other landholders combined, including the government.

The land thus owned includes the bulk of the rainforest. Although Europeans may think of the rainforest as unoccupied and wild, the indigenous people of Africa consider it a resource to be used and managed by humans, and the forest is crisscrossed by human boundaries. As a Nigerian friend told me, "No matter how far you go into the bush in my country, somebody owns that land."

This system of ownership is itself a result of the predominance of shifting cultivation as a subsistence base. To farmers, fallow forest plots remain valuable, and so usage rights on them are maintained tenaciously. Much of the Guinean rainforest, in fact, is not virgin— as we tend to imagine rainforest to be—but secondary or tertiary recolonizations of forest farms. Much more of the Zairean rainforest is virgin, but the traditional system of ownership there is similar to that of West Africa.

In sum, the key problem is not increasing population, the expanding market economy, or the shifting of farmers to poorer land. These may be seen as accelerating factors, but not, or at least not yet, as the immediate factors behind the rainforests' destruction. Rather, the crucial problem is that subsistence farmers are unable to convert to continuous cultivation on fixed sites. Continuous cultivation poses a new set of requirements that farmers are too poor to meet, and their debt-plagued governments cannot aid them enough.

CONVERSION TO CONTINUOUS CULTIVATION

Indigenous slash-and-burn cultivation takes advantage of tropical conditions effectively. Slashing and burning reduces the trees to highly nutritive ashes, which supplement the notoriously poor tropical soil for a few growing seasons. Traditional forest plots are somewhat protected from erosion by the surrounding trees. In the typical kitchen-garden patchwork of these plots, foodstuffs and cash crops, vines and shrubs and low trees and unpulled stumps mingle in messy abundance, shading and protecting each other. This imitates the rainforest's diversity and complexity. The countless interdependencies of its plants and animals, many of which are still mysterious to us, are to some extent retained.

Continuous cultivation is both more labor-intensive and more capital-intensive than traditional methods. It requires more diligent weeding, more extensive irrigation and erosion control. It requires cash for fertilizers, seeds or seedlings, draft animals, and machinery. For farmers new to it, it entails an element of unfamiliarity and risk. But subsistence farmers are constrained by their immediate circumstances. They are typically in debt for seeds and equipment, and for living expenses in the half of the year during which their crops are growing. The prices their produce can get in the market are rarely high enough to pull them from debt. Because they need to produce so much to both eat and fend off debt, they tend to overexploit their land.

In much of sub-Saharan Africa, women bear the burden of farmwork: by some estimates, up to 70 percent of the actual labor, including the hoeing, weeding, harvesting, transporting, and storing. In addition, their domestic tasks—food processing (pounding or grinding roots or grains into usable form), cooking, hauling water, and collecting firewood—require many hours every day, cutting seriously into time for farmwork. Increasingly, men migrate to the cities to work during much of the year, leaving their families behind. Yet, since in many African nations women cannot own land or take out loans, men remain in charge of farm planning, often deciding to plant cash crops—and pocketing the proceeds—rather than planting foodstuffs. Women therefore are reluctant or unable to invest in long-term, potentially risky improvements.[7]

Similarly, the increasing number of African tenant farmers have little incentive to invest the capital and labor necessary for long-term cultivation into land that belongs to others. When fertility drops, they can always move on.[8]

For successful conversion to intensive subsistence cultivation, these difficulties must be addressed. This requires cheap, dependable methods by which farmers can replicate the protective, restorative roles played by trees in the natural forest. Over the past two decades, agricultural scientists have developed methods that work, not by imitating alien forms of agriculture, but by adapting indigenous practices.

These methods, collectively known as agroforestry, basically consist of imitating the structure of the natural forest, with its diversity and intermingling of species. Food crops are planted together with tree species selected for various special qualities. The most important are fast-growing leguminous trees, such as Leucaena and Gmelina. (Legumes fix nitrogen in the soil, restoring its fertility.) At the same time, the trees protect the soil from erosion. They can also provide fodder for livestock, green manure for crops, and firewood for sale.

Because it is better suited to tropical conditions, agroforestry typically achieves a production more sustainable, cheaper, and often greater than transplants of high-input Northern-Hemisphere agriculture. But conveying these new methods from scientists' experimental fields and U.N. pilot programs to the masses of poor farmers has proved a difficult problem. The chronic poverty of African nations has often inhibited agroforestry programs, as well as other conservation efforts.

On the other hand, there have been some notable successes. Farmers readily adopt the new methods when suitable technologies and materials are available, and when short-term subsistence needs do not have to be compromised. Women have been at the forefront of many conservation efforts. One example is the Green Belt movement, a reforestation program set up by the National Council of Women of Kenya. Other important projects have been organized and carried out by local, volunteer, women-run mutual-aid societies. Such societies permeate African life, from dance clubs to investment pools; they represent one of the most positive forces in African conservation.

THE TIMBER INDUSTRY:
TREES AS A NONRENEWABLE RESOURCE

The tropical timber industry treats trees as a nonrenewable resource, like oil or gold, simply to be plucked from the earth. In the Northern

Hemisphere, intensively managed tree plantations dominate the industry, but most tropical logging is from virgin or uncultivated secondary forest. Worldwide, only about 10 percent of logged tropical forest is reforested.[9] The percentage for Africa is lower: of the dozen or so African nations with considerable rainforest, only one, Ghana, has any managed forest at all.[10] Treating the rainforest as a nonrenewable resource is in fact a self-fulfilling prophecy: once the trees are gone and the soil turns infertile, the forest in all of its diversity cannot be renewed.

The tropical timber industry is replete with wasteful practices. Only a few of the many potentially useful tropical woods are recognized in the global market, so only the best trees of a few species are singled out for cutting. Since rainforest trees are interwoven by their canopies and by vines, felling one prize giant pulls down its neighbors, opening a wide swath of ground to erosion. Much of such incidentally felled timber is wasted. Up to one-third of forest cover is removed just for logging roads, and more wood is lost to inefficient processing. Since profits are not being maximized, more timber is cut.

Historically, the timber industry has been confined to areas near rivers and roads, along which loggers can get in and wood can be hauled out. Increasingly, however, loggers are opening up the deepest forest areas. In fact, the first tracks into remote areas are often the roads blazed by huge logging corporations, which are soon followed by local, land-hungry farmers—a graphic example of the interplay of wealth and poverty underlying the rainforest's destruction. Such "development" has often been promoted by governments eager for the profits of timber.

The most striking example of such development in Africa is the Transgabon Railway, the continent's largest single construction project and its equivalent of the Transamazonian Highway. The Transgabon's avowed purpose is to civilize and commercialize Gabon's 215,000 square kilometers of mostly virgin rainforest. The World Bank studied the project in its proposal stages, and advised against it. But this negative recommendation was ignored by the 30 entities—

national governments, international funding agencies, and European logging companies—that financed the project. The first leg of the railway was completed in 1983, and Gabon's timber exports rose 16.7 percent that year.[11]

A LEGACY OF EXPLOITATION

The world market for exotic hardwoods may be traced in history at least as far back as the harvesting of the celebrated cedars of Mount Lebanon, praised in the Song of Solomon. (Mount Lebanon is now a stony hill.) The ancient Mediterranean knew the ebony of Africa and the teak of Southeast Asia. For centuries, African woods followed the trans-Saharan trade route to Europe, remaining luxury items. By the early 1700's, transatlantic trading had created a market in the New World for wood from Gambia, Senegal, and Côte d'Ivoire. Thus, African timber, along with gold, was integrally linked to Africa's prime export of the period: slaves. (The poet Coleridge, among others, called for a British boycott on mahogany because of its ties to slavery.) Logging increased markedly during the African colonial period, and, after the end of World War II, it boomed in the international market.

The modern timber industry is dominated by the huge tree plantations of the industrialized North, which account for about 85 percent by value of its annual trade. But the underdeveloped world's 15 percent amounts to billions of dollars annually, and includes most of the trade in hardwoods. The market favors the exporting of raw logs from the tropics to the North, because, as with most commodities, unprocessed products command lower prices and face fewer trade barriers. In 1984, raw logs comprised 59.5 percent of the value of Africa's timber exports.

Africa accounts for only a small fraction of the total global timber trade (1.6 percent by value in 1984, for example). But timber is extremely important to the economies of those African nations that export it. In 1982, timber accounted for 13 percent of Côte d'Ivoire's export earnings, 10.5 percent of Liberia's, and between 6.8 and 7.5 percent for Cameroon, Gabon, Congo, and Ghana.[12]

For most of the 1980's, Côte d'Ivoire and Gabon were, after Malaysia, Indonesia, and the Philippines, the world's largest tropical hardwood exporters. But Côte d'Ivoire will become a net wood importer within the next few years, as its remaining forests are destroyed, and Nigeria is already a net importer. Of the Guinean rainforest nations, only Liberia and Sierra Leone still have extensive tracts available for logging. Meanwhile, Gabon, Cameroon, and Zaire are stepping up their logging operations as the depletion of West Africa's rainforests causes the industry to shift southward.

Virtual client relationships exist between certain European nations, especially France and Germany, and their former African colonies. Most exported African hardwood winds up in European-made furniture and paneling. Japan, the world's largest wood importer, has recently begun exploring a major increase in imports from Central Africa. The United States (the second-largest importer by value, third by volume) imports little wood directly from Africa.

However, indirect imports by the United States may be greater than indicated in industry statistics, because the United States imports far more already processed products than any other nation or region, including a good amount of European-made furniture and paneling. And we should not underestimate the ramifications for Africa of the United States' powerful role in the modern global economy, particularly as a home for and subsidizer of many major international moneylenders.

African (as well as Southeast Asian) forestry is organized by the concession system, in which vast plots of land are deeded to corporations for exploitation. Such corporations are often foreign, and are often headquartered in the land of their host nation's former colonial master. British concessions dominated logging in Ghana and Nigeria until the early 1970's, when those nations began clamping down on the industry. French concessions thrive in Côte d'Ivoire, Gabon, and Central African Republic; German in Cameroon, and also in Congo and Zaire. Concessionaires often control such sawmills, pulp plants, and plywood and veneer factories as exist in their host countries. In short, much of the wealth generated by African timber winds up in foreign pockets.[13]

Some nations have begun taking steps to control the logging industry, such as banning the export of endangered species of trees, establishing minimum quotas of domestic processing by foreign logging concerns, or requiring that concessionaires contribute to reforestation. Also, certain international trade alliances have sought to redress some of the logging industry's chronic economic imbalances. These include STABEX (a fund within the European Development Fund) and the fledgling International Tropical Timber Organization, an advisory body of both timber-exporting and importing nations. The ITTO has included conservation principles in its articles of incorporation, but what policies it may recommend based on those principles, and how it proposes enforcing them, remains to be seen. The timber industry's potentially increased involvement in rainforest protection could place more of the burden on the logging companies and on developed countries that have the funds to do something about the situation.

PROTECTION OF THE FOREST

All contemporary African nations have established at least minimal restrictions on forest use. But the laws ostensibly establishing protected areas are full of ambiguities and concessions to the demands of loggers and the subsistence needs of the poor.[14] Indeed, the poverty of African nations subverts most attempts at enforcement of protective laws. Such ministries of conservation as exist are mere departments within ministries of forestry or agriculture, and subject to their philosophies and budgets. Africa's politicians are often blamed for failing to address environmental concerns adequately, but this can be seen as a result of the indebtedness that drives African economies.

Protected forests cover only about 69,200 square kilometers (including 57,900 square kilometers in Zaire), or 3.7 percent of the mainland's rainforests.[15] Because of the lack of funds, they cannot be patrolled against agricultural encroachment or poaching. A single elephant tusk may fetch $1,000 on the black market, more than a forest warden earns in a year. Illegal logging and timber smuggling also are rampant.

The incorporation of rainforests into national parks has sometimes proved problematic. Because much "unoccupied" rainforest is, or was, traditionally owned, governments have had to purchase park lands from their own people at great expense—where they have not appropriated it outright. They have found that the very idea of a national park—a reserve owned by the government and set apart from human use—is literally foreign, imported from North America and Europe. To many Africans, such reserves have appeared as the invention of their former oppressors. In fact, some colonial governments used reserves as a political weapon, to deprive unruly communities of their land. The creation of parks has forced some indigenous peoples to leave their ancestral lands or, if they have remained put, to eke out their living as tourist attractions. It has also been discovered—too late—that the ecological balance and beauty of certain areas made into parks had been maintained by the practices of the people who formerly lived there.[16]

Yet there are some promising signs. In Rwanda, the last wild homeland of the mountain gorilla, which is in rainforest, has been made into a preserve that funds itself through vigorously promoted but closely supervised tourism. Creative solutions such as this are likely the best hope for the preservation of any wild areas.

The problems facing Africa's rainforests are immense: farmers shifted onto poor land and unable to convert to better cultivation methods, population growth, the difficult position of African women, the expanding market economy and increasingly insecure land tenure, the inability of African governments to grant sufficient aid. Without sweeping changes addressing the underlying global inequities perpetuating African underdevelopment, it is hard to imagine that the steps necessary to save Africa's rainforests can be taken.

But for centuries, Africa's spiritual and cultural wealth has transcended its material poverty and historical vicissitudes. The African spirit is resilient. As the proverb puts it, "No condition permanent." This slogan, born in Nigeria's cities in the 1960's, in a tense time of rapid modernization, connotes a willingness to embrace fortune and misfortune alike, and to change. Today, at Africa's ancient holy shrines, praise singers raise chants to the orishas while accompanied by bands of electric guitars and synthesizers. Given a chance, farmers adopt new methods. Women pool time and labor to move earth and raise trees. If these human resources can be tapped and reinforced, much may be accomplished.

PART THREE

BAD MANAGEMENT

•

"If we believe absurdities, we shall commit atrocities."
VOLTAIRE

"but this, this is something other.
busy monster eats dark holes in the spirit world
where wild things have to go
to disappear
forever"
BRUCE COCKBURN
"IF A TREE FALLS"

•

7

EXTINCTION

Life in Peril

ANNE H. AND PAUL R. EHRLICH

•

Suppose you are about to fly to Brazil on Growthmania Airlines, an airline with the ambition of doubling its size every year until it eventually fills the entire universe. As you walk out to the jet, you notice a man on a ladder using a crowbar to pry rivets out of the airplane's wing. Curious, you ask him what he's doing. "I'm popping these rivets," he replies, "it's a good job. Growthmania pays me 50 cents for each one I pop, and they sell them for 75 cents each."

"You must be crazy," you reply. "You'll weaken the wing; the plane will crash."

"Relax, I've already taken 200 rivets out of this wing, and nothing has happened yet. Lots of planes fly with missing rivets. They build a lot of redundancy into jet aircraft, partly because they don't completely understand the materials and stresses involved, so nobody can prove that taking another rivet out will weaken the wing too much."

Now, if you have any sense, you'll walk back into the terminal, book a ticket on another airline, and, if you're civic-minded, report Growthmania to the aviation authorities. You know it is quite true that airplanes can and do fly safely with some missing rivets or some minor equipment malfunctions. But no one in his or her right mind would fly on an airline that continually removed rivets as a matter of policy, simply because no one can prove that popping one more rivet would lead to a wing's separating. The end of the rivet-popping trend is clear, but exactly when it will happen is obscure, both because the design of the wing is not completely understood and because the future stresses to which it will be subjected cannot be predicted.

Similarly, natural ecosystems—the communities of plants, animals, and microorganisms that live in an area and interact with each other and with their physical environments—are continually having their "rivets popped": populations and species of innumerable organisms are going extinct today, largely because of human intervention.[1] In the last quarter of this century alone, biologists have estimated, as many as 20 percent of the species existing at midcentury may disappear.[2]

No one can predict the exact consequences of those losses, just as the consequences of rivet-popping can't be predicted; exactly how an ecosystem works, what its most vulnerable elements are, and the stresses it may face in the future are unknown. But any biologist worth his or her salt can assure you that, if species are continuously removed, sooner or later a breakdown will occur.

Like the aircraft of responsible airlines, natural ecosystems ordinarily are under "progressive maintenance." The extinction of populations and species is a normal part of the evolutionary process, representing, in a sense, nature's failed experiments. When an organism with a particular genetic makeup leaves more offspring in the next generation than does another type, it's an evolutionary success story. Eventually, the less successful types go extinct. But these occasional extinctions are balanced naturally by the constant founding of new populations and the creation of new species through the evolutionary process of speciation—just as rivets are always being replaced and malfunctions corrected in properly maintained aircraft.

This process has been going on since life began on Earth perhaps four billion years ago, but during most of that time, more species were being created than were going extinct, ultimately producing the vast panoply of biotic diversity we see today. On a few occasions, each within a relatively short period of time, a "mass extinction event" occurred. At each of these times, a substantial portion of the existing complement of species disappeared from the fossil record.

The last such event, about 65 million years ago, finished off the dinosaurs, among other major groups of organisms.

Some biologists think that in the last episode at least, and possibly the others as well, the extinctions were caused by a cataclysmic event. A giant meteor or comet striking Earth's surface would have raised a huge cloud of dust high into the atmosphere. Lingering for many weeks or months, the dust would have prevented sunlight from reaching the surface. With no sunlight, green plants, algae, and bacteria could not carry out photosynthesis, and many of them perished, as did many of the animals dependent on them for food. Regardless of what caused the extinctions, however, or whether the losses occurred within months or over millennia, it certainly took many millions of years for the biosphere to recover from the losses.

THE ROLE OF HUMANS

Now, unfortunately, another global epidemic of extinctions is occurring on a similar scale. This time, though, the agent is not some uncontrollable extraterrestrial body colliding with Earth: it is the behavior of a large and expanding population of one organism, *Homo sapiens*. To make matters worse, the same activities that are causing the extinctions are, if anything, suppressing the processes that normally give rise to new species and populations. The current rate of species loss can be only roughly estimated, but biologists think that losses of bird and mammal species in the last few centuries have been about 5 to 50 times the normal rate, while toward the end of this century they have risen to about 40 to 400 times normal rates.[3]

What have human beings been doing to cause the demise of so many species and how long has this been going on? Even before agriculture was invented, expert human hunters seem to have exterminated many of the large mammals that inhabited Europe, Asia, and North and South America—animals such as a huge North American dromedary, giant sloths, mammoths, aurochs, and the saber-toothed cat. In historic times, people have been responsible for the loss of the dodo, the Tasmanian wolf, giant moas, the passenger pigeon, and Carolina parakeet. And today, we are all aware of endangered species such as rhinos, elephants, cheetahs, tigers, wolves, ferrets, and numerous birds.

For these and many other species, hunting has been the primary direct cause of disappearance. Many less-conspicuous organisms such as rare cacti and other plants have also been pushed toward extinction, if not always quite over the brink, by human collectors. And some species have been targeted for extermination because they were considered pests; many large cats, wolves, grizzly bears, and even elephants are in this category—although the market value of the tusks of one elephant could support an entire African village for a year.

Still other species, such as predatory birds at the top of a food chain and some fishes, have been decimated by poisons intended to kill pests or by spills of oil or other toxic substances. Indeed, we may be underestimating the role of poisoning from various kinds of pollution in causing extinctions. Acid rain may prove to be an effective, if insidiously slow exterminator—especially in combination with other agents such as climate change and other pollutants.

But by far the most effective way in which human beings have caused extinctions is indirectly, through habitat destruction. People have modified to some extent more than two-thirds of the planet's land area—including much of the most productive land—and have had a significant impact on aquatic ecosystems, both freshwater and oceanic. Of Earth's land, more than 10 percent has been converted to cropland; perhaps 2 percent is paved over in urban development, roads, airports, and so forth; 25 percent is pasture; and the 30 percent still forested is rather heavily exploited or is just tree farms—monocultures of exotic (non-native) tree species.

This vast replacement of natural ecosystems with human-dominated ones, as human population has expanded in a few centuries from several hundred million to five billion, has inevitably spelled disaster for the organisms that share the Earth with us. Millions of populations of unsung, inconspicuous organisms—small plants, vertebrates, insects, and other invertebrates—have been pushed to extinction, or at least have been drastically reduced in range, genetically impoverished, and thus endangered.

Current estimates suggest the loss of three or four species a day in tropical moist forests alone. Even though tropical forests are far and away the world's most species-rich ecosystems, as well as among the most endangered ones, this is surely a gross underestimate. Earth's remaining tropical forests are being cut down or significantly degraded at the rate of 25 hectares per minute—a loss of an area about the size of North Carolina every year. There simply is no way to count the losses of myriads of still undescribed tiny plants, insects (especially the millions of species of beetles dwelling in the forest canopy), nematodes, mites, fungi, and other obscure creatures that have been displaced. And further losses occur as vast unbroken tracts of natural area are reduced to small fragments that simply cannot support the variety of species that large ones do.

The change from a natural ecosystem to a human-directed one also commonly results in reduced productivity. Green plants and other photosynthesizing organisms have the ability to capture and use the energy in sunlight and convert water and carbon dioxide into carbohydrates; those materials are the source of energy on which virtually all other organisms, including ourselves, depend for life. This energy is known as net primary production (NPP); it is the sum of the energy produced through photosynthesis minus what the photosynthesizing organisms use for their own growth and life processes.

In just the last few decades, the conversion of forests and grasslands to cities, cropland, or pastures, and other processes such as desertification have reduced the worldwide NPP on land by an estimated 13 percent.[4] At the same time, the share of the planet's terrestrial NPP used directly by human beings and their domesticated animals (as food, fodder, and fiber, including wood) is about 4 percent; from the oceans the share is about 2 percent.

This seems modest enough, although disproportionate for one of as many as 30 million species with which we share the planet's bounty. But that 4 percent by no means accounts for all our impact on terrestrial life. By altering natural ecosystems or replacing them

cial ones, we change the flora and fauna and divert most of
's energy into a different array of organisms (some of which
sts). Some NPP is destroyed in human-caused fires, and
some is simply wasted.

When this cooption and diversion are calculated, humanity accounts for nearly 30 percent of the NPP on land and about 19 percent globally (including that 2 percent of the oceans' NPP). If the
roughly 13 percent of potential NPP on land that has been lost because of human action is included in the calculation, human impact
on terrestrial systems rises to nearly 40 percent, and that on the entire
biosphere to about 25 percent.

Small wonder an epidemic of extinctions is occurring. *Homo sapiens* has literally taken the food from the mouths of other species
and the homes out from under their feet (or roots). We use, lose, re-
direct, or spoil 40 percent of the energy produced by all of Earth's
land ecosystems and wonder why our favorite birds, butterflies, or
flowers are hard to find these days. Perhaps more relevant, the persistent and prevalent human poverty in certain regions is reinforced by
both the reductions in productivity caused by the degrading or replacing of ecosystems and the limits to possible photosynthetic production in any one area.

THE IMPORTANCE OF BIODIVERSITY

Why is it so important to preserve species or different varieties of
plants and animals, let alone microorganisms we can't even see?
Many people want to preserve a particular species just because it is
beautiful or interesting. People have probably always appreciated the
beauty of such organisms as flowers, butterflies, and birds. The advent of the microscope enabled us to see and appreciate even more.

In the last century, it has also increasingly been felt that at least
domesticated animals had rights and deserved to be treated well. Indeed, the gradual extension of "rights," exemplified at one extreme
by animal rights activists, has also led to a belief that other organisms
have a right to existence equal to that of human beings and that so-

ciety has an obligation (because of its power to destroy) to preserve and protect other species—a stewardship duty.[5] •

The aesthetic and philosophical reasons for preserving other life-forms besides ours are convincing to some people, but not the majority. There are hardheaded types who heed only pocketbook issues. If they could see the living things around them as resources—rather than just part of their surroundings, of no more consequence than roadside pebbles—they would find it easier to understand why preserving all species is essential for the lasting well-being of just one. All our food and the products we use every day originally came wholly or in part from a plant, animal, or microbe: consider for instance wool, silk, or cotton clothing and furnishings, paper, medicines, spices, rubber tires, oils in cosmetics and lotions, paints and dyes, shell buttons, ivory keyboards, or wooden houses and furniture.

• Tropical forests in particular are rich potential sources of valuable foods, medicines, and products of all kinds—if we don't destroy them before their potential can be discovered. When we selectively remove species and damage or destroy entire ecosystems (as in deforestation), resources of enormous potential value are lost. •

Tropical forests, more than other kinds of ecosystems, remain un-catalogued treasure houses. Of the approximately 1.4 million species that are known to science, only about one-third are in tropical forests. This is mainly because science has explored those forests less extensively than other environments. Although tropical forests occupy only about 7 percent of the Earth's land surface, they probably contain the great majority of the estimated 10 million to 30 million species on the planet. Of the tropical species so far recognized by Western science, most are little known and their potential economic value is yet to be explored.

Another argument for the special value of rainforests is the high level of endemism—the occurrence of a species in only one or a few localities—that exists there. Forests in temperate zones, such as those throughout eastern North America, tend to contain the same dozen or so species of trees and a similarly limited array of smaller plants, mammals, and insects. But destruction of any moderate-sized tract of tropical forest is quite likely to cause the extinction of several species that exist nowhere else.

The human population today is increasing rapidly and is expected by demographers to double its current size before growth stops. About 20 percent—over a billion people—are chronically hungry and living in "absolute poverty."•Since humanity is quickly depleting its resources, the logic of preserving species that could become valuable resources should be clear even to confirmed urban canyon dwellers.• Yet even that argument is not persuasive enough to withstand the economic pressures behind the loggers, land-clearing settlers, and developers who continue to convert land to "more profitable" uses.

Yet there is an even more compelling, if much less widely understood reason to preserve other life-forms besides their intrinsic and potential economic values.•Natural ecosystems, with their component species, are our life-support system? Since the Earth was formed over four billion years ago, other species have played an essential part in creating the conditions that permit human beings to exist and survive. Natural ecosystems are still actively involved in maintaining those conditions; they provide essential supporting services to civilization that we cannot do without and could not adequately replace even where we know how to do so.

Among these indispensable services are: maintaining the quality and composition of the atmosphere; moderating climates and weather; supplying fresh water; replenishing soils, cycling nutrients essential for life, and disposing of wastes; pollinating plants (including numerous crops); controlling the vast majority of pests and vectors of disease; providing food from the sea; and maintaining that vast "genetic library" of organisms from which has been drawn the very basis of civilization.

Most often we are not aware of these essential services until we lose them. People have noticed that the disappearance of a forest has often been followed by the drying up of formerly dependable streams in the area. When the forested area in the Virunga Mountain National Park in Rwanda was reduced by 40 percent in the 1970's, for instance, several streams that had provided water to the rest of the intensively farmed nation disappeared.

Similar observations have been made throughout the world, especially when mountain watershed forests were removed. A forest particularly, but any kind of vegetative cover, tends to soak up, slowly release, and recycle moisture through the atmosphere. Rainwater that falls on the Amazon forest, for example, is recycled an average of nine times as the moisture-laden air mass passes across the continent. With no forest to absorb and respire it, most of the water would simply run off the bare ground, washing away thin topsoil and flooding the river. Further downwind, the air would be dry, producing drought.

Deforestation or removal of other kinds of vegetative cover (such as scrubland or savanna) thus commonly leads to intensification of both droughts and floods. The frequent catastrophic floods of lowland India and Bangladesh are directly traceable to the deforestation of the Himalaya mountains in Nepal. The diminished river flow in the Nile in recent years, which threatens the agriculture of overpopulated Egypt, is due to deforestation in the watershed of the Nile's headwaters.

The same process is responsible for silting up the Aswan Dam, which will be rendered useless in a few decades. That silt is the result of accelerated soil erosion from the same deforested hillsides, a universal problem. Worldwide soil losses from erosion—much of it from deforestation and devegetation as well as from careless farming technologies and overgrazing—are an estimated 26 billion tons per year.[6] This is a loss civilization cannot afford. Soil erosion, although it can be temporarily masked by increasingly heavy applications of fertilizer, will sooner or later lead to declines in agricultural yields.

Desertification is the five-dollar word that covers the entire process of devegetation, soil loss, local climate change, and loss of productivity in arid regions; and the resultant degradation of the land is not reversible in practical terms. The impoverishment of the people dependent on desertified systems is among the great tragedies of this era. A prime example, and a possible harbinger for other vulnerable areas, is the continent-wide drought and famine in sub-Saharan Africa.

When we become aware of such changes, we can begin to have an inkling of our dependence on natural systems. When pest problems get out of control, and crops suffer attacks from blights and rusts, we notice the loss of pest- and disease-control services. A change in the weather (rarely for the better) is another clue that services have been disrupted. Most often, after deforestation, weather downwind becomes noticeably warmer and drier. Such changes can occur in any region, from the equator to the poles, but they are almost always most severe in the tropics.

Although these lessons have been clear since ancient times, when Greek philosophers recorded their observations and connected what they saw with the impoverishment of the land, they never seem to remain learned. The demise of any number of once-flourishing civilizations, from the Mesopotamians to the Khmers, can be traced to a failure to maintain ecosystem services. Perhaps every society must learn for itself that massive conversion of landscapes, the pollution of waters, and other abuses lead to losses of productivity in the long run.

Usually the motivating influence is a short-term gain or a very localized change made without considering the impact if many similar changes were made on a large scale (such as incremental forest-clearing for a series of farms). Nature most often is not vanquished in one mighty battle, but is taken in a series of minor skirmishes. Today we have a global civilization, a network of increasingly interdependent societies, heedlessly destroying ecosystems everywhere, one bit at a time.

If the ancient lessons are not applied soon, humanity just might follow the dinosaurs to oblivion. Only someone who did not know what rivets are for would knowingly patronize an airline with the rivet-popping practices of Growthmania, and only such a person would want to ride on Spaceship Earth when the rivets in its ecosystems were always being removed. But here we are, with no other spaceline offering transport, so let's educate the world to save those rivets.

8

INDIGENOUS PEOPLES

The Miner's Canary
for the Twentieth Century

JASON W. CLAY

•

~~~~~~

Miners going into the mines often used to carry small birds, such as canaries, which were highly sensitive to the buildup of toxic gases. If the birds died, the miners quickly fled. Today, the world's 500 million indigenous peoples, living in some 15,000 distinct groups, are the miner's canary; and the Earth—particularly the tropical rainforest—is the mine. That the canary is dying is a warning that the dominant cultures of the world have become toxic to the Earth. In this case, however, we cannot flee the mine.

This century—considered by many to be an age of enlightenment, progress, and development—has witnessed more genocides, ethnocides, and extinctions of indigenous peoples than any other in history.[1] In recent years, no groups have been more threatened than those living in the rainforests. In Brazil alone, an average of one Indian culture per year has disappeared since the turn of the century. The survival of such groups depends on the survival of the forests;[2] and the policies and lifestyles of dominant cultures are destroying both.

STATE BUILDING: LOST CULTURES, NEW EMPIRES

States are the largest and most powerful political units in the modern world. Most of the world's more than 160 states have been created since World War II, and the boundaries of the vast majority have been created by Westerners to fulfill their own economic and political interests.

In contrast, most indigenous peoples—or "nations," as many prefer to be called—have existed for centuries. An indigenous nation is characterized by its distinct language, culture, history, defined territory, and political organization. Its boundaries are defined by natural geographical features and by traditions that have been rooted in the land for generations.

But today, indigenous peoples everywhere find themselves living in states that they had no hand in creating, controlled by groups that do not represent their interests. Many indigenous nations also find themselves split between states. The arbitrary boundaries of modern states do not define "nation-states" but, rather, little empires,[3] each of which encompasses dozens if not hundreds of tribal groups.

The loss of indigenous cultures around the world is neither accidental nor historically inevitable. Modern states, and the citizens who hold power in them, covet land and resources that have long been managed by indigenous peoples. The states and individuals who can ultimately claim control of these resources stand to gain considerably; and since they have the power to do so, they persecute and kill the indigenous peoples who stand in their way.

There appears to be no correlation between ideology and state efforts to centralize power and control resources. Indigenous peoples are attacked by states representing the left, right, and center of the political spectrum—religious as well as secular. The size of the target is not determinative either. Some persecuted groups are tiny minorities; others are majorities.

Many indigenous peoples live in some of the most remote and least explored areas of the world, areas containing Earth's last "unclaimed" resources.[4] Since World War II, the increasing awareness of the finite nature of the Earth's resources has led to a relentless assault on the land and resources of indigenous peoples. Many Third World states are interested in exploiting these resources to pay their foreign debts. At least half of these debts, on average, have resulted from the purchase of weapons, some of which are used to remove indigenous peoples from resource-rich regions.

Modern technology in the form of helicopters, satellite surveys, and telecommunications equipment has enabled states and corporations to make detailed surveys of the Earth. Even the most isolated indigenous societies are now being probed in a one-sided, involuntary exposure to the rest of the world. Once an item of value—trees, minerals, agricultural land, oil, hydroelectric potential—is identified, the real onslaught begins. At this point the canary begins showing signs of stress.

For example, in late 1987 gold was found on the lands of the 8,000 forest-dwelling Yanomami Indians of northern Brazil. Within eight months nearly 30,000 Brazilian prospectors had invaded the region to seek their fortunes. The government claimed that it could not prevent this massive, illegal invasion. It also admits that at least one Yanomami a day has died since the gold rush began—but the figure could be two to three times that high.

Prior to World War II, smaller forest-dwelling indigenous groups attempted to avoid sustained contact with the outside world by moving into even more isolated areas. Although this strategy worked to some extent (often, however, precipitating conflict between such groups), today no truly isolated places remain.

For smaller indigenous societies mere contact with outsiders can be devastating. Although the largest groups living in the Amazon contain tens of thousands of people, most number only a few hundred. Brazil's 200 ethnic groups, for example, include only 220,000 Indians. Historically, in North, Central, and South America, contact with "civilization" caused the deaths of 60 to 90 percent of the inhabitants. Most died from common diseases such as influenza, measles, malaria, or venereal disease introduced into their areas by colonists.[5] Most who died never had direct contact with outsiders, but were infected by neighboring tribes.

Besides the diseases that mere contact brings, even greater hazards follow state-led development. Many indigenous peoples are poisoned or even killed by the unannounced and unexplained introduction of new technologies into their areas.[6] The plants, animals, and even the water that Amazonian Indians depend upon are now being contaminated by the mercury used in gold mining. Nambiquara Indians in Brazil have been poisoned by drinking water stored in empty 2,4-D and 2,4,5-T herbicide cans that were sold to them for that purpose by neighboring ranchers. Fishermen in Ghana use a lindane-based insecticide to "catch" fish, unaware of its effects on the Brong or Ewe peoples who live downstream or on the urban consumers of the fish. In Sarawak, Malaysia, natives who take jobs with logging companies are not told of the health hazards—chain saws, falling trees, and shifting loads of logs—associated with the logging industry.[7]

We in the industrialized states are finally learning how to avoid poisoning our environment and ourselves. But the threats that we have successfully avoided often are transferred to indigenous peoples. Our attempts to reduce pollution frequently result in the export of hazardous industries or wastes to countries where they are dumped on unsuspecting peoples. In West Africa, the president of Benin was paid recently to allow European firms to dump toxic waste in his country. He was at least somewhat aware of the health risks posed by the waste, so he had the dump site located near the land of an ethnic group opposed to him. Only international criticism stopped the project.

Beyond being infected, poisoned, and mutilated, indigenous peoples are also discriminated against, denied political voice, deprived of their lands, and displaced. Some of the larger groups, in a desperate attempt to defend themselves and their land, have taken up arms; more than 80 percent of the armed conflicts in the world today are between nations and states. Most of the casualties in such conflicts are indigenous civilians, primarily women, children, and the elderly—more than five million since World War II. In addition to the deaths, more than 75 million indigenous peoples have been displaced as a result of such conflicts, and 13 million more have fled to neighboring states as refugees.[8]

Such conflicts did not occur only in the distant past. In 1988 more than 200,000 indigenous people were killed, and more than two million more—that we know of—forced from their homes in Brazil, Burma, Burundi, Ethiopia, Guatemala, Indonesia, the Philippines, and Thailand. In most instances the violence is not random: it is directed by states against indigenous peoples.

Due to the large numbers of people displaced, state versus nation conflicts are also the main cause of famine. Most of the million or so famine-related deaths in Ethiopia from 1984 to 1987 resulted from government policies aimed at relocating farmers from distinct indigenous nations into new villages where their movements and food production could be controlled by the state.[9] In addition to killing more than 100,000 people, Ethiopia's forced relocation programs have moved more than ten million people and are now the leading cause of famine in the country. They are also one of the major causes of deforestation, causing the destruction of 8 percent of Ethiopia's remaining forests in one year.

More often than not, state versus nation conflicts do not take the form of conventional wars or rely on the use of conventional weapons. In the 1960's, Brazilian colonists dropped grenades from helicopters on Indian villages and gave measles-infested blankets to newly contacted tribes as a way of creating "unoccupied" land, which they then could claim. In 1974, six ranchers in Colombia were acquitted of murdering Cuiva Indians living in that country's Amazon region on the defense that killing Indians in the rainforest was the same as killing animals. In Burma, U.S.-provided herbicides for opium eradication have been sprayed from helicopters on the household gardens of those who dwell in the country's rainforests.

THE LEGALITIES OF MAINTAINING THE EMPIRE: BUILDING THE CANARY'S CAGE

Most states are, at best, indifferent to what happens to indigenous peoples. Many states want such groups to disappear quietly, but others are more active in their attempts to eliminate or assimilate indigenous peoples through legal manipulations, which can take many forms.

In Brazil, members of ten indigenous groups were killed during 1988 by miners, ranchers, construction workers, farmers, timber merchants, policemen, and local and state politicians, none of whom have been brought to justice.[10] The government does not attempt to prevent or prosecute such actions, for two apparent reasons. First, Indians are not regarded as people. Legally, they are not citizens of Brazil; they are "incompetent," having the same legal status as retarded people. As long as they choose to remain Indians and hold resources communally, they have no rights as citizens. Second, indigenous peoples are in the way. They are seen as an obstacle to Brazil's development, or more specifically, to generating the resources the state needs to pay its debts. Furthermore, it is assumed that the inevitable destiny of the country's indigenous peoples is to become Brazilian; that Indian identity belongs in the dustbin of history.

States also attempt to limit the legitimate rights of indigenous peoples to engage in debate on issues that are important to their own survival or to the survival of the forests upon which they depend. Recently two Kayapo Indians from Brazil came to the United States to speak at a rainforest conference. Later they were invited to Washington, DC, to meet with members of Congress and officials at the World Bank and explain their opposition to proposed hydroelectric dams that would flood their lands. Upon returning to Brazil the Kayapo were charged with committing subversive activities, i.e., practicing free speech in the U.S. Their true crime, however, was obstructing a $500 million loan to Brazil that could be used to pay part of the interest due on Brazil's huge foreign debt.

In some countries indigenous peoples have rights to land but not to other resources that are necessary for them to continue or improve their way of life. For example, indigenous peoples frequently own the land that they occupy but not the trees on it; yet, without the forest, the land is virtually worthless. Members of the Penan and other indigenous groups in Malaysia have been arrested and are standing trial for blockading logging roads to prevent the clear-cutting of their ancestral forests. But, as in many countries, Malaysian government officials are major investors in the timber companies that are destroying the Penan's land and culture. In most countries indigenous peoples also have no mineral or water rights, so that mines or dams can destroy the resources necessary for a viable way of life, which is the situation that the Kayapo face.

In many countries, state policies are intended to force indigenous peoples to destroy their communal landholding patterns and systems of resource management. In such countries, land that is not "improved" is not owned. In rainforest areas, improving the land often means cutting the trees and practicing modern agriculture. In addition, the banking laws of such states do not allow indigenous people to borrow money against communal property, which effectively keeps indigenous peoples from altering their ways of life or forces individuals to push for the privatization of communal property rights. In all these ways, considerable pressure is placed upon indigenous peoples and the forest resources upon which they depend.

Once robbed of their means of livelihood, the land and its resources, indigenous peoples are forced to adapt to state societies whose language and customs they do not know. Without educational, technical, or other skills, indigenous groups generally suffer from permanent poverty, political marginality, and cultural alienation. Their societies disintegrate, and the surviving individuals become the flotsam and jetsam of the modern world. Debt-ridden states, as they unravel the social net of indigenous communities, create dependent populations that they can ill afford.

Contact between indigenous peoples and the rest of the world is a *fait accompli*. Extermination, however, is not. Indigenous societies recognize the benefits of increased interaction with the state society and the international economic system, but they want to preserve their own resource base and identity in the process. Furthermore, it is increasingly clear that indigenous peoples know best how to live within and yet sustain the most fragile areas of the Earth. If such regions are to be incorporated into the global economy without being destroyed, we must first learn and then adapt the indigenous methods of sustainable resource management.[11]

STATE DEVELOPMENT VERSUS NATION DEVELOPMENT

For some people, the right of indigenous people to exist is an open and shut moral issue. Unless such people infringe upon the rights of others, it is argued, they should have the right to practice their culture or retain or abandon aspects of it as they choose. Others argue, however, that development and state building will eventually create a better world (this can best be described as trickle-down equality). These people argue that to make an omelet, one must break a few eggs. And so it is the canary's eggs that are broken.

Though rarely included in development planners' calculations, there are tremendous costs incurred by displacing or dismantling the cultures of indigenous peoples. In the same way that they convert lush rainforests into depleted land, development and state-building activities inevitably convert self-sufficient indigenous populations into refugees and displaced people. These groups become dependent not only on the states that create or receive them, but on the international community as a whole.

Refugees, displaced people, and famine victims not only divert scarce resources from more appropriate development activities; frequently they are forced to degrade the environment in order to survive. Most Third World countries cannot repay their foreign debts, much less provide social services to uprooted and impoverished people or fund reclamation projects for devastated ecosystems. Thus, the destruction of rainforests and indigenous cultures not only squanders resources and destroys lives, it mortgages the future of generations to come.

Furthermore, top-down development programs—those funded by bilateral or multilateral agencies and implemented in the Third World—do more harm than good. They take the initiative and responsibility for improving a group's livelihood out of its hands and make it dependent on outside ideas and funding, all the while ignoring the fact that indigenous peoples have been managing their resources on their own for generations.

What indigenous peoples need most of all is the enforcement of their legal rights; and much could be gained by including indigenous peoples in development efforts if their constitutional rights were guaranteed. As examples from around the world have demonstrated, resource conservation is most successful where people have guaranteed land tenure and control over their livelihood, especially those who depend solely upon and know the resources of the forest best. Both development and conservation would be better served if states reinforced rather than undermined local systems of tenure and resource use. The next section cites some examples.

Indigenous people have an intimate knowledge not only of the specific flora and fauna of their areas, but of the soils and climatic factors that affect production as well. This knowledge is the major difference between tribal peoples and immigrant newcomers who lack an adequate understanding of the forest's processes, or government planners whose knowledge is based on controlled experiments, textbooks, and bureaucratic paper-pushing.

The most appropriate development activities, then, could well result from developing indigenous nations rather than destroying them. Such efforts would complement existing indigenous resource management strategies, health care, or educational systems, rather than imposing alien models. "Nation development" would require assistance agencies, whether international, state, or nongovernmental, to work through local indigenous organizations. It also would require indigenous organizations to be in charge of projects in their areas, with outsiders providing advice and only limited funds to help a group over a specific hurdle. Appropriate development, in other words, would maintain or promote self-sufficiency and self-reliance.

INDIGENOUS PEOPLES' DEVELOPMENT:
THE CANARY HAS FOUND ITS VOICE

A number of forest-dwelling indigenous peoples have begun to assert their rights over land and resources.[12] Some groups have been so successful that they call into question a number of assumptions about development, sustainable resource management, social change, and even the way people will live together in the future. The few examples that follow demonstrate the wide range of appropriate development strategies employed by these peoples to protect their ways of life. In each instance, there is a behind-the-scenes role for international organizations but the indigenous groups call the shots. Each of these examples has provided a model for other groups desiring to initiate similar projects.

Parks, Tourism, and the Kuna Indians

The Kuna Indians of Panama recently established the world's first internationally recognized forest park created by an indigenous group. The reserve not only provides revenue to the Kuna from tourists who come to learn about the rainforest, and from the sale of research rights to scientists, it also protects and preserves an important part of the Kuna's heritage.

The Kuna control access to research sites and demand reports from all researchers before they leave the area. They also require each scientist to hire a Kuna assistant to accompany him or her throughout their stay, which allows the Kuna to patrol remote areas while protecting and learning from the scientists. In this way, they have established a precedent for other indigenous groups, and even countries, regarding research undertaken on their land.

Indian-run Education Programs Among the Shuar

The Shuar live in remote rainforest villages in Ecuador's eastern Amazon region. Within living memory, Shuar participated in intratribal warfare and head hunting. As they came into contact with the expanding state society, they put their differences aside and formed the Shuar Indian Federation, one of the strongest indigenous organizations in Latin America.

They soon realized that their children needed an education if they were to compete in Ecuador. In order to keep their children at home, maintain their traditions, and avoid assimilation, the Shuar have set up a radio education program. Each remote village has its own portable receiver and a trained teacher's assistant. Not only do the children excel in Ecuador's formal education requirements, they also study Shuar history, resource management, and science in the Shuar language. The radios also provide adult education and news about events outside the region.

CRIC—Environmental Restoration in Southern Colombia

CRIC, composed of 56 Indian communities in Cauca, Colombia, was formed in 1971 to protect Indian lands, resources, culture, and human rights in a region whose forest cover was destroyed by mines and cattle ranches. In 1984 CRIC began a forestry program with three tree nurseries, run by local communities, to supply seedlings to communities that agree to plant a minimum of 1,000 trees, all native species. One community has completed nine reforestation programs, and nearby peasant communities have sought advice about setting up similar programs. Now the major objectives are watershed reforestation and the planting of shade and fruit trees, as well as stands for firewood. CRIC's member communities realize that reforestation is a long-term project. They have come to believe, however, that such a commitment to forests is essential to the future viability of Indians in the area.

LET THE CANARY SING

Indigenous peoples throughout the world have been quick to see the advantages of becoming part of the world economic and political system. The groups that have survived contact and adapted successfully have sought to maintain their identity while picking and choosing from what is available from the outside. Most realized long ago that they, like the rest of us, can maintain their identity while incorporating new ideas or aspects of material culture. Indigenous peoples realize, too, that they can often use advice about the implications of the adoption of certain technologies. Ultimately, such groups, like ourselves, must have the freedom to make their own decisions and to accept responsibility for the consequences.

Within the next few decades, the fate of the world's remaining indigenous peoples, the fragile environments they occupy, and the valuable knowledge that they embody could well be decided once and for all. A number of individuals, corporations, and states are already pursuing their own "final solutions." The 20th century will be remembered either as the century when we destroyed much of the Earth's genetic and cultural diversity, or the century when peoples learned to live together and share their knowledge in order to maintain the diversity upon which we all depend. Working together, we can make a world of difference.

9

MULTILATERAL
DEVELOPMENT
BANKS
AND TROPICAL
DEFORESTATION

BRUCE RICH

•

Deforestation in the moist tropics is not merely a local phenomenon, but is inextricably linked to national and international institutions, especially those affecting economic development policy and financing. The most important institutions in this field are the four multilateral development banks (Mdbs). The Mdbs are unique public international institutions that loan more than $25 billion annually for development projects in 151 countries. Besides the World Bank, which lends to all developing areas of the globe, there are three regional Mdbs operating specifically in the regions for which they are named: the Inter-American Development Bank (IDB), Asian Development Bank (ADB), and African Development Bank (AFDB). The Mdbs, especially the World Bank, play a critical role in financing development activities and influencing development policies that affect tropical forests.

The four Mdbs are governed by executive boards of directors, which must approve every loan and every major policy. The directors represent individual member countries or groups of countries, and their voting power is roughly proportional to the financial contribution of the country they represent. For example, the executive director of the World Bank, an American, has by far the greatest voting power on its board—about 19 percent; and the four other major donor countries, Japan, West Germany, the United Kingdom, and France have voting shares ranging between 4.8 percent and 7 percent.

Over half of MDB loans in recent years have gone to support projects in sectors that can seriously affect tropical forests: agriculture, rural development, energy (mainly hydroelectric dams), and transportation (mainly roadbuilding). The projects and policies of the MDBs have a much greater ecological impact on the developing world than even their huge loan commitments indicate. For one thing, funds lent by the MDBs are complemented by even greater sums provided by recipient countries, other development agencies, and private banks. For every dollar they lend, the MDBs attract about two extra dollars through co-financing arrangements.

Secondly, the MDBs are a critical force in influencing the whole pattern and direction of economic development in tropical forest countries. Their loan conditions can be extremely specific and often have policy impacts that go far beyond the implementation of a single project. The World Bank prepares highly influential economic analyses of a country that shape planning discussions among the development banks, other aid agencies, commercial banks, and governments. Such direct policy leverage is becoming increasingly important for the MDBs. Indeed, these "structural adjustment" and "sector" loans seek to alter entire national economies so that they will be more integrated with international markets and more export oriented. Exports commonly are linked to the use of forested lands.

The adverse environmental impacts of MDB-financed activities on tropical forests have been well documented for over a decade and a half. More than half of the Earth's remaining tropical moist forests are in Latin America; one-third in Brazil alone. In certain parts of this region, multilateral loans for agricultural colonization and energy and mining infrastructure have abetted a scale and rate of deforestation that are without parallel anywhere else on the planet. Another 20 percent of the tropical forest biome is located in Southeast Asia, with Indonesia alone containing nearly 10 percent of the Earth's remaining rainforests and Malaysia approximately another 3 percent. In this region, too, loans from the World Bank and ADB have played a significant role in the conversion of tropical forests in recent years. The two countries that contain nearly half the Earth's remaining rainforests—Brazil and Indonesia—are the second and third largest cumulative borrowers from the World Bank, and the biggest borrowers from the IDB and ADB, respectively. Thus, multilateral banks play a key role in influencing the economic and political dynamics of deforestation, a matter of the highest concern for all who wish to ensure the future of life and the biosphere.

PROJECTS AND THEIR IMPACTS IN SEVERAL SECTORS

Agriculture

MDB agricultural policies and projects contribute to accelerating deforestation in at least three major ways. First, the capital-intensive, high-input model of modern, mechanized agriculture promoted by national governments is reenforced by MDB support. This pushes smaller farmers out and concentrates land in large holdings where labor needs are reduced. Given the absence of effective land reform in most tropical countries, the major escape valve for this displaced population is migration, either to increasingly overcrowded large cities, or to frontier areas, principally tropical forests.

Second, MDB lending to tropical forest countries for agriculture promotes both economic inefficiency and ecological destruction: governments use these loans to subsidize development activities that encourage deforestation. In many cases, forest conversion likely would not occur if not for these subsidies, the effects of which are made worse by laws that base land ownership on clearing. Moreover, the dynamics of land speculation and profiteering in highly inflationary economies—Brazil is a leading example—guarantee that much of the international financing of agriculture in tropical forest nations directly or indirectly fuels virtual deforestation machines, unless stringent regulations are enforced.

Third, the MDBs are continuing to finance agricultural projects that directly cause deforestation, particularly forest colonization schemes and cattle ranching. Each of these is discussed below.

Cattle Projects

Over the past 20 years the MDBs have financed cattle projects on a large scale, especially in Latin America and Africa. Though MDB support for livestock was greatest in the 1970's, both the World Bank and the IDB continue to finance the livestock sector. Livestock projects and credits have contributed both indirectly and directly to accelerating deforestation. In many areas, large, consolidated cattle ranches have replaced smaller, subsistence-oriented farming, contributing greatly to concentrated land ownership and the migration of uprooted people to tropical forest areas. In other regions, large areas of pristine tropical forest have been destroyed for cattle pastures.

Livestock development is one of the least suitable and most wasteful of all conceivable development alternatives for tropical forest regions. In Latin America pastures occupy huge areas of land with low concentrations of cattle per hectare. Worse, pastures in former tropical forest areas often become wasteland after a few years because of declining soil nutrients, weed invasions, overgrazing, and soil compaction. Finally, livestock projects generate very little employment compared with most investment alternatives.

Colonization Projects

The environmental and economic justifications for MDB-financed forest colonization projects are even more dubious. A decade and a half ago, a study of 24 colonization projects in Latin America noted that "few spheres of economic development have a history of, or a reputation for, failure to match that of government-sponsored colonization in humid tropical zones."[1] A 1988 survey of several settlement projects in the Amazon showed an average rate of attrition among colonists that exceeds 65 percent.[2] The major ecological factor in their abysmal performance is the preponderantly poor quality of soil in tropical moist forests. Public health problems, particularly malaria, also take a toll beyond the most pessimistic expectations of planners.

Given the relentless record of failure for agricultural settlement in tropical forests, it is appalling that the MDBs have continued to support such projects substantially over the past two decades, and indeed made some of their largest and most destructive investments in this area in the early and mid-1980's—at a time when evidence of the collapse of such resettlement schemes was overwhelming.

One of the most notorious and destructive examples of such MDB-financed resettlement programs is Transmigration in Indonesia, for which the World Bank alone committed some $560 million in seven separate loans between the mid-1970's and late 1980's. Transmigration is the most ambitious resettlement scheme of the postwar era, involving the eventual resettlement of millions of people: from the densely populated inner islands of Indonesia, such as Java, Lombok, and Bali, to pristine tropical forest areas sparsely inhabited by indigenous peoples in the Indonesian outer island provinces such as Kalimantan (Borneo) and Irian Jaya (Western New Guinea). According to the World Bank's own estimates, 500,000 families were relocated by the government of Indonesia to forest regions in the outer islands since 1980 alone; as many as 500,000 other families migrated spontaneously, attracted by the settlement centers and infrastructure created by numerous Transmigration sites. In the 1980's, well over 4.5 million people have colonized what are mostly extremely poor tropical forest soils, resulting in the deforestation of at least two million hectares, and possibly somewhere between four million and six million hectares.[3]

Both the World Bank and the Indonesian government have acknowledged the crisis in the Transmigration program and are responding with huge investments in so-called "second stage" Transmigration, which is a euphemism for attempted ecological and economic rehabilitation of failing Transmigration colonies.

The World Bank's biggest, most disastrous involvement in forest colonization in the tropics is its financing of the now infamous Brazil Northwest Development Program (Polonoroeste). The bank approved six loans totaling $457 million for Polonoroeste from 1981 to 1983. In addition, as of early 1989, the Bank was preparing two more loans for the region that could total an additional $350 million: a loan of some $200 million to attempt to promote sustainable agricultural development in settlement areas where the first loans have up to now manifestly failed; and an emergency malaria control loan of $150 million, focusing principally on alleviating the malaria epidemic that earlier bank loans abetted. The total cost of this mammoth Amazon colonization, settlement consolidation, and road construction scheme is now well over $1.6 billion.

The most lasting impact of the World Bank's involvement in Polonoroeste is the highest rate of deforestation in the world, threatening the ruin of a tropical forest area three-fourths the size of France by the mid-1990's. Other consequences are an epidemic of highly resistant and virulent malaria unprecedented in scope, the threatened physical and cultural extermination of the more than 10,000 Amerindians belonging to over 60 different ethnic groups, and a complete economic debacle, since most of the tree-crop, export-oriented agriculture planned for the region never materialized.

Polonoroeste is an international scandal. The second most heavily indebted country in the world is borrowing hundreds of millions of dollars from an institution that purports to be the world's leading source of economic development expertise for a fundamentally ill-conceived scheme that has already brought about incalculable human misery, death, and irreversible environmental destruction with global implications.

In March, 1985, in response to pressures from environmental groups, the World Bank suspended disbursements for Polonoroeste because Brazil was not meeting the Bank's conditions for the protection of Indians and the environment—the first time the Bank had ever halted disbursements on a loan for environmental reasons. But just as the World Bank was preparing to halt disbursement on its Polonoroeste loans, the IDB proposed $72 million more in loans for the paving of 300 miles of the extension of the Polonoroeste penetration road, BR-364, from Porto Velho, Rondônia, to Rio Branco, the capital of the adjacent state of Acre. Although the U.S. executive director abstained on environmental grounds, vetoing $13.5 million of the loans, the project was nevertheless approved.

Once disbursements began, the same process occurred in Acre as in Rondônia: construction of the road proceeded on time or even ahead of schedule, but implementation of environmental and Indian lands protection measures was nonexistent or extremely dilatory. Again, under great pressures from the U.S. Congress and environmental groups, the IDB halted outstanding loan disbursements on the Acre road improvement project in December, 1987, for noncompliance with loan conditions specifying environmental and Indian lands protection.

Lessons to be learned from the Polonoroeste and Acre experiences are simple and bitter: the most basic is that in any infrastructure project opening up new areas of tropical forest, environmental and indigenous lands protection measures must not only be planned, but be implemented, before construction is allowed to proceed. In addition, it is folly to promote massive agricultural colonization in such areas. Finally, the MDB financing of projects such as Polonoroeste and Transmigration appears to be a grotesquely expensive way to make certain that developing countries go more deeply into debt without making any economic progress.

Energy Sector Lending

Large-scale hydroelectric projects funded by the MDBs also contribute to tropical deforestation, both through direct inundation and by opening up areas around new dams and reservoirs for spontaneous colonization. In the latter instance, the lack of measures to control deforestation in reservoir watersheds gravely shortens the lifespan of projects and undercuts their economic viability. In the 1970's, for example, the IDB loaned over $400 million dollars for three giant hydroelectric dams in Central America: El Cajon in Honduras, Chixoy in Guatemala, and Arenal in Costa Rica. These loans did not include watershed management plans, and as a result, agricultural colonists began clearing the forests. Subsequent soil erosion is now silting up the reservoirs at an alarming rate.

An ongoing World Bank program to lend well over a billion dollars to Eletrobras, the Brazilian state electric utility, threatens to wreak further environmental havoc. The bank-approved Eletrobras master investment plan, the "Plan 2010," calls for the construction of 136 new dams by that year, of which about 60 percent will be in the Amazon rainforest area and affect indigenous peoples. In particular, the bank loan will help finance feasibility studies for a series of proposed dams on the lower Xingu River, which would inundate thousands of square kilometers of pristine tropical forests, creating the largest human-made lakes in the world.

In India, World Bank–financed energy projects pose considerable threats to some of that country's remaining forests. In 1989 the bank was considering loans totaling $420 million to finance the Narmada Sagar Dam on the Narmada River, India's biggest westward-flowing river. The dam would inundate 40,000 hectares of prime hardwood forest in central Madhya Pradesh state, destroying one of the most important remaining wildlife habitats in central India and forcibly displacing an estimated 80,000 indigenous inhabitants.

THE IMPACT ON THE BANKS OF PRESSURE FOR REFORM

Any review of the environmental policies and procedures of the World Bank must distinguish between those conceived before and after May, 1987, the date the bank's president announced sweeping reforms in dealing with environmental matters. Previously, the World Bank's environmental expertise was concentrated in an Office of Environmental Scientific Affairs, which had seven staff members out of the bank's more than 6,000 employees.

Before 1987, it was clear that the tiny staff of the environmental office was woefully inadequate to effectively implement the bank's environmental policies. In 1983, environmental groups in the U.S. began to look closely at the World Bank and other MDBs, using a variety of information-gathering techniques including case studies of specific projects and expanding contacts with a growing network of nongovernmental organizations (NGOs) in the Third World. This research and advocacy resulted in, among other things, some 24 separate hearings in the U.S. Congress that addressed the environmental performance of the MDBs.[4] The hearings produced an overwhelming public record of negligence and led Congress to enact legislation that required the U.S. executive directors of the MDBs, beginning in late 1985, to promote far-reaching environmental reforms in the banks and to report back to Congress regularly on progress. The recommendations focused on greatly increasing environmental staff, funding more projects that were environmentally beneficial, and on consulting regularly with representatives of local community groups, NGOs, and the ministries of environment and public health in borrowing countries.[5]

The MDB campaign, as it began to be known, worked extensively through the media to call attention to MDB-financed environmental disasters. The campaign also worked with NGOs and parliamentarians in Western Europe to pressure major European members of the MDBs to promote similar environmental reforms through their MDB executive directors. The result of these pressures was World Bank president Barber Conable's 1987 announcement of sweeping environmental reforms.

More than a year and a half later, little has been implemented and even the blueprints have been cut back. The number of staff promised for the new environment department shrunk with each public pronouncement on the subject—from 100, a figure cited by a bank senior vice president the day after Conable's speech, to a final figure of about 23. In addition to reinforcements in the central department, 22 positions have been authorized for the four environmental assessment units in each of the bank's operational regions. But these assessment units have not been given sufficient budget or power to influence proposed projects at an early stage.

In Brazil, the World Bank has refused and/or has been incapable of acting effectively to avoid needless deforestation and environmental devastation in several of its largest lending programs. Even more flagrant, until late 1988, was the hesitancy of the bank's operations staff in Asia on issues such as forced resettlement and consultation with local NGOs. Only after years of criticism by NGOs in the United States, and mass on-site demonstrations by tens of thousands of displaced people has the bank finally been prodded into close scrutiny of the environmental and social impacts of a number of its projects in India. Thus, the advances are mainly on paper. Although the bank in recent years has promulgated several policies that seem exemplary, implementation has lagged far behind.

The IDB's record is no better. With over 1,800 professional staff, the IDB has only three professionally trained ecologists or environmental experts to review an average of over 60 new projects and scores of ongoing projects a year. In at least two cases, projects publicized as models of IDB environmental commitment have been targets of massive protests by Latin American environmental groups for gross environmental negligence.

Clearly, the bottom line in evaluating MDB environmental policies is the environmental quality of what comes out of the project pipeline—and there, with some isolated exceptions, improvement has been minimal and agonizingly slow.

PRESSURING THE BANKS: THE PATH AHEAD

Pressure on the MDBs from NGOs has resulted in damage control—as in World Bank loans for Polonoroeste and IDB loans for Acre. Congressional and media critics have made clear the need for systematic reform. The MDBs have responded with some increases in environmental staffing and awareness. But there has been little change in the overall environmental implications of the banks' operations. Indeed, deforestation in major MDB borrowing countries is accelerating at an unprecedented rate.[6]

Pressure to modify or halt destructive projects works. However, the dynamics of deforestation cannot be separated from the overall framework of development and underdevelopment. A campaign to save tropical forests must focus on identifying and promoting less destructive, more clearly sustainable development options. Regionally, this means identifying and strengthening local constituencies—such as Amazon rubber tappers, indigenous peoples, nongovernmental groups of various kinds, and forest farmers, all of whom have a vested interest in conserving forest resources. Internationally, this means reducing the overwhelming economic pressures on developing countries to overexploit their natural resources, pressures fueled by their external debt. The public international financial institutions, which include the International Monetary Fund (IMF) in addition to the MDBs, are the only existing institutions that have the potential to deal with all of these matters in a coordinated fashion.

In some sectors, such as energy, the argument for less destructive alternatives is overwhelming. For example, there is no justification for the World Bank's ongoing support for a power sector investment plan in Brazil that calls for dozens of new dams that will inundate large areas of Amazon rainforest and will open up even larger areas to spontaneous migration. A study published by the World Bank in late 1986 concluded that *one-half* of all the new energy-generating infrastructure projected to be needed in Brazil by the year 2000— some 22,000 megawatts—could be obviated by investments in industrial and urban end-use efficiency and conservation at a quarter of the cost.[7]

In agriculture, unfortunately, the alternatives are less well developed and the need for them is even more urgent. One of the most important and pressing alternatives to settlement of tropical forest regions is land reform, an issue that poses enormous political difficulties to its proponents within Latin America and elsewhere. The MDBs and the IMF have not been shy, to say the least, about firmly insisting on "adjustment programs" that include other politically difficult and unpopular measures, such as cuts in social services and elimination of food subsidies, to ensure that Latin American countries continue to service their external debt. If there were worldwide pressure on these institutions to exercise in the cause of land reform even a fraction of the political will they have demonstrated in these highly controversial adjustment programs, major progress would result.

Indigenous peoples in tropical forest areas have developed a wide range of sustainable agroecological systems that researchers have only begun to document and analyze. The MDBs should be helping to harvest this knowledge, critical for the future of sustainable development, rather than plowing it under.

But it is also in the controversy surrounding the World Bank and IDB projects in Northwest Brazil that we can see the beginnings of an alternative approach to rainforest development based on the knowledge of forest-dwellers. This approach is based on the full participation of local communities—in this case rubber tappers—who harvest rainforest products such as natural rubber and Brazil nuts. Following the debacle of Polonoroeste, rubber tapper communities in the region proposed in 1985 the establishment of "extractive reserves" that they would administer, where the forest would be conserved and sustainably harvested. The long-term economic returns from the extractive harvesting of rubber and other products such as fruits, medicines, and ornamental plants are greater than those from either cattle ranching or colonist agriculture. Under pressure from environmental groups in the United States, who steered the rubber tappers' proposal to top-level management in the World Bank and IDB, the World Bank and IDB gave their political and financial support for the proposal. This in turn helped to catalyze Brazilian federal and state authorities to facilitate the establishment of the first such reserves. Already, 12 extractive reserves totaling more than five million acres are being established in four Brazilian Amazon states.[8]

Increasingly NGOs are recognizing that in order to promote sustainable development alternatives in the MDBs, local communities must participate in project planning and have access to information on economic development activities that will affect them. In the United States one vital element in the environmental impact assessment process involves public hearings where alternatives can be put forth and discussed. But currently, MDB project documents are confidential; and the centralized, hierarchical structure of these institutions militates against the free flow of information. Although both the World Bank and the IDB have made rhetorical commitments to the greater involvement of NGOs and local community groups in their operations, this is not taking place. It is time for nongovernmental groups in developed countries and in the Third World to call for "glasnost" in the MDBs.

For most tropical forest countries, particularly in Latin America and Africa, the most urgent macroeconomic issue of all is the catastrophic burden of its foreign debt, which creates overwhelming direct and indirect pressures to destroy tropical forests. NGOs and all people concerned about the rainforests' future must press the World Bank and IMF to play a key role in debt relief efforts for developing nations, despite the reluctance of both institutions, as of early 1989, to consider promoting large-scale debt forgiveness or write-downs as an option. One concept of potential debt relief is "debt for nature" swaps, where part of a country's external debt is forgiven in exchange for the country's agreement to protect a portion of its natural resources, typically forest land.

Real reform in the MDBs will not occur without steady and increased political pressure. What has been won so far is an unprecedented and undeniable place for citizen activism, the only force that can bring accountability to the agencies controlling the international development agenda. But the fact that the World Bank and the IDB have undertaken some bureaucratic reforms does not mean that environmentalists can assume that their case is won, or even that their ideas will get a sympathetic hearing. New posts have been created in the past without disrupting "business as usual." Environmentalists should remember that for any bank or bureaucracy, let alone the MDBs, nothing is cheaper than words.

10

TAKING POPULATION SERIOUSLY

Power and Fertility

FRANCES MOORE LAPPÉ

AND

RACHEL SCHURMAN

•

Since 1950 the world's population has doubled, and 85 percent of that growth has occurred in the Third World, where today's population growth rates are unprecedented. Because the fastest rates of growth are in many rainforested countries—Brazil, the Philippines, Indonesia, Guatemala—we cannot hope to protect rainforests without asking, What set off this population explosion? And how can we defuse it to help bring human population into balance with the Earth's ecology?

To answer these questions, we present a "power-structures perspective,"[1] focusing on the multilayered arenas of decision-making power that shape people's reproductive choices, or lack of them. This perspective shows how the powerlessness of the poor often leaves them little option but large families. Indeed, high birth rates among the poor can best be understood as a defensive response against structures of power that fail to provide—or actively block access to—sources of security beyond the family.

When we ask what can be learned from the handful of Third World countries that have been extraordinarily successful in reducing fertility, we find this thesis reinforced. In each, far-reaching social changes have empowered people, especially women, thereby facilitating alternatives to child bearing as a source of income, security, and status.

POPULATION: WHAT'S THE PROBLEM?

In the most widely held definition of the population problem, growing numbers of people are pitted against limited amounts of resources. In this food-versus-resources perspective, humanity is fast overrunning the Earth's capacity to support us; indeed, current environmental degradation and hunger prove that in some places we've already pushed beyond the Earth's limits.

Our prior work has demonstrated that it is incorrect to explain hunger by blaming high population density when the two are not demonstrably related.[2] China, for instance, has only half as much cropped land per person as India, yet Indians suffer widespread and severe hunger and the Chinese do not. Costa Rica, with less than half the cropped acres per person of Honduras, boasts a life expectancy—one indicator of nutrition—14 years longer than that of Honduras, and close to that of the industrial countries.[3]

Obviously, many factors other than sheer numbers determine whether people eat adequately, such as whether people have access to fertile land to grow food, or have jobs providing them with money to buy it.

The same simplistic formulation must be rejected when it comes to environmental destruction. Within this century, forests in the tropical Third World have declined by nearly half. Much of the damage is attributed to peasants practicing slash-and-burn agriculture. But if land in Brazil, for example, were not the monopoly of the few—with 2 percent of the landowners controlling 60 percent of the arable land—poor Brazilians would not be forced to settle in the Amazon, destroying the irreplaceable rainforest.[4] In Indonesia, commercial logging is a major source of the destruction. There, lumber multinationals Weyerhauser and Georgia-Pacific have leveled an estimated 800,000 hectares a year—at least four times more than the area affected by peasant slash-and-burn farming.[5]

Surely in some locales populations already exceed the size at which they can coexist healthily with the environment, but "to blame colonizing peasants for uprooting tribal people and burning the rainforest," write two rainforest ecologists, "is tantamount to blaming soldiers for causing wars."[6]

THE EMERGING "POWER STRUCTURES PERSPECTIVE"

Over the past two decades, a more sophisticated social analysis of the population problem has begun to emerge. It points to economic, social, and cultural forces that keep Third World fertility high: among them the low status of women, the high death rates of children, and the lack of old-age security. From this social perspective, high fertility becomes an effect more than a cause of poverty and hunger.

This chapter seeks to synthesize crucial insights emerging from this perspective, while adding a critical dimension: social power. By social power we mean, very concretely, the relative ability of people to have a say in decisions that shape their lives. To understand why populations are exploding in the Third World, one must understand how choices about reproduction—those most personal, intimate choices—are influenced by structures of decision-making power. These structures include the distant arena of international finance and trade, and extend downward to the level of national governments, on through the village, and, ultimately, to relationships within families.

"Power structure" is not a mysterious concept. It simply refers to the rules, institutions, and assumptions that determine both who is allowed to participate in decisions and in whose interests decisions are made. The decisions most relevant to the population question are those governing access to and use of life-sustaining resources— land, jobs, health care, and the education needed to make the most of them—and contraceptive resources.

Decision-making structures can most usefully be characterized as

falling along a continuum from what we call democratic to antidemocratic. By democratic we mean decision-making structures in
which those most affected by the decisions have a say, or that mini-
mally include consideration of the interests of those affected. In no
polity or other social institution is power shared in completely equal
measure, but in our definition, democratic organization exists to the
extent that power is dispersed and no one is utterly powerless. In contrast, antidemocratic structures are nonparticipatory when those
most affected have no say, or unequal when power is so concentrated
that a few decide exclusively in their own interests. Our thesis is that
antidemocratic power structures create and perpetuate conditions
keeping fertility high.

In Western societies one tends to think of democracy as strictly a
political concept, and of power as exercised only in the political
arena. We in the West also assume that because the communist state
is the antithesis of political democracy, any use of the term *democratic* is inappropriate when describing communist societies. However, power is a critical variable in both political and economic affairs, as well as in social and cultural life. And the labels *democratic*
and *antidemocratic*—describing structures of decision-making
power in a multiplicity of social institutions—are most usefully applied not to societies *in toto*, but to the many arenas of life within
societies.

Within any given society, power is not necessarily structured along
the same lines throughout the political, economic, and social sectors. These varied sectors influence each other, but asymmetry is
more the norm: a society might be highly antidemocratic in the way
political power is wielded but might allow considerable sharing of
economic control over essential resources. Take China. Under the
former collectivized system, everyone had the right to participate in
economic life and share in the fruits from the land. At the same
time, political leadership was not freely chosen and people's right to
political expression was not protected.

The converse is probably more common. In a number of societies—the United States is an example—political participation and

expression are protected, but citizens' rights to economic resources are not. So a significant share of the population goes without enough income to provide adequate food, housing, and health care.

Structures of economic and political power differ by level as well: although they may be relatively participatory at, say, the national political level, they may remain grossly unequal at another level—for example, when it comes to relations between men and women within the family.

When this power-structures perspective is applied to the population problem, it reveals the ways in which structures of power—interpersonal to international—influence reproductive choices.

POWER AND REPRODUCTIVE CHOICE

In largely agrarian societies, the most accurate indicator of the economic power structure is the control of farmland, for access to land determines a family's security.

What are the consequences for fertility when at least one billion rural people in the Third World have been deprived of farmland? In many countries, including Brazil, Mexico, the Philippines, India, and most of the Central American countries, landholdings have become increasingly concentrated in the hands of a minority during the period of rapid population growth. When the more powerful have an incentive to expand—such as the chance to grow lucrative export crops—and have military backing, they can quite easily seize the land of the less powerful. They might do it legally, by calling in the loan of a heavily indebted peasant family, or not so legally, by simply bulldozing the peasant's land and laying claim to it. The peasant family has no legal title or lawyer to back up its claim in court.

In this context, without adequate land or secure tenure—and with no old-age support from the government or any other source of support outside the family—many poor people understandably view children as their sole source of power. Indeed children can be critical to their very survival.

For those living at the economic margin, children's labor can augment meager family income by freeing adults and elder siblings to earn outside income, or by bringing in money directly. Furthermore, in most Third World societies, parents rely on their children to care for them in old age. Children's earnings also provide insurance against risk of property loss for many rural families for whom a bad crop year or unexpected expense can spell catastrophe.

Adding pressure for high birth rates are high infant death rates in the Third World, for to enjoy the possible benefits of children eventually, the poor realize they need to have many children initially.

Of course, the value of children to their parents cannot be measured just in hours of labor or extra income. The intangibles may be just as important. In community affairs, bigger families carry more weight and status. And for poor parents—whose lives are marred so much by grief and sacrifice—the role children play in fulfilling the very real human need for joy and satisfaction cannot be underestimated.

High birth rates reflect, moreover, the disproportionate powerlessness of women. With no say in many decisions that determine their role in the family, as well as in the society at large, many women have little opportunity for pursuits outside the home. Perpetual motherhood becomes their only "choice."

Women's subordination to men within the family cuts to the core of the population issue because it often translates into a direct loss of control over their own fertility. After several births, many Third World women want to avoid or delay pregnancy. But they simply do not have the power to act on their desire. As one doctor in a Mexican clinic explained, "When a wife wants to . . . [try] to limit the number of mouths to feed in the family, the husband will become angry and even beat her. He thinks it is unacceptable that she is making a decision of her own. She is challenging his authority, his power over her—and thus the very nature of his virility."[7] Patriarchal family and community attitudes may also pressure a woman to keep having children until she gives birth to a son, regardless of her own wishes or even possible jeopardy to her health.

The power-structures perspective helps explain the high birth rates where women are subordinated within the family and the society, but also it recognizes that the men who hold power are often themselves part of a subordinate group—those with little or no claim to income-producing resources. Denied sources of self-esteem through productive work and access to the resources needed to shoulder responsibility for their families, such men are likely to cling even more tenaciously to their superior power vis-à-vis women. In many cultures, men unable to earn enough money to support dependents feel inadequate and unable to maintain a permanent household. The resulting self-blame can contribute to a behavior pattern of men moving in and out of relationships, fathering even more children.

TAKING THE BROADER VIEW

Thus, the power-structures analysis stresses the impact on fertility of women's subordination to men, a condition that contributes to the social pressure for many births. But it places this problem within the context of unjust social and economic structures that deny women realistic alternatives to unlimited reproduction, structures that encompass far more than the family or even the community. From the level of international trade and finance, down to jobs and income available to men as well as women, antidemocratic structures of decision-making set limits on people's choices, which in turn influence their reproductive options.

Consider the global "debt crisis." In the 1970's, Third World governments received large loans from banks in the industrial nations and invested the money in big-ticket projects—airports, arms, nuclear power plants, and so on—responding to the interests of their wealthiest citizens. In the 1980's, many of these loans came due, just as the interest rates climbed and prices of raw material exports from the Third World hit a 30-year low. As a result, between 1982 and 1987, the net transfer from poor countries to banks and governments in the rich countries totaled $140 billion, or the equivalent of two Marshall Plans.[8]

How did Third World countries come up with such sums? Health and welfare budgets and food subsidies got slashed first. And, to earn foreign exchange, land and credit increasingly went toward export crops. But reduced health care budgets mean that more babies die and fewer resources are available for comprehensive family planning care. More resources devoted to crops for export means that, locally, food becomes more scarce and more expensive. Understandably, nutrition and health worsen.

Thus, the "international debt crisis," seemingly remote from intimate reproductive behavior, ends up affecting the conditions of basic family security, health, and nutrition known to influence fertility.

This discussion of the layers of decision-making power shaping rates of human reproduction might make the reader draw back with skepticism, for could not virtually every economic, political, and cultural fact of life be viewed within such a broad perspective? Our response is that to achieve a holistic understanding, one's view must necessarily be far-reaching. But such an approach need not lack coherence. The pivot on which our perspective turns is the concept of power. Without it we believe it is impossible to understand the complex, interrelated problems of poverty, hunger, population growth, and ecological stress, much less act effectively to address them.

SOLUTIONS FROM THE POWER-STRUCTURES PERSPECTIVE: THE EVIDENCE

A power-structures perspective holds that far-reaching economic and political change is necessary to reduce birth rates to replacement levels. Such change must enhance the power of the poorest members of society so that they no longer feel the need to cope with economic insecurity by giving birth to many children. Social arrangements beyond the family—jobs, health care, old-age security, and education (especially for women)—must offer both security and opportunity. At the same time, acceptable birth control devices must be made universally available.

Consider the population trends over the last 20 years in the 70-odd countries designated "low" and "lower-middle" income by the World Bank, countries that are home to three-fourths of the world's people.[9] Although average annual population growth rates in the industrial countries have been below 2 percent a year for decades, among the more than 70 poor countries only six had both reduced their population growth to less than 2 percent by the period 1980–85 and cut total fertility rates by one-third or more since 1960. The six are China, Sri Lanka, Colombia, Chile, Burma, and Cuba. Although not a country, the Indian state of Kerala also meets these criteria.[10]

Population growth in these seven societies has slowed at a much faster rate than occurred in the now industrialized countries during their transition from high to low growth. What do these population success stories tell us?

Is it that these seven have carried out the most aggressive family planning programs? In general, no. A 1985 study rated most Third World countries according to what demographers call "family planning effort"—the prevalence and strength of organized family planning programs. The study included the six countries we are focusing on here (Kerala was not included because it is not a country). It found that two had weak or very weak family planning effort (Chile, Burma); one showed moderate effort (Cuba); and three showed strong effort (China, Sri Lanka, Colombia).[11]

What made the strong family planning efforts in those three countries so successful were the social changes introduced that allowed people to take advantage of birth control programs. What significant developments took place in these disparate societies that may hold the key? For one thing, in striking contrast to most Third World societies, four of the seven have assured their citizens considerable security through access to a basic diet: China, Kerala, Cuba, and Sri Lanka.

Of these seven societies, to us the most intriguing demographic case study is that of Kerala state in India. Its population density is three times the average for all India,[12] yet commonly used indicators of hunger and poverty—infant mortality, life expectancy, and death rate—are all considerably better in Kerala than in most low-income countries as well as in India as a whole. Its infant mortality is less than one-third the national average.[13]

Other measures of welfare also reveal the relatively better position of the poor in Kerala. In addition to a grain distribution system that keeps the cost of rice and other essentials within their reach, social security payments, pension, and unemployment benefits transfer resources to the poorest groups. Expenditures on public health in Kerala have historically been high, and the female literacy rate is two-and-a-half times the all-India average. Although land reform left significant inequality in land ownership, it did abolish tenancy, providing greater security to many who before were only renters.

But perhaps the most fundamental difference is that from the 1950's onward, political organization among Kerala's poor led to greater self-confidence. The poor came to see health care as their right, not a gift bestowed upon them. And among agricultural workers, grassroots political organization has also been the key to making land reform meaningful, to keeping wages relatively high, and to securing old-age pensions.

Although more complex, China's recent demographic history is equally telling. From 1969 to 1979, China achieved a dramatic transition from high to low rates of fertility, often attributed simplistically to an aggressive family planning program. Through a network of "barefoot doctors," family planning programs reached into every village, making birth control freely available and relying on group persuasion to change attitudes toward childbearing and family size.

Unarguably, such a concerted effort helps explain the dramatic fall in China's fertility rate in the 1970's. But China's family planning program did not arise out of thin air; it reflected prior, massive political change. We can unequivocally condemn China's totalitarian features while recognizing that a shift in power from a leadership long ignoring the needs of the Chinese peasantry to one attempting to address those needs was a prerequisite to China's population success record.

It was in 1979 that China's family planning policies took a new tack, when the Deng Xiaoping government instituted the world's most restrictive family planning program. Material incentives and penalties began to be offered to encourage all parents to bear only one offspring, and enormous pressure was brought to bear on those who become "unofficially" pregnant. At the same time, China's post-1979 approach to economic development began to undercut guaranteed employment, and old-age and medical security. In agriculture, the "individual responsibility" system replaced collective production; private entrepreneurship is now encouraged.

Thrown back on their own family's resources, many Chinese again see having many children—especially boys—as beneficial, both as a substitute for lost public protections and as a means of taking maximum advantage of the new economic system.[14] Since 1980, in fact, China's birth rates have *risen*.[15] This fertility rise is not due solely to these economic and social changes, but surely these underlying changes add to pressure for higher fertility.[16]

REFLECTIONS AND IMPLICATIONS FOR ACTION

In our view, the population puzzle is impossible to solve without employing the concept of social power. The very great diversity of these societies underscores our earlier point that power is not a monolithic concept, moving uniformly through the many sectors and levels of a society. It is diverse, characterized by uneven development. But within each of these successful societies, shifts in power relations in key aspects of family, community, and national life have made lowered fertility possible: the enhanced power of women, through basic literacy, education, and employment; the heightened power of peasants to provide food and income for themselves because of land reforms; the bolstered power of consumers to secure adequate nutrition where deliberate policies have been implemented to keep basic food staples within reach of all; the enhanced capacity of people to protect their health as medical care becomes accessible; and the heightened power of women to limit their births through birth control. These are some vital measures of changes needed for people to be able to choose fewer children.

In recent years, however, especially with the advent of the debt crisis, some have suggested that Third World countries are just too poor to address rapid population growth through economic and social development. Surely our examples demonstrate the fallacy of this easy out. Of the seven societies we cite for their exceptionally rapid drop in fertility, four are among the world's poorest: China, Sri Lanka, Burma, and the Indian state of Kerala. Poverty is no excuse for the continuing violation of basic human rights to essential resources.

EFFECTIVE RESPONSES TO THE POPULATION PROBLEM

Since the 1960's, those operating from the people-versus-resources perspective have linked the specter of famine to overpopulation and, in challenging this view, structural analysts have understandably focused on food, too. They have shown that hunger is not caused by inadequate resources.[17] Those using the power-structures perspective must now make clear that although hunger is not caused by too many people, for many other reasons one might well judge a nation to have too many people.

To thrive, human beings need a pollution-free environment to protect health, and enough physical space to allow for intellectual and spiritual growth. Ecosystem services such as adequate clean water, cool breezes, clean air, and diverse natural resources all support humans in their day-to-day activities. Human well-being is also enhanced by the opportunity to enjoy an environment undefaced and untransformed by human manipulation. The power-structures perspective emphasizes the quality of human relations but this can hardly be described without attention to the larger natural world we inhabit.

This analysis can therefore serve all those concerned about the quality of life for yet unborn generations. At the same time, it can incorporate the insights of ecological thinkers who challenge the assumption that if humans are thriving, then everything is all right. The accelerating destruction of irreplaceable rainforests is only one example of environmental assault, which threatens far more than humanity's well-being. This perspective can affirm that the infinitely rich biosphere itself must be considered of innate worth.

In other words, the power-structures analysis can show how the same antidemocratic structures that keep fertility high also play a central role in environmental destruction. Further, it can incorporate the insights of those questioning *any* model of development that perceives the environment merely as a pool of resources for human use.

In recent years it has become commonplace to acknowledge the complex social roots of the population problem. But when attention turns to solutions, this social analysis is foregone. It is assumed that regardless of the real roots of the problem, better birth control programs are all that the industrial West can offer.

We do not accept this view, especially as U.S. citizens. As a major world power, the U.S. government directly and indirectly shapes the behavior of many foreign governments. It is inconceivable that the United States would ever stop using its foreign policy to aid those governments it deems supportive of its own interests. But until our government transcends its deep fear of redistributive change abroad, our tax dollars will go on supporting governments that block the very changes we outline in this chapter as necessary to allow people the option of smaller families.

U.S. policy toward the Philippines illustrates our point. The population growth rate in the Philippines is among the highest in Asia, and its people are among the poorest and hungriest. Seventy percent of the rural people either lack land altogether or lack secure tenure to the land they farm. The United States supplied billions of dollars to maintain the former martial law government of Ferdinand Marcos, which not only refused to reform this gross imbalance in access to resources, but furthered economic concentration. Since 1986, the Philippines' new government remains unwilling to confront the underlying insecurity at the root of hunger and high birth rates; yet, it too receives enormous U.S. military, economic, and diplomatic support.

Unfortunately, the Philippines is the rule, not the exception. Rarely has the United States made its economic and political support conditional on domestic policies addressing the undemocratic economic structures that stand in the way of a significant drop in birth rates.

We argue that such a change in policy cannot come about until U.S. citizens reorient their government's understanding of what is in our own interests.[18] Simply funding a family planning initiative in the Philippines or in Honduras, for example, is woefully inadequate. If U.S. citizens are serious about confronting the worldwide population problem and related ecological problems, we must be willing to do that which is much more controversial: explicitly to identify the link between U.S. policies and the antidemocratic structures of decision-making power that keep birth rates high to begin with, and to use our rights as citizens to alter those policies.

Taking population seriously thus means incorporating the concept of social power as an indispensable tool of analysis and facing the logical consequences. It means learning from the historical evidence: without more democratic structures of decision-making power, from the family to the global arena, there is no solution—short of dehumanizing coercion or plagues—to the population explosion. The fate of the Earth hinges on the fate of today's poor majorities. Only as they are empowered to achieve greater security and opportunity—can population growth halt.

11

CENTRAL AMERICA

Political Ecology and U.S. Foreign Policy

JOSHUA KARLINER

•

The United States government sees Central America as a strategic bridge between two oceans and two continents. These geographic characteristics, which have contributed historically to deep U.S. involvement in the region, also account for the extraordinary biological diversity on the isthmus. A wide variety of life forms from both North and South America, including migratory birds and rare, often unidentified plant species, meet in Central America's lush tropical forests. But since World War II, U.S. security and development imperatives have been the primary force behind the rapid deterioration of this biological wealth. And since the early 1980's, the steep escalation of U.S. military involvement in the region has threatened to irreversibly destroy Central America's ecological equilibrium.

The region's biologically rich and fertile yet fragile natural resource base, upon which its economies depend, is suffering from decades of development policies that have promoted export agriculture over basic human needs, creating a pattern of unequal land distribution. This has enriched local elites and foreign corporations while forcing the majority of the population off the prime agricultural land. When the Central American people rebel against these unjust conditions, the region's governments and the U.S. government respond with repression and militarization, fueling a downward spiral of poverty, war, and environmental destruction.

More than two-thirds of Central America's original forests have been felled, with most of the destruction occurring since 1960. Deforestation continues today at a rapid rate of more than 4,000 square kilometers a year. Deforestation of the region's rainy, steep-sloped uplands has caused the siltation of downstream potable water sources, hydroelectric dams, irrigation projects, and coastal fisheries. Soil erosion has impoverished more than half of all the agricultural land, causing farm productivity to decline sharply.[1]

In Costa Rica, deforestation is so bad that the government, once an exporter of timber, is beginning to import wood. The Choluteca region of Honduras, almost completely deforested by cattle ranchers and cotton growers between 1950 and 1980, has been undergoing a process of desertification, which contributes to increasing hunger. In El Salvador, the most ecologically deteriorated nation in Latin America, every major watershed and river basin suffers siltation, droughts, and floods. Only a tiny percent of the original forest remains.

Yet despite environmental deterioration and its dynamic, spiraling relationship to socioeconomic deterioration, few policy makers or activists make the connection between the interwoven issues of poverty, ecological destruction, and war in Central America. Those debating U.S. policy in the region have not only failed to recognize that there are environmental dimensions to the region's deepening crisis, but have also neglected the widespread environmental impacts of U.S. foreign policy itself.

Many mainstream environmental organizations have also failed to see the relationships between these issues, singling out rapid population growth as the "underlying problem" in Central America.[2] Although population, likely to double in the next 25 years, does contribute to crisis in the region, it is not the root cause. Neither is deforestation, although almost all the region's rainforests will disappear in roughly the same amount of time. Both population growth and deforestation are rather symptoms of a much deeper, underlying structural crisis (see Chapter 10). This crisis has roots in Spanish colonialism, a highly stratified class structure, a myopic U.S. foreign policy, and an unjust international economic order that treats the Third World as a gigantic resource reserve.

THE ROOTS OF DESTRUCTION

Since the Spanish Conquest, Central America's natural resources have helped fuel the development of the North's economies. Wood, minerals, and luxury crops have been extracted or cultivated and shipped to colonial Spain, England, and later, the United States. Early efforts by Central Americans to control this exploitation of natural resources ran into strong resistance from the Northern powers. During the first half of this century, U.S. troops intervened repeatedly to defend strategic and corporate interests in the region.

In the 1950's the United States began pursuing a more sophisticated strategy that used multilateral and bilateral aid agencies to consolidate its political and economic grip on the region. This "new and improved" development model was designed to increase production of agricultural crops for sale to transnational corporations on the world market. This agro-export strategy promoted economic growth by intensifying banana and coffee production, and diversifying agricultural exports to include non-traditional products such as cotton, beef, sugar, timber, rice, and later, fruits and flowers.

This agro-export development focus has increasingly skewed what was already an unequal land tenure system by further concentrating fertile land in the hands of a few Central American families and multinational corporations. By the mid 1970's, 4 percent of the population owned 73 percent of the land, and the poorest 77 percent of the region's people owned just 7 percent of the land.[3] Impoverished Central Americans have been forced into farming forested hillsides and colonizing the region's rainforests, where they have no option but to cut down the forest to grow corn and beans for survival.

Such inequity has inevitably led to widespread movements for land redistribution and other economic reforms. The U.S. response to these reform movements has been to bolster its alliances with the local militaries and the export growers in order to defend the status quo. The result has been increased poverty and environmental destruction, as well as the emergence of repressive, military-dominated governments that fortify the agro-export model.

ECOLOGICAL DESTABILIZATION POLICIES

Perhaps the single most environmentally destructive policy the United States ever implemented in Central America was the Latin America–wide Alliance for Progress. In the name of development and economic growth, the Alliance pushed wave after wave of agricultural export crops from Central America's fertile Pacific shores eastward across its diverse terrain. The Alliance did promote agrarian reforms, but in reality these reforms turned out to be rainforest colonization schemes, designed to make room for more export crops while easing pressures for redistribution of the most fertile lands. While these export crops were booming, food production in Central America sank and malnutrition soared. Militarization, aimed at assuring "stability and security," enforced these social and economic policies.[4]

The two most destructive commodities promoted by the Alliance were cotton and cattle. By the mid-1960's, pesticide-drenched cotton covered most of the region's fertile Pacific plain, where corn and forestland had dominated just ten years earlier. Throughout the 1960's and 1970's a cattle boom, financed by multilateral and bilateral loans (see Chapter 9), stampeded Central America, pushing more peasants off their land and overrunning the region's rainforests. By 1980, 22 percent of the land mass, more land than was utilized by all other agricultural commodities combined, was in permanent pasture.[5]

Once again, movements for social change, which threatened the stability of the agro-export model, grew out of these economic inequities. In response, the Alliance fostered militarization to keep these movements down. Gruesome stories abound of peasant communities that were literally blown away for organizing resistance to cattle ranchers who were evicting them from their lands and pushing them deeper into the rainforest.

In the mid-1960's, for example, Guatemalan peasants organized to keep their land. An armed guerrilla movement emerged at the edge of the rainforest to challenge both the government and the ranchers. In response, a U.S. Special Forces team directed a Guatemalan counterinsurgency campaign that used helicopter gunships, fighter bombers, and napalm to destroy a 500-person guerrilla insurgency. It is estimated that the army killed an additional 6,000 to 8,000 people in the process. Once the resistance was virtually eliminated, military officers were rewarded with huge cattle ranches, the rainforest continued to disappear, and multinationals began to exploit mineral and oil resources. Similar conflicts occurred in Nicaragua and Honduras, and—with less violence—in Costa Rica.[6]

In this context the "hamburger connection" (the import of Central American beef by the U.S. fast-food industry), a frequent target of U.S. environmental activists, can clearly be seen as merely another symptom of the larger Central American nightmare of export agriculture, unequal land distribution, repression, and U.S. military intervention. U.S. environmentalists would be wise to move beyond their current fast-food fixation and consider allying themselves with movements that address fundamental power relations in Central America.

Peasant movements fighting for land redistribution are challenging these power relations and may become the fundamental force that can reverse the surging tide of rainforest destruction in Central America. For while they are not driven strictly by ecological considerations, genuine land reform movements are inherently environmental movements in that they seek to bring food production out of the forests and off the hillsides.

YA SEEN ONE RAINFOREST, YA SEEN 'EM ALL

The U.S. government response to Central American movements for social change during the late 1970's and 1980's has been to increase intervention in the region. U.S. policy in the Reagan years was dominated by a campaign to roll back the socialist-oriented Nicaraguan revolution through a combination of the contra war and economic pressure. At the same time, the United States has spent billions of dollars in military and economic aid on a policy aimed at containing revolutionary movements in the rest of the region and building a "military shield" to provide a stable environment for "development" and "democracy."[7] "Development" of course means maintaining the agro-export formula; "democracy" is the name in which any challenges to this export formula, and ultimately to U.S. power in the region, are squelched.

Annual U.S. foreign assistance to El Salvador, Honduras, Guatemala, and Costa Rica increased nearly sixfold between 1980 and 1987, jumping from $150 million to $895 million a year. The U.S. spent two-thirds of the aid it gave Central America and the Caribbean on direct military and "security" assistance, and roughly 1 percent went to environmental protection.[8] This pattern of escalating military spending in Central America, combined with nearly total neglect of environmental problems and their root causes, is foreclosing future options for sustainable economic development in the region. In its effort to save the region from supposed communism, the United States is literally destroying Central America.

Nowhere is this clearer than in El Salvador.[9] Its economy has all but collapsed, and is being sustained only by the $1.3 million that the United States pumps in daily—more than 50 percent of the country's national budget. According to a report by the U.S. Congress Arms Control and Foreign Policy Caucus, 75 percent of U.S. aid to El Salvador is directly related to the war, even though the majority is called funds for "economic support." This military-oriented spending overwhelms the $1.5 million—or .005 percent—of aid annually spent on environmental and natural resource management. In fact, in 1988 the U.S. spent almost two hundred times as much on war-related aid in El Salvador as it did to protect and restore the environment.[10] Rather than addressing the roots of crisis in El Salvador, U.S. tax dollars have brought about more than one million refugees and 70,000 Salvadoran deaths (many were killed by right-wing death squads).

The U.S. war in El Salvador has also claimed a direct ecological toll. For example, El Pital, El Salvador's only lower montane forest, has been reduced to a series of charred remnants. Once targeted as a national park, El Pital was more recently the target of a U.S.–backed counterinsurgency bombing campaign. Counterinsurgency has also turned vast areas of Morazan and northern Chalatenango provinces into virtual wastelands—crops destroyed, forests charred, and landscapes scarred with bomb craters. In 1982 the paramilitary death squad ORDEN killed four park rangers at the Montecristo Cloud Forest National Park and assassinated 30 other community members who were cooperating with the park service.

A similar situation exists in Guatemala, where the army has carried out a scorched-earth counterinsurgency campaign destroying forests, fields, livestock, and at least 440 villages. Between 1982 and 1987 more than one million Guatemalans were displaced from their land. Many of these refugees have fled to the lowland rainforests of neighboring Mexico, where they practice slash-and-burn agriculture.

In Honduras, the second poorest nation in the Western Hemisphere, a massive infusion of U.S. aid made the country a staging ground for the contra war as well as a command post for counterinsurgency in El Salvador and Guatemala, earning it the nickname "Pentagon Republic." Honduras' share of development assistance actually declined in the 1980's, while military aid and environmental destruction increased. In 1986, for example, according to the government-run Honduran Forestry Corporation (CORFOP), Honduras lost more than 1,000 square kilometers of forest. This was due to U.S. military maneuvers and construction, the flight of Nicaraguan refugees from the contra war, and the presence of more than 10,000 contras themselves. This military-induced deforestation more than doubled Honduras' normal deforestation rate.[11] According to information obtained by the Environmental Policy Institute, a United Nations and Honduran government report charges that these activities have caused more than $125 million in damages to Honduran forests. According to the director of CORFOP, "The contras are changing the whole ecology of the zone—the vegetation, wildlife, soils, and water sources are being damaged."

In Nicaragua, international attention has focused on contra atrocities against doctors, teachers, and agricultural extension workers. However, the war dealt a series of blows to Nicaragua's innovative environmental policies as well. For example, the contras assassinated more than 30 employees working in the environmental and forestry sectors between 1983 and 1987, and kidnapped at least another 75. Sandinista efforts to fight back are also causing some environmental damage; the army's ground-based mobile rocket launchers and MI-24 helicopters, for example, have destroyed patches of forestland.[12]

Perhaps the most devastating impact of the conflict was the indirect economic effect. Nicaragua's huge per capita foreign debt, the U.S. economic embargo, U.S. economic pressure to halt all multilateral loans to Nicaragua, and the contra war combined with internal mismanagement to create a severe economic crisis that crippled the country's social and environmental programs. A 1987 World Wildlife Fund report noted that "The drain on the economy from the continued conflict has had a far-reaching negative impact. Government conservation programs are severely reduced and local people are increasingly tempted to exploit natural resources for fast, hard currency."[13]

The U.S. rollback policy in Nicaragua and its containment policy in the rest of Central America have effectively blocked some of the fundamental changes that are necessary if Central Americans are to begin building environmentally sustainable, socially just societies. Nevertheless, the Sandinista revolution has taken some significant steps toward creating this ideal.

REVOLUTION IN THE RAINFOREST

The Sandinista revolution succeeded in 1979 by violently overthrowing the 42-year-old, U.S.–created and –supported Somoza dictatorship. Since then the government has pursued some environmentally destructive policies such as promoting agricultural development on forestry land. Overall, however, the revolution's structural reforms and efforts to break with the traditional agro-export patterns have given the Sandinistas unprecedented potential for implementing comprehensive environmental reforms. Since 1979 Nicaragua has moved toward a more ecologically sustainable style of development that could save its rainforests—the largest remaining in Central America.[14]

During their first month in power, the Sandinistas nationalized all of Nicaragua's forests, which Somoza had previously doled out in concessions to multinational timber corporations. They also quickly moved to implement a program of land reform, which within five years had successfully halted all rainforest colonization projects and redistributed more than one-fifth of the nation's productive farmland.

During their second month in power Sandinistas created the Nicaraguan Institute of Natural Resources and the Environment (IRENA), the first environmental agency ever in Nicaragua. In addition to implementing a broad spectrum of other programs, by 1982 IRENA had targeted 18 percent of Nicaraguan territory for national parks and reserves, including the largest pristine rainforest north of the Amazon Basin, the 10,000 square kilometer Bosawas forest on the Honduran border. It was in Bosawas that IRENA began managing the country's first rainforest national park, Saslaya, in 1981.

In 1982, however, in one of the opening salvos in their war against the environment, the contras kidnapped Saslaya's administrator and two rangers, forcing the closure of the park. Further contra attacks burned numerous reforestation projects, destroyed vehicles and buildings, and made it unsafe for environmentalists to work in many rainforested areas.

Nevertheless, Nicaragua continues to maintain some of its innovative environmental programs—including environmental restoration, development of alternatives to pesticides, and a sea turtle conservation program. These programs and others, along with a small but vocal nongovernmental environmental movement, receive support from international environmental organizations as well as some Western European governments. One of the outstanding programs is an effort to create a rainforested "peace park" on the border with Costa Rica which, on the Nicaraguan side, combines land reform, forestry, and rainforest conservation. U.S. support for this kind of "long-range conservation and development program," writes John B. Oakes in the *New York Times*, is "the surest way to help the Central American people restore their economy and stabilize their politics." Yet, despite broad international support for the project, he notes, "our government is conspicuously absent."[15]

A ROLE FOR U.S. ENVIRONMENTALISTS

When we consider the U.S. role in Central America, it becomes clear that environmentalists who want to save the region's rainforests must work to shift Washington's policies away from supporting militarization and export agriculture and toward peace, social justice, and ecologically sound development in the region.

If we are serious about saving the rainforests of Mesoamerica we must go beyond supporting national parks and tiny environmental groups. We must not merely join consumer campaigns to boycott beef, or efforts to make multilateral development banks' loans more environmentally sound. We can no longer afford to be single-issue environmentalists.

These specific efforts are important. But if the World Bank continues to direct 80 percent of its loans to the export sector—with or without environmental safeguards—farmers will be pushed off their land and rainforests will fall. If the global debt crisis is not resolved, Central American nations will continue to ravage Nature in order to service their loans. If the United States does not reverse its promotion of militarization and agro-exports, any environmental programs that the U.S. Agency for International Development may introduce are in effect a smoke-and-mirrors distraction from the real damage U.S. policy is causing.

The bottom line is that if the basic needs of Central America's population are not met, if there is not enough land to grow food, the

rainforest will continue to disappear. If the demands of the subordinated for land and social change continue to run up against brutal
repression, people will fight back. If the United States continues to
undermine all efforts at structural change that might allow a more
socially just, economically viable, and ecologically sound development model to emerge in Central America, the United States will
also continue to undermine the very stability it claims to be seeking
in Central America.

Although it is important for environmentalists to organize consumer boycotts, keep pressure on the MDBs, and support parks and
environmental organizations in the region, it is imperative to build a
broader environmental movement, one that supports social change
in Central America and allies itself with movements throughout this
hemisphere that are working for such change. A broader environmentalism must address such issues as peace and equity, while also
contributing an environmental perspective to both land reform
movements in Central America and the growing U.S. movement to
change our government's policies in the region. It is through this
broader environmentalism that we may ultimately be able to save the
rainforests.

12

THE CONSUMER CONNECTION

Psychology and Politics

SUZANNE HEAD

•

At least once a month I find in my mailbox a large envelope offering the chance to win millions of dollars by entering the sweepstakes of one corporation or another. The Publishers Clearing House sweepstakes are a good example of these blatant provocations to conspicuous consumption. In case we can't imagine what we would do if we were to win fabulous wealth, PCH's full-color brochure graphically illustrates how we could enjoy "life's richest rewards":

> *Picture yourself living in luxury and comfort . . . with everything you want at your fingertips, thanks to your oversized bank account. Well, you can live this enviable lifestyle—guaranteed— provided you return your entry by the deadline. . . . Move into the house of your dreams! Join the jetset as you globetrot around the world! Indulge yourself with expensive jewelry and clothing! Relax aboard the luxury yacht you've always wished you could own! Get behind the wheel of your dream machine . . . or hire a chauffeur!*

The Publishers Clearing House literature plays upon the assumptions that money can buy life's richest rewards, that money and a luxurious lifestyle are the only ingredients needed for a fulfilling life, and that nothing else in the world matters. These are the myths of an obsessively materialistic society. Greed-baiting is so common in our mass culture that it often goes unquestioned. But unquestioned assumptions are at the very core of our society's addiction to consumption. They are the social equivalent of the addict's denial; for, until very recently, they have blocked serious consideration of the destruction that results from compulsive consumption.

When money is the only thing that matters, we find it easy to disconnect the ways in which we acquire and spend money from the effects of doing so. With such monocular vision, we become blind to the interdependence of all life. Yet, as we have seen in previous chapters, economics, politics, and ecosystems are all interdependent. Politics is inseparable from economics, and economics is inseparable from the Earth's productivity. Similarly, consumerism is integral to those social structures that destroy rainforests and other cultures. How we get and spend our money, or cast our "dollar votes," inevitably affects the rest of the human and natural world for good or ill.

On a deeper level, consumerism also is closely linked to social ills within the United States, for our patterns of consumption reflect social, psychological, and—ultimately—spiritual conditions here at home. We express many things about ourselves in the way we cast our dollar votes: our personal integrity, our worldview, and our relationship with ourselves, our society, and Nature—even our commitment to life on Earth.

THE GREAT AMERICAN CONSUMER RELIGION

Until about 30 years ago, before the advent of shopping malls, ladies used to dress up in suits, hats, and white gloves to go shopping in the great urban centers such as New York and San Francisco. They prepared themselves to enter the hallowed halls of Saks and I. Magnin in the same way they prepared for church. Looking back, I realize that in dressing up and going shopping with my mother and grandmother, I was being initiated into what was to become a major religion during my lifetime.

Among the *Oxford English Dictionary's* definitions of religion are these: "Action or conduct indicating a belief in, reverence for, and desire to please, a divine ruling power; the exercise or practice of rites or observances implying this"; and "Devotion to some principle; strict fidelity or faithfulness; conscientiousness; pious affection or attachment." If the frequency and magnitude of U.S. consumption are any index of devotion, then consumerism is definitely a religion, and the divine ruling power is the dollar.

By the end of 1988 there were 32,180 shopping centers gracing our landscape. According to the International Council of Shopping Centers, 94 percent of the adult U.S. population visits these places at least once a month.[1] They have ceased to be merely places to shop—they have become major centers of community life, not only for wage-earning age groups, but for large numbers of teenagers and the elderly. Sociologist Mark Baldassare says that "Malls provide what little civic identity exists in the suburbs. They are places to go— if not to meet people, then to see other people, to feel you are a part of things."[2] For many people, hanging out in the local shopping mall is the only collective ritual available.

In her *Wall Street Journal* article on these "icons of contemporary culture," Ellen Graham interviewed numerous shoppers in New Jersey's Garden State Plaza and New York's Hudson Valley Mall. She found that many regulars "drop by as often as once or twice a week, finding amusement and banishing boredom in the pursuit of goods." Mall regulars call shopping their hobby or their favorite pastime. With the fervor of a true religious devotee, one woman declared: "I have to buy something every week. I could shop every day. I think stores should set up cots so you could take nap breaks and start all over again."[3]

Now even organized religion has started to come to the shopping malls. In a mall in Paramus, New Jersey, shoppers can shop and attend mass at St. Therese's Catholic Church in a single trip. "It's convenient," says one such shopper. "I can do my shopping, then come to confession." One of the priests at St. Therese's explains that the idea is to take religion where the people go—shopping malls.[4] All of St. Therese's 100 folding chairs are often occupied during the 25-minute mass conducted several times a day—an indication, perhaps, that the religion of consumerism may not fully meet our spiritual needs.

A NUMBERS GAME OR SURVIVAL?

In 1987, U.S. consumers spent $584 billion at shopping centers, representing 54 percent of the nonautomotive retail trade. This concentration of consumption gratifies the retailers at shopping malls, but few of them are independent entrepreneurs. Because of the high rents and competition, most mall tenants are retail chains—which accounts for the uniformity among shopping malls. As Graham says, shopping malls constitute a "homogenized chain-store sprawl from coast to coast" that blurs regional distinctions.

Purchasing 54 percent of our consumer goods in shopping centers means that at least 54 percent—although it seems more like 99 percent—of what we buy is mass produced, mass marketed, and controlled by massive corporations. If Americans hang out in shopping malls "to relieve loneliness, alienation or boredom," as Graham says, one has to wonder to what extent our need for a personal connection to our world is fulfilled by the choices presented in the plastic, impersonal monoculture brought to us by corporate America.

It is hard to deny that corporate productivity builds a wall between us and Nature's productivity. Over the last 30 years, since the malling of America began, goods and services have reflected less and less their biological and cultural origins. At the same time, psychologically and spiritually, we have become more and more detached from the Earth. Our culture long ago abandoned the idea that the Earth is alive and that we owe gratitude and respect for all life. Any sense of sacredness and decency toward living beings has been overpowered by our obsession with abstract wealth, which values the Earth's fertility only in terms of numbers. Having withdrawn our faith from the processes of life and invested it in money's power to buy all human happiness, we have become evermore dependent upon such conveniences as disposable diapers, automobiles, and hermetically sealed buildings. In the process, we have surrendered our personal and social power to the corporations that deliver our goods and services.

Motivated only by the short-term view of profit, corporate America extracts raw materials from biological and cultural environments with all the detachment of a machine: human laborers, other species, and resources are considered only in terms of numbers, inputs, and quotas for production. The procedures that convert raw materials into the goods we buy are likewise abstract, more numbers and quotas. Infected by this factory mentality, consumers join in the numbers game by focusing upon the consumption of life rather than on life itself. Our society's fascination with the mounting numbers has resulted in the unaccountable and mindless destruction of the Earth's ecological fabric, and rainforest destruction is the starkest case in point.

The United States is the world's greatest consumer and equally the greatest despoiler of our planet's natural resources. With less than 5 percent of the world's population, we consume 25 percent of the world's energy each year, generating 15 percent of the world's acid rain—causing sulfur dioxide emissions and 25 percent of the nitrogen oxides and carbon dioxide, the gases that contribute to the greenhouse effect.[5] By comparison, Western Europe contributes 17 percent of the worldwide emissions of carbon dioxide, and Japan merely 5 percent.[6] Everything considered, the average U.S. family's consumption has 40 times the environmental impact of the average Indian family and 100 times that of the average Kenyan family.[7]

What we consume we also discard. Since 1960 our annual accumulation of trash has increased by 80 percent; in 1987 the United States produced 160 million tons of solid waste, including an average of a half-ton of residential garbage per person. Within four years, one-third of the country's 6,000 landfills will be full. But, despite the prospect of drowning in garbage, we still recycle only 10 percent of what we dump.[8] By contrast, Japan recycles over 50 percent of its waste and Western Europe around 30 percent.[9]

. Meanwhile, our consumption of wood and paper products contributes greatly to rainforest destruction. According to the Rainforest Action Network, the United States imports about $2.2 billion worth of tropical hardwoods each year, over one-fourth of the $8 billion annual trade in tropical timbers. For every foot of tropical plywood or paneling we buy, much more forest is destroyed in the logging process.[10]

However, tropical hardwoods—teak, mahogany, rosewood, meranti, ebony, lauan, and others—are luxury woods much prized by U.S. consumers. Furniture, picture frames, tableware, and paneling made of these woods are status symbols for homes and offices, signs of wealth and power; so are boats made of teak. And what are status symbols, if not projections of our self-esteem and position in the world? Perhaps if we were more committed to our bodies and our planet, we would rely less on the symbols of conspicuous consumption, and therefore consume less.

Our consumption of tropical wood and wood products—in effect our consumption of tropical rainforests—is something that we in the North definitely can change. But it will require a change within ourselves, a change of attitude and perspective. The same is true of our beef consumption. The U.S. ranks third in the world in per capita beef consumption. We chewed our way through 108.5 pounds of meat per person in 1985.[11] But asking Americans to cut down on their beef consumption seems to be quite impertinent, for the meat myth runs deep in Western civilization. As John Robbins writes in *Diet for a New America*:

> We are deeply conditioned in our attitudes towards meat. We have been taught to believe that our very health depends on our eating it. Many of us believe our social status depends on the quality of our meat and the frequency with which we eat it. . . . Males have been conditioned to associate meat with their masculinity, and quite a few men believe their sexual potency and virility depend on eating meat.[12]

This kind of conditioning is actively fostered by the National Livestock and Meat Board and other corporate interests that spread their propaganda through the schools. As the Meat Board wrote in its 1974–75 Report: "The 37 million elementary and 15 million high school students in the United States constitute a special Meat Board audience."[13] Accordingly, the Meat Board, Oscar Mayer, Mc-Donald's, and the National Dairy Council, among others, provide schools with free "nutritional education" materials. These "hucksters in the classroom," as Robbins calls them, make sure that America's children get hooked on meat and dairy products.[14]

The educational materials, including coloring books, encourage kids to associate meat and dairy products with the healthy and wholesome old-time farm. What they don't tell kids or their parents is that factory farms now produce meat and dairy products with dangerously high levels of antibiotics, hormones, pesticides, and other unhealthy additives. The meat and dairy industries not only feed us deceptive, false, and misleading nutritional information—they also feed us four times more of these additives than we consumed in 1960.[15] Animal flesh and fat now carry high concentrations of these toxic chemicals.

It isn't just human health that is endangered by the consumption of beef. The forests of North, Central, and South America are being cut down to provide grazing land for cattle. In 1985, a typical year, we purchased 52,000 metric tons of beef from Central America. This demand speeds the conversion of rainforests into cattle pasture.[16] Cattle grazing is extremely destructive to the land. Tropical rainforest soils that have been grazed by cattle and pummeled by their hooves erode quickly. The richest of life systems become biological deserts, a cost not accounted in our numbers game.

It is worth noting that if the agricultural grains that are fed to livestock in the United States were fed to humans, we would need only one-fifth of this grain to sustain us. There would be plenty of food for all the world's people, 60 million people would not have to starve each year, and the rest of the land could regenerate itself. In addition, for every person who switches to a pure vegetarian diet, an acre of trees is spared every year.[17] By venerating the beef myth we pay ten times as much for a pound of protein as we would if we ate a vegetarian diet; we also provide enormous profits and power to an industry that is destroying land, ecosystems, and cultures. We reinforce industry's desire for short-term profits with a counterpart: our own desire for short-term gratification—in the form of fast-food hamburgers, for example. By casting our dollar votes for beef we shorten our own lifespan and that of the planetary life-support system.

INSATIABLE CRAVINGS: CONSUMPTION AS ADDICTION

That factory farms and shopping malls have grown up together is less a coincidence than an indication of the ravenous growth of consumerism during the last 30 years. It has been a time of unprecedented materialism and disconnection from natural processes, marked by the prevalence of stress, alienation, drug abuse, and many other social ills. These three decades have also seen an unprecedented acceleration of tropical deforestation. The major lesson of the rainforests—that all things are connected—applies not only to ecological conditions, but to personal and social conditions as well.

Consumerism is relentlessly promoted through the mass media in order to maintain the continuously high levels of consumption upon which our economy depends. Observers of human behavior are becoming increasingly aware that consumerism is, in fact, an addiction, driven partly by Madison Avenue myths and partly by our own emptiness and alienation. The television commercials and magazine ads of mass culture present images of a warm and magical world full of love and assure us that we will gain access to that world if we buy the product—whether toothpaste, long distance telephone service, or jeans—being advertised. The implication is always that our own life is less perfect than the lives of those who wear this fragrance or that label. It is our own gullibility that empowers advertising, which in turn triggers cravings through visions of a world that doesn't exist.

Psychologist Luigi Zoja is one of those who regard consumerism as the dominant religion of our times. He argues that when a society lacks meaningful rites of passage, unsatisfied longings for sacredness and belonging are expressed as obsessive consumption.[18] If we think that the mythical, perfect world of Madison Avenue is reality, our attempts to belong in that world and play by its rules inevitably lead us to consume. The fact that money can't buy love seems to have been stricken from the rulebook of consumer society. So we consume more and more, trying to find ultimate fulfillment in the dominant collective ritual: the orgy of consumption. We become addicts.

Marion Woodman, another psychologist, holds a similar view. "Addictive behavior," she says, "begins with a yearning to belong—to be a real person in a real situation. But in our society, perfection is confused with reality. Unless you pretend to be perfect, you don't belong. . . . Addicted persons . . . can't trust reality. The ground of reality—their ability to rely on their own perception of what is real—has been pulled out from under them."[19]

Woodman says that children in our culture are conditioned from infancy to perform, conform, and please others, rather than to live by their own needs and feelings. "Pummeled by mass media and peer group pressures, their identity may be utterly absorbed by collective stereotypes. In the absence of adequate rites of passage, ad-men become the high priests of an initiation into the addictions of consumerism."[20]

The view that obsessive materialism is the root of addiction is shared by numerous psychologists. Another, Stanislav Grof, M.D., has said that "Addiction to chemical substances is only the most extreme expression of a much larger phenomenon. In the broadest sense, addiction can be defined as dependence on various aspects of the external world as exclusive sources of satisfaction. Addiction, understood in this way, represents a prominent feature of the entire Western civilization, which has lost connection with the inner world and shows fascination with material pursuits."[21]

Many of our society's addictions are to substances and products that originate in the tropics—not only drugs such as cocaine and heroin, but also chocolate, coffee, tobacco, tea, and sugar. Huge tracts of rainforest have been cleared for plantations of these export crops. As with meat, our addictions to these latter products are pushed by advertising and bring enormous profits to the powerful industries that deliver them to us. And these industries in turn exert considerable influence on U.S. foreign policy.

So this is the destructive cycle: addictive consumers support industries that lobby for policies that enable corporations to extract wealth from the Earth in ways that destroy forests, other ecosystems, and indigenous cultures. With the profits thus gained, these corporations advertise their products worldwide, so that more people become addictive consumers, which keeps the vicious cycle going.[22]

BREAKING THE ADDICTIVE CYCLE

Any addiction by definition is self-destructive, whether practiced by an individual or a society. Addictive consumerism is destructive not only to individuals and society, but to the Earth. According to Woodman, Grof, and many others, our addictive society is on a suicidal course that is, in Woodman's words, "a spiritual journey that's become perverted." Grof says, "In the last analysis, the psychological roots of the crisis humanity is facing on a global scale seem to lie in the loss of a spiritual perspective."

The needs that we try to satisfy with things are insatiable because they cannot be fulfilled with things: they can be fulfilled only by a personal shift from materialism to a spiritual perspective. The idea that the cycle of addiction can be broken only by genuine spiritual experience is also supported by the founders of Alcoholics Anonymous and such authorities as Carl Jung and Gregory Bateson.

Spirituality in this sense is unlike conventional religion in that it rests on the direct, personal experience, unmediated by priests of any kind, of belonging within the sacredness of all life. True spiritual experience transcends the cycle of abstraction, alienation, and addiction resulting from the dominant worldview. As an integral part of the vast living whole, one rediscovers one's reciprocal relationship with, and responsibility to, the web of life.

This view supports the perspective of the deep ecology branch of environmentalism, which asserts that spiritual experience is essential for changing behaviors and dismantling institutions that are environmentally destructive. For deep ecologists, the rediscovery of the spiritual reciprocity between humans and the rest of Nature is the basis for restructuring contemporary societies in ecologically harmonious ways.[23]

THE LESSONS OF HISTORY

We have no other choice than to restructure our relationship with the Earth in ecologically harmonious ways. Because the resources of the Earth are limited, our consumeristic culture simply cannot continue as it is. If we do not change our perspective and our way of life, we will leave nothing but a wasteland for our descendants. One way or another, whether we choose or Nature chooses for us, we must change our ways. In the next century, our grandchildren, and certainly their children, will view the deserted remains of shopping malls with dismay. How could their ancestors have spent so much time in these ugly places without a thought for what would remain for future generations? These temples to the false god of abstract wealth will be abandoned as chemically and spiritually toxic, and only feeble grasses will reclaim the vast parking lots. Spiritual gathering places will surround the modest marketplaces of the future. Here the surviving elders will tell stories about the unfortunate mistakes of former generations, whose patterns of overconsumption were a more pernicious excess than the explosive fertility rates of what used to be known as the Third World.

The elders will teach the youngsters the lessons of history: how no civilization has ever destroyed its resource base and survived. How, out of greed and the lust for power, the political and economic power structures of the 20th century separated Third World people from the means to fulfill their survival needs and First World people from the means to fulfill their spiritual needs, and pitted the people of both worlds against each other through the myth of scarcity, which became a self-fulfilling prophecy. And how, out of arrogance and disrespect for the Earth, the dominant power structures of industrial nations nearly rendered the planet unlivable. The elders will teach the youngsters never to forget that humans are dependent on the Earth and that their relationship with the Earth must be reciprocal: they must give back at least as much as they receive.

Then the elders will gather the people to go out and plant trees, and pray that the Earth will regain its fertility. They will celebrate each sign of life with gratitude. And they will greet the other creatures of the Earth with gladness, as harbingers of regeneration.

PART FOUR

WISE
MANAGEMENT

•

Can we rely on it that a "turning point"
will be accomplished by enough people
quickly enough to save the modern world?
This question is often asked, but whatever
answer is given to it will mislead.
The answer "Yes" would lead to complacency;
the answer "No" to despair.
It is desirable to leave these perplexities
behind us and get down to work.

E. F. SCHUMACHER
A GUIDE FOR THE PERPLEXED

•

13

THE
DEVELOPMENT
OF TROPICAL
RAINFOREST
ECONOMICS

RICHARD B. NORGAARD

•

Tropical rainforests are being destroyed because our theories of economic development are naive. Whether one is concerned with the immediate subsistence needs of peasants, the livelihoods of indigenous peoples, the profits of capitalists, or the forests themselves, economic development in the tropical rainforests has almost always been a disaster. Clearly, it's time we admitted that our economic thinking, the system of beliefs that has led us into such massive environmental destruction, is incompatible with the survival of tropical rainforest ecosystems.

These unfit ways of economic thinking are deeply rooted in Western thought and are thus common to both neoclassical and Marxist economics. An elaboration of these unfit elements provides some insights into how economic theory and development could be made compatible with the complex dynamics of social and ecological systems in the tropical rainforest.[1] Such insights in turn suggest how the development of a "tropical rainforest economics" might occur.

MISCONCEPTIONS IN ECONOMIC THINKING

Development as Manifest Destiny

The idea of progress is deeply rooted in Western thought and has been widely incorporated in the beliefs of many in the Third World. The assumption of the inevitability of progress has been extended by economists to the inevitability of economic development. If we assume that development is inevitable, there is no point in fretting over values, indigenous peoples, other biological species, or environmental features that are "in the way" of, or sure to disappear with, development.

Because we believe that development is inevitable and basically desirable, we—through our economists and development planners—have concentrated on making it happen more quickly. Schools, water supply systems, small hospitals, and eventually highways were built in the Amazon during the 20th century with the hope that they would release the development potential inherent to the region. Of course, it was recognized that more than these particular things were needed, but the conditions that would promote development were still thought of as discrete entities, as specific steps. The list has become longer and longer, with more difficult steps constantly being added as development planners have attempted to remove the obstacles and unleash the inevitable development potential inherent in the rainforests.

But, as we know, the obstacle that is being removed is the rainforest itself. How has this happened? The concept of development as a process of removing obstacles has created a mind-set that blocks serious thinking about system dynamics, both social and ecological. In order to effect desirable changes, we must understand both this mind-set and the social and ecological system dynamics of the rainforest—and, in the process, create alternatives to the worldview of the economist.

Development as Modernization

The Western idea of progress, as nebulous and abstract as it may be, has presumed only one general course of development for all. Development has been modernization: the adoption of Western science, technologies, material inputs, social institutions, and values. Economic planners thought development meant the development of modern industry. Agricultural specialists thought it meant the adoption of modern inputs and techniques. Political scientists argued that Third World bureaucracies needed to be modernized to make them efficient. Underlying all of these thrusts was the presumption that development would come through technologies and institutions rooted in Western science.

The myth of development as modernization follows from several myths of Western science. For example, we believe that science is an accumulation of linked universal truths that eventually lead to one unified understanding of everything, and that this knowledge can be used to determine the best solutions to "problems." This overarching belief is questionable in itself, but we make things worse by interpreting the problems narrowly so that they conform to our solutions. Agricultural problems are simplified to problems of crop productivity, for example. If we ignore the social and ecological context, it becomes arguable that fertilizers and chemical pest controls, the modern inputs used in the First World, are the solution.[2]

The myth of modernization led to early overinvestment in modern industry, the misuse of temperate zone agricultural technologies, and excessive development of centralized, Western-style bureaucracies. Local resources were used poorly. Indigenous knowledge, cultivars, and farming practices were lost. Governments became centralized and rational by Western standards, but irrational given the social and ecological systems with which they were supposed to interact.

Much has been learned from the mistakes, but a correction is only beginning to get underway. A great many of the educated people of

Third World countries, as well as all of those in international assistance agencies and most in the legislatures and public interest groups affecting the policies of the international assistance agencies, have been trained to think like Westerners and work with Western technologies, inputs, and social structures. The cumulative inertia of this mind-set creates considerable resistance to change. But today, a few nongovernmental organizations, academic institutions, and assistance agencies are beginning to explore alternative directions in development that build on indigenous knowledge, technologies, and social organization. For rainforested regions and the people who live there, the real development potential lies within these alternatives.

Development as Capital Accumulation

Capital accumulation—the net transformation of resources and labor into more and more productive assets such as factories—can lead to higher levels of well-being, but misconceptions arise when economists think of capital only in the abstract. The accumulation of capital has been subsidized by governments to accelerate development, with little attention to the specific capital that might be effective in particular social or ecological settings. In the Amazon, this tendency to abstraction allowed capital to be defined as investments in the clearing of forest, planting of grasses, and purchasing of cattle. Although it is possible to make a tropical rainforest behave like a cattle pasture for a while, the short life of pastures makes them a very poor investment in real capital. The subsidization of "capital investments" in forest clearing has not only grossly simplified the ecosystem; it has not even led to economic development. Amazon planners wanted to establish permanent agriculture as an alternative to shifting slash-and-burn cultivation. But by subsidizing clearing, they hastened the slash-and-burn cycle by making the opening up of new land more economical than more intensive management of already cleared land.

One must be very imaginative or awfully naive to think that a simple pasture ecosystem with wispy grass and exposed soil is better capital than the complex rainforest with all of its biomass and its ability to capture the energy of the sun and recycle nutrients. Frederick Soddy tried to convince economists half a century ago to pay closer attention to the difference between financial and real capital.[3] Financial capital is simply a promise for a share of the returns from real capital—from the returns on investments in machinery and equipment, buildings, and land improvements. Real capital is Nature's capital: natural resources transformed into a more productive state for people through labor and ingenuity. Financial capital—with government subsidies rather than real capital supporting it—has been created in the Amazon and other rainforested regions.[4]

One example of investment in real capital can be seen in certain forms of rice cultivation. The transformation of wet tropical ecosystems into rice paddy has been successful throughout much of Southeast Asia. Paddy systems keep weed competition down and retain nutrients as effectively as the "best" of natural ecosystems. Caboclos, the peasants of the Brazilian Amazon, cultivate rice along the banks of the Amazon River simply by planting as the river drops after flood season. This approach could be improved through gradual investments in dikes and drains by the caboclos themselves. Investment incentives would help, and of course, they would need title to their property. Diking and draining for paddy rice could be a creation of real capital. But until only recently, the people along the river have been viewed as backward by economic development planners in Brasilia, the capital of Brazil, because they combine agriculture, fishing, hunting, and gathering. In reality, their lifestyle is successful and has the potential for development. It is simply not modern.

Development as Specialization and Exchange

The concepts of comparative advantage, specialization, and the gains from exchange are central to economic theory for both free markets and for centralized planning. Comparative advantage results when people in one region have trading advantages that enable them to produce specific goods more cheaply than those in another region. Such advantages stem from differences in the productivities of people, tools, and land in various economic activities. It immediately follows that total output can be increased through specialization of people, tools, and land in those activities for which they have a comparative advantage. Specialization in particular activities leaves each producer with a surplus of one or more products and deficits of others. Producers then barter with each other until they have a mix of goods that makes each as happy as possible given the willingness of others to trade. Comparative advantage, the efficiency of specialization, and the gains through exchange are basic to our understanding of economic systems and to our understanding of the development process.

The "gains from trade" argument underlies many development policies and is the basis for many projects in rainforest ecosystems. Road construction has been justified on the grounds that it facilitates trade. Some farmers who once planted diverse crops for subsistence have specialized and have become part of a global exchange. But other subsistence farmers have been bought out or forced out by larger commercial ventures attracted to the now more accessible region. And these large ventures inevitably replace ecologically based, biodiverse agricultural systems with extensive single-species monocultures.

The problem is that environmental services atrophy under monoculture. Locally specific nitrogen-fixing bacteria, mycorrhizae that help plants absorb nutrients, predators of pests, and pollinators and seed dispersers—all of which coevolved over millennia and provide environmental services to traditional ecosystems—have gone extinct or had their genetic base dramatically narrowed by monoculture technologies. Deprived of the flora with which they coevolved, soil microbes disappear. Insecticides, herbicides, and fertilizers, as well as genetically selected seeds of little variability, have replaced biodiverse life systems. In this way, specialization, exchange, and the consequent regional homogeneity of crop species have destroyed environmental services.

The global exchange economy also induces temporal variation, which is environmentally destructive. Factors beyond the rainforest—crop failures, new technologies, changing tastes, variations in interest rates, changes in the strengths of cartels, and variations in trade barriers—all of these redefine comparative advantage. This redefinition is accommodated, at least in theory, when people, tools, and land shift their specialization to different lines of production, redefining the pattern of exchange. Economists assume that factors of production are mobile, that labor, capital, and land can shift between the lines of production in a way that optimizes the good of all.

If these adjustments to exogenous change could be undertaken without individual hardship or social or ecological system transformation, economic well-being would be maximized. With all producers adjusting to best compensate for a change, the change in the aggregate is minimized, keeping aggregate well-being as close to the undisturbed maximum as possible. In aggregate, production is more stable than it would be if the adjustments did not take place. But this stabilizing process for the whole increases the amount of change at the individual level in terms of who does what and with which tools and land. Variation in aggregate production is reduced through increasing the variation for the individual components in the economic system. For example, landless peasants move from place to place to harvest various crops for export. These people, despite theory, pay dearly to move around.

The economic model used for designing exchange policies makes other implicit assumptions. It assumes that not only can people move around in order to minimize aggregate fluctuations, but land can move freely between uses, too. However, relatively few environments can freely shift to support rice, then cotton, then cattle pasture, and back to rice, in the way that a reasonably adaptive person might shift from one type of agriculture to another. Thus development through exchange simplifies agroecosystems but increases their variation from year to year. In the process, real environmental capital—soil fertility, nutrient and water cycles, and so forth—and the services thereof are lost.

Comparative advantage, specialization, and the gains from exchange are the very core of both microeconomic theory and the linear programming models of socialist planners. This core presumes an atomistic world. If everything could be divided up and assigned as property, if the existence of one thing were not dependent on the existence of another, if things could be traded in discrete units instead of amorphous globs, if processes including trade could be reversed, the theory would not get us into trouble. But such is not the nature of the world. Economists have adapted the theory to account for linkages and irreversibility, but when more than one or two things are connected and irreversibility is recognized in full, the economic model is intractable.

Economic development plans rely on theory for guidance. Nevertheless, planners know how reliance on free trade policies can hurt laborers in specialized regions under particular conditions, perhaps leaving lasting effects on subsequent generations. (Capitalists, of course, are cushioned from the shocks of change through favorable tax policies.) But development planners have yet to incorporate into their thinking the fact that analogous damage to portions of ecological systems can lead to irreversible losses.

Development as manifest destiny is at best an excuse for not thinking. The development concepts of modernization, capital accumulation, and the gains from specialization and exchange have proven unfit as a basis for development planning. Nevertheless, we need not throw these economic concepts out of our tool kit of approaches to understanding economic systems. Capital accumulation can lead to development when the right capital and supporting institutions are added. Exchange theory gives quick insights and raises interesting questions about possible gains. However, economic planners should use these theories only in conjunction with broader frameworks that offset their shortcomings.

UNDERPINNINGS OF A
TROPICAL RAINFOREST ECONOMICS

Economists and planners will eventually accommodate the broader objectives and systemic understanding demanded for sustainable tropical rainforest development if enough people hound them and show them how. The transition will certainly, however, take too long. In the meantime, the sorts of mistakes that economic thinking and practice are making today will have to be prevented through political vigilance. Even when economic thinking is more developed, new problems will have evolved beyond the capabilities of theory and institutions. Thus I am optimistic about the development of economic models and practice, but not so naive as to think that a revolution in thinking and institutions will occur early and rapidly enough to prevent the destruction of a significant portion of the remaining tropical forest and her peoples.

Dismantling the Dominant Worldview

I am particularly concerned that the advance of economic thinking has been slowed by the dominant epistemological beliefs of Western society. Logical positivism, with its emphasis on objectivity and the accumulation of linked universal truths, is losing its grip. Even economists are beginning to wax epistemological.[5] Nevertheless, economists, natural scientists, and the educated public generally hold to 19th century beliefs about science and public action that are at the root of the development crisis.

Early Western scientists set out to understand a static world as God had created it. They envisioned the acquisition of knowledge as a process whereby individual minds investigated Nature's parts and processes. In this model, the mind itself is conceived to be an independent entity that merely perceives and interprets: asking questions, thinking, and acting neither influence the underlying principles that govern Nature nor affect the mind itself. And like the mind, Nature in the dominant worldview also just exists. The world just is and the mind just perceives and interprets. In this way, mind and Nature, people and the natural world, have been juxtaposed and considered separate from the beginning of Western thought. The emphasis on the objectivity of knowledge stems from this static juxtaposition of mind and Nature.

Logical positivism might best be illustrated diagramatically as in Figure 1. We begin by observing what we have a priori decided are the universal parts and relationships of Nature, we derive theories

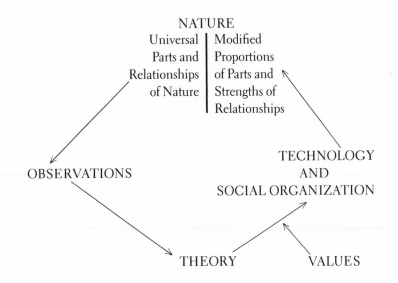

Figure 1. The Worldview of Logical Positivism

about these characteristics, we test theories against Nature, we design technologies and social organizations based on theories and values, and thereby modify Nature. The assumption that the proportions of Nature's parts and the relative strengths of Nature's relationships can only be modified is based on the assumption that the universal nature of the parts and relations, as well as human values, must remain unchanged. For, if they changed, our knowledge would become obsolete through its very use, and prediction and prescription would not be possible.

This worldview supports the application of "universal truths" through large centralized institutions. Following the belief that the only good knowledge is universal, we assume that the knowledge arrived at in temperate climates with temperate values must be true for all cultures and ecosystems. Then urban bureaucracies headquartered in Rome and Washington, DC, go to great lengths to apply this knowledge to the rural tropics. The results have been disastrous, of course, for tropical ecosystems in general, and particularly for the rainforests.

Fortunately, the dominant Western worldview has come increasingly under attack. Two major criticisms are relevant to our discussion. It is to be hoped that criticisms such as these will help to break up the epistemological logjam that has prevented consideration of realistic and sustainable alternatives.

First, it must be acknowledged that logical positivism cannot accommodate complexity. The physical laws of motion, gravity, and heat are universal, and the ways in which molecules chemically react are invariant. But the numbers of ways that the simple parts and relationships studied by the physicist and the chemist can combine to form complex biological organisms, let alone ecological systems with human participants and cultures, are infinite. Hence, it is unreasonable to expect to find universal principles for renewable resource systems even apart from people, let alone with people involved.

Second, there is the problem of evolution. In biological and social systems, new parts and relations evolve rather rapidly. The application of knowledge through institutional change and new technologies exerts new selective pressures on biological and social systems, changing the fitness of different parts and interactions. Thus the use of knowledge changes the nature of social and ecological reality. For example, the application of our knowledge of the chemicals that are toxic to insects led to the evolution of resistant insects. Likewise, our consciousness of the difference between modern and indigenous agricultural technologies may lead to the evolution of new technologies that blur the original differences. Given these considerations, the static worldview of logical positivism is obviously untenable in a world of accelerating social and ecological change.

The Emerging Coevolutionary Worldview

In the emerging worldview, people are included as a part of evolving local systems. The characteristics of each system have evolved to reflect the nature of the people—their social organization, knowledge, technologies, and values. Indeed, humans have actively selected the characteristics of species and assisted in maintaining desirable bio-

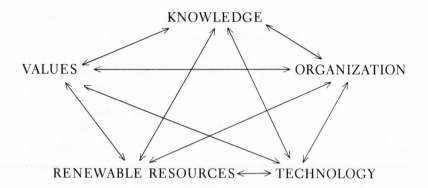

Figure 2. The coevolution of knowledge, values, social organization, technology, and the biological system

logical relationships for centuries. The species and varieties selected and the relationships assisted depend on people's values, what they know, how they are socially organized to interact with their environment, and the techniques available to them.

And just as ecosystems bear the imprint of our activities, human cultures reflect some of the characteristics of their physical and biological environments. Different physical terrains and climates and their associated biological systems—alpine, tropical rainforest, savanna, and desert—lead to different ways of knowing, select for different forms of social organization, support different technologies, and encourage different values. Cultural diversity reflects ecosystem diversity.

The diagram in Figure 2 illustrates a coevolutionary worldview. Innovations or changes occur in each of the components of the ecosystem: knowledge, organization, values, technology, and renewable resources. Whether these innovations or changes are maintained depends on whether they prove fit with respect to the other components, as indicated by the arrows in the figure. Since each component puts selective pressure on the others, each reflects characteristics of the others; therefore, each part can be understood only in the context of the whole. This coevolutionary explanation of the development of knowledge, technology, and social organization indicates that at best, economic planners can work with the process. Given the nature of knowledge and the implications of its use, one can readily see how top-down planning based on one understanding of economics has led to unexpected consequences and frequent failure.

If economists and development planners begin to adopt a coevolutionary worldview, we can expect a move toward decentralization to accommmodate differences in values, social organization, and ecological systems between places. Indigenous peoples could evolve in their own way. Development planners would take an adaptive approach, experimenting with small changes and monitoring how these affect the course of development. Big projects will be fewer. The role of global exchange will decrease. Rainforest technologies will evolve out of the subjective experience of those involved, rather than being imposed from afar and based strictly on "objective" knowledge.

We must hope that these lessons from the rainforest will be incorporated into our understanding of economics over the coming decades. The myths of logical positivism, embedded in the design of our bureaucracies and in our concept of responsible bureaucratic behavior, must be replaced with realistic bases for social organization. The myths justify hierarchies of expertise and centralized power that are modern guises for old class structures as well as sources of biological and cultural destruction. The future is unclear, but the general directions we need to take are becoming clearer and the political will is becoming stronger.

14
WHY
SUPERNATURAL
EELS MATTER

KENNETH IAIN TAYLOR

•

The world's remaining rainforests are being cut down at a disastrous rate. Often the local people, whether indigenous or colonists, are blamed for this, because of what is said to be their irresponsible practice of slash-and-burn agriculture. But, in fact, all serious studies of natural resource use by indigenous peoples show that their traditional ways of life have been brilliantly conservationist.

The Yanomami and Kayapo Indians of Brazilian Amazonia, for example, each in their own ways, have been extremely successful in preserving their tropical forest territories. Both groups make use of an astonishing diversity of the rainforest's plants and animals. At the same time, they manage forest life in such a way that the plants, animals, and they themselves—the human beings—thrive and flourish. They live in the forest and use the forest's resources, but they also leave the forest intact for the future.

What makes them so remarkably successful where we, the outsiders, seem always to fail and to end up destroying the forest and its natural resources? The answer to this question seems to lie in their entire way of life, in their traditional ways of knowing and living within the ecology of the rainforest. The Amazonian Indians are already doing, and have been doing for centuries, what we would like to know how to do. And yet, their ways of knowing and being are so different from our own that we hesitate to consider them conservationists. Because of the discrepancies between their cultures and our own, we tend to overlook what may be the key to preserving the rainforests. Therefore, let us take a closer look at how they do it.

YANOMAMI LIFE IN THE FOREST

The Yanomami Indians live in northern Brazil and southern Venezuela, on both sides of the divide between the northernmost part of Amazonia and the southernmost part of the Orinoco River basin. There are 22,000 Yanomami, speaking four closely related languages. The linguistic subgroup with which I have lived, the Sanuma, are in the northwest of the Yanomami territory.[1]

Unlike the outsiders who have tried to profit from the forest's natural resources, the Yanomami do not just cut down and sell the lumber of their forests, they do not just clear-cut the forest to raise cattle, they do not just plant exotic trees to produce cellulose for sale, they do not just plant some cash crop to sell for a living. Instead, the Yanomami use and depend on their forest resources for their entire livelihood: for hunting, fishing, and collecting forest resources, and for farming their small fields and gardens in the style known as "shifting cultivation." They cull from the forest everything they need for food, clothing, shelter, good health, and prosperity. All of these activities vary in intensity and regularity from season to season and from everyday to ceremonial, ritual, or magical occasions. Such precise uses of their forest resources are possible only because they possess a deep and extensive understanding of the natural processes of their environment and a way of life that respects those processes.

Yanomami villages are situated in small clearings. They build houses with tree trunks, poles, leaves, and vines, which they easily get for themselves in the forest. Every few years, for one reason or another, they move their village to a new site, where they build themselves brand new houses in a matter of days. Radiating out from the village are major trails that lead to fields in current use, to "abandoned" fields, to places where they regularly hunt, fish, and gather food, and to campsites in the forest. The forest around the village is also crisscrossed by lesser trails used on hunting or collecting trips for food and raw materials of all kinds.

This complex and fluctuating network of changing sites and locations and the shifting tracery of trails that link them to each other are not, of course, evenly spread out over a uniform and homogenous circle of forest. In the Yanomami area, when you travel through the forest for even a few minutes, you are struck by its diversity. On a short walk from a Sanuma village, for example, you will find high ridges topped with tall trees and little undergrowth, low swampy areas choked with almost impenetrable vegetation, river banks where hanging lianas impede your easy progress, sandy-bottomed clear forest streams, and wider rivers interrupted by rapids and waterfalls. Each of these environmental variations, or biotypes, provides the Yanomami with a particular set of natural resources. Access to each biotype is essential; without it, Yanomami life would not be possible.

It is normal for a Yanomami community to move its village every few years as the best sites for preparing fields get used up in the area immediately surrounding the village site, and new fields have to be made at greater and greater distances from the village. Also, the fabric of the house structures deteriorates, becoming intolerably infested with cockroaches, crickets, fleas, and *bichos-de-pe*, or chigoe fleas. When things reach this point the community moves.

First new fields are prepared close to the new village site. When these begin to produce food, building the new houses begins. This need not be done in any particular hurry, of course, since the old village is still perfectly inhabitable, but within a few days or weeks of hard work things are ready and moving day arrives.

It is a tremendously exciting moment when everybody packs up everything they possess in the world, loading it all into baskets and backpacks. With pet animals and supplies of food for the trip itself, as well as for the first day or two at the new village, they set out. Some of the old people carry smoldering embers from the hearths they are leaving behind forever. With children on top of basket loads, in baby slings, or running along beside the grown-ups, the entire community begins what may be a trek of several days through the forest to the new village site.[2]

Yanomami life also requires constant interaction between village communities. Some communities need to trade with others for commodities not available locally, and some people have to look for a spouse in other communities. Each dry season, everyone takes part in a number of intervillage festivals, either as visitor or host. In the rare event of a severe shortage of field crops, it helps to be able to visit, en masse, a friendly neighboring community where food can be found until the visitors' new fields begin to produce. Likewise, the shamans are not limited to curing only fellow villagers. Patients may visit a renowned shaman in a neighboring village and, in a difficult case, a shaman may be invited to attempt a cure in a village other than his own.[3]

All of these activities—hunting, collecting, farming, relocating villages, and intervillage festivals and visits—require and ensure that the Yanomami know their territory and its assorted biotypes intimately. This knowledge allows them to make full use of the resources to be found within their forest environment.

HOW THE SANUMA USE THE FOREST

It is impressive to see the variety of plants and animals that the Yanomami use in one way or another. The Sanuma I lived with for two years in the upper Auaris river valley of Brazil consider most of the animals of their environment to be "edible fauna," or *salo bi* (the Yanomami terms used in this chapter are always those of the Sanuma I lived with). Virtually all *salo bi* are considered worth hunting or fishing or collecting. Among the Sanuma I knew, only the *pumodomi*—possum, mice, and lizards—are taboo to everybody.

A number of other species, which belong to several categories of "supernatural fauna," are outside the *salo bi* category and it is out of the question to intentionally hunt them or eat them. Otherwise, the Sanuma use virtually all the fauna of their environment, including some insects, for food.

Most ground-going and tree-climbing animals are prey to Sanuma arrows, and some are even caught by hand. With the paralyzing juice of a vine, or with hook and line, the Sanuma bring a wide variety of fish to the hearth. Various other creatures are also considered worthy meals, such as snakes, frogs, crabs, and caimans.

Their extensive use of the fauna is matched by their use of forest vegetation. While I lived among them, I saw the Sanuma use the wood, leaves, fibers, and other parts of the long list of forest plants and trees to build, make, weave, or prepare most of their material possessions and equipment. Several species of trees are used for housing structures, for dueling poles, in the preparation of their hallucinogenic snuff, and for firesticks and the constantly needed firewood. Palm and other kinds of leaves are used to thatch shelters and permanent houses, to bundle food, as sunscreens, fans, temporary mats, or as wrappings for foods baked in the embers of the fires. Palm trees, bamboos, and canes are used for bows, arrows, arrowheads, and quivers. Lianas are used for fish "poison"; canes and vines for basketry, hammocks, and lashings of all kinds; barks for hammocks, cords and tump lines; fibers for making rope. Flowers, leaves, and seeds are used for personal adornment; resins for adhesives and flammable torches. Some plants are used for medicinal and magical purposes, and as both contraceptives and aphrodisiacs.

When we add to that list the fruits, nuts, roots, seeds, shoots, palmitos, and mushrooms that supplement the many food crops grown in their fields and gardens, we end up with a lengthy list of plants of which the Sanuma make good use. Among this Yanomami subgroup, more than 400 wild plants are known and named, with more than 180 of these used for one purpose or another. Of these 180 plants, some 135 are used regularly. Sixty of these are edible, with some 20 forming a staple part of the normal diet.[4]

For the Sanuma to use all of these species of plants and animals, they must, of course, have a very detailed knowledge of their territory. They also require a very considerable knowledge of the diets, behavior, and daily and seasonal routines of these animals and a constantly updated mental inventory of the supply and locations of the plants they use. This is the basis of their vast ecological knowledge but, as I discuss below, their successful preservation of all these plant and animal species depends on more than just knowledge.

HOW THE KAYAPO MANAGE

How the Kayapo know, manage, and use the plants and animals of their forests is also astonishingly subtle and complex. These Indians also live in Brazil, but far to the south of the Yanomami, in the basin of the Xingu River. Their territory, near the southern limit of Amazonia, is a region of forests interspersed with areas of more or less open *cerrado* (similar to savanna).

Like the Yanomami and almost all the Indian groups of Amazonia, the Kayapo hunt, fish, and gather a great many species of forest plants and animals and practice shifting cultivation. They also concentrate useful plants by transplanting and then cultivating them in "resource islands" in midforest, forest fields prepared beside camping sites, natural forest openings, agricultural plots and old fields, and along the sides of their many kilometers of trails through the forest. They also select and transplant a number of semidomesticated native plants and "manipulate" a number of animal species (birds, fish, bees, mammals) for sources of food.

Perhaps the most impressive of all their techniques is their ability to create patches of forest (*apete*) in the open *cerrado*.[5] Darrell Posey, an ethnoecologist, became aware that these isolated patches of forest were human-made only after almost seven years of research among the Kayapo. As he has pointed out, "perhaps the most exciting aspect of these new data is the implication for reforestation. The Indian example not only provides new ideas about how to build forests 'from scratch,' but also how to successfully manage what has been considered infertile. . . ."[6]

As a result of the Kayapo's presence and their remarkable way of life, the plants and animals of their area are more diverse, more locally concentrated, of greater population size and density, and more youthful and vigorous than they would be in a forest that lacked these indigenous resource managers.

IS IT KNOWLEDGE OR IS IT WISDOM?

The Yanomami and the Kayapo, each in their own way, make full use of the diversity of the rainforest's plants and animals. Yet, they also manage the life of the forest in a sustainable manner that allows human and nonhuman life to flourish.

In the Sanuma case, we see a cultural system in which there is an extremely widespread, or "extensive," use of a truly enormous range of resources, both animal and vegetable. When they want or need any of the great number of resources that they use on a regular basis, the Sanuma simply to go to the specific biotype within their territory where they know the item may be found.

The Kayapo undoubtedly know their forest and "cerrado" territory at least as well as the Sanuma know theirs. But the Kayapo manage their plant and animal resources in a different and much more "intensive" way, with their constant transplanting of not just a few, but a very considerable number of wild plants.

Both the extensive system of the Sanuma and the intensive one of the Kayapo work well to preserve the plants and animals of these Indians' forest environments. The Sanuma system is an appropriate one for an expanding group which, in living memory, has been able to move into new areas of forest and now has a very large territory at its disposal. The Kayapo system, traditionally, appears to have been their way of supporting an extremely large population—much larger than today—in a part of the country where they were surrounded on all sides by neighboring indigenous groups.

Although we may readily admire the ecological knowledge of tribal peoples like the Yanomami and the Kayapo, we nevertheless tend to ask whether they are really conservationists. This question, although it has been addressed from a number of perspectives, usually betrays an ethnocentric bias: the implication is that indigenous peoples are conservationists if and only if they do their conserving in our way. However, whatever they are doing to so effectively preserve the forests, we may be sure that it is done in their own way.

In our way of life, ecological knowledge is considered a highly technical speciality that scientists acquire through long years of study and many months of research in the field. We do not expect everyone to have this knowledge. Similarly, conservation is an emerging science for which most of us recognize the need, but which we tend to leave to the specialists—the ecologists and environmentalists whom we essentially employ to do the job for us. Not only do we compartmentalize tasks in this way, but we also, following the bias of Western science, expect this knowledge to be explicit, conscious, something that can be rationally articulated.

It serves no purpose, however, for us to expect the indigenous peoples' ecological and conservation skills to be likewise compartmentalized, specialized, and articulated. On the contrary, theirs is an ecological wisdom that is intricately woven into the very fabric of their cultures; for the most part it is not an articulated, conscious "body of knowledge." The accounts I have given of the Sanuma and the Kayapo indicate that they not only possess systematic ecological knowledge, but that their entire way of life expresses an ecological wisdom that enables them to take care of their forest environment. However, it is not expressed in ways that our scientists have been able to recognize or accept as an ecological science or system of knowledge.

Here are two examples of the ecological wisdom of the Yanomami with whom I lived. To have a successful intervillage festival in memory of an important dead person, the hosts have to provide a generous supply of roasted game meat for their visitors. To do this requires a hunting expedition of several days. A group of men, some of them from the host village and some of them visitors, goes hunting in areas that are quite far away from the village and are hunted only on these special occasions. These are the areas of "no man's land" between neighboring and sometimes hostile villages. In between festival hunts, these areas are left alone and function as "game preserves."[7]

But the Yanomami do not speak of these areas as game preserves (though they do enjoy telling you about the great quantities of game to be found in them). They speak of this aspect of their hunting life in terms of commemorating the dead, honoring their visitors, and staying away from possibly contested areas between their own and their neighbors' villages.

Another example is seen in the Yanomami's constant mobility. Every few years communities change the location of their villages, sometimes dividing into smaller units, other times joining together and moving into temporarily larger, multiple communities. As a result, the areas of forest used by the communities are constantly changed and rotated, allowing both plant and animal populations to recuperate from the intensive use of the previous years.

Once again, as the Yanomami see it, it is not only ecological considerations that bring about their villages' splitting, coming together, and mobility. From their point of view, these shifts and movements are motivated by the desire to get away from the rival factions with whom they have been quarreling, or to move further away from feared enemies to "safer" parts of the forest.

Some of the Kayapo's expressions of ecological wisdom are similarly oblique. They believe in an enormous supernatural electric eel that they call *ru-ka-uk*. They say that it "raises" certain species of fish. Since its shock can be lethal over a range of some of some 500 meters, the Kayapo carefully avoid the waters where the *ru-ka-uk* lives. These waters happen to be where the fish spawn, and, as Darrell Posey expressed it, this belief is thus an "important ecological management mechanism." In fact, Posey suggested that we try to understand this belief and its ecological function by thinking of the *ru-ka-uk* not as an eel but as a concept—a concept, perhaps, of protecting fish spawning beds.

Posey also provides the text of a Kayapo myth that he calls "Why women paint their faces with ant parts."

> *The trails of the fire ant . . . are long. They are ferocious . . . like men. But the little red ant of our fields . . . is gentle like women; they are not aggressive. . . . Their trails meander like the bean vines on the maize. The little red ant is the relative/friend of the manioc. This is why women use the little red ant to mix with*

urucu *to paint their faces in the maize festival. The little red ant is the guardian of our fields and is our relative/friend.*[8]

Posey goes on to say, "The myth begins to make sense when we understand the coevolutionary complex of maize, beans, manioc, and the *Pogomyrmex* ant." It turns out that the ants are attracted to the nectar of the young manioc plants. In getting to the nectar, they use their mandibles to trim away obstructions, including any bean vines that are beginning to climb up the young manioc plants and would eventually prevent them from growing. The twining bean plants, thus unable to grow on the manioc plants, are left with the maize plants as their natural trellis. In the process, they provide valuable nitrogen, which is needed by the maize. The ants, then, are the natural manipulators and "facilitate the horticultural activities of the women," who admire the ant for its industrious and organized activity and mix bits of the ants in their body paint "in order to aquire the perceived qualities of the insect."

In neither case—eels or ants—do the Kayapo articulate these matters in ecological terms. The beliefs and practices in question contain and communicate important ecological wisdom, but they are expressed by the Kayapo as myth or supernatural belief, and in body painting techniques.

ARE THE INDIANS CONSERVATIONISTS?

Most discussions of Indians as "conservationists" ask whether or not these people consciously and intentionally practice conservation. On the one hand, as the Yanomami and Kayapo examples show, it does seem that these people—like so many other indigenous peoples around the world—do, somehow, preserve their environment and its natural resources. On the other hand, there is no reason to suppose that they do so consciously, in the way that we Westerners might. On the contrary, what the examples show is that the desired result can be achieved in the most extraordinarily roundabout ways.

Indigenous forest-dwellers who were lucky enough to be left alone by the outside world took good care of their forests for centuries, and, in recent years, they have shown their willingness and ability to do so in the context of modern state societies—if they are allowed to. We who advocate the preservation of the rainforests need to recognize that these expert environmental custodians have an important role to play in the future of the world's remaining tropical rainforests. We do not yet know how to conserve the rainforests and, in fact, seem to be able only to destroy them.

Our best, and perhaps last, remaining option may be for us to swallow our pride and concede that it is the indigenous peoples who know how to take care of the rainforests—and let them go on doing it. Taking this option, however, means not doing things in our customary way. It is not enough for scientists to learn from these people some bits of explicit ecological knowledge that they can then apply on our behalf whether or not the indigenous peoples survive. For the wisdom necessary to save the rainforests is contained only in the complete traditional systems that these people practice. Nor can we expect these ancient ways of forest preservation to be continued by acculturated, integrated, or assimilated people stripped of their traditions and crashing around the forest with firearms and chainsaws and outboard motors. Our Western compulsion to "civilize" or "modernize" the Indians is an indulgence and a luxury that neither we nor the forests can any longer afford.

Taking this last remaining option, then, means leaving the Indians alone to the greatest extent possible (while accepting the responsibility to protect and cure them of *our* diseases), leaving them alone to decide for themselves which, if any, of their traditional practices they may want to change. If we are lucky, they will opt to continue their traditional ways of forest conservation.

And we must also continue to learn from them. They do know the forest best, and though we may not be able to live their culture we can learn valuable lessons—from how to grow biodiverse forest from depleted cattle pasture, to how to select species that will meet the needs of non-indigenous people, to how to respect the forest's processes. If deforestation is to stop, "intensification" of the forest's productivity must occur for the benefit of those rural peasants living in, or colonizing, any areas of the forest that are not already occupied by Indians.

Protecting and learning from indigenous people is an option we cannot forgo. If we do anything else we will be condemning the forests to virtually total destruction. But if we can find the good sense to let the indigenous peoples look after the rainforests on behalf of us all, then the winners will be not only the Indians and the rainforests, but all of humanity and the planet as a whole.

15

AGROECOLOGY

Reshaping Agricultural Development

STEPHEN GLIESSMAN

AND

ROBERT GRANTHAM

•

Imagine traveling through the Southeast Asian rainforests of Sumatra in a beat-up old bus. As it scrapes to a halt in a muddy gravel pullout, defeated-looking people—the only ones in sight—move toward it, loaded with sacks, cases, and bundles, their eyes withdrawn behind wraps and hats to ward off the steady drizzle. Muddy sacks are flung up onto the roof of the bus to be tied down with the other luggage, while wet, big-eyed children jump aboard, followed by their parents.

Across a grassy ditch lies an agricultural field, wet and eroding in the tropical rain. Reddish brown runoff streams through parallel rows of crops, defying their mechanical neatness. Although the cool rain is a relief in the tropical heat, it is a mixed blessing, for it is washing away what fertility is left in the land that is being abandoned.

The new arrivals pack the aisles, attempting to converse above the engine's roar as the bus resumes its journey. The driver's knowing questions draw sadness and uncertainty from the men standing near him. Three years ago they arrived here as settlers, hoping for a new and better life in the developing agricultural frontier where new roads penetrate previously undisturbed forest. But these soils did not compare to the rich volcanic soils of their home in Java. After a few seasons of cropping, the land could give no more. And the tools that were needed to grow the abundance of rice they were used to—the fertilizers and seed varieties and insecticides—were not easy to come by, and, if found, they were too expensive.

Now these people have no specific destination. They will move further on down the road toward primary rainforest, seeking new land to burn in order to gain the nutrients of the forest's ashes for their crops. These passengers are not travelers; they are rootless, destitute victims of unsustainable agricultural development in the tropics.

This scene is repeated along much of the 500 kilometers of Trans-Sumatran Highway in Indonesia—and, likewise, the Transamazon Highway in Brazil and the Transgabon Railway in Gabon. Colonists around the world are converting tropical rainforests into farmland. Many are purposely shifted from densely populated regions into rain-forested lands by government-sponsored transmigration projects. The governments' remedy for overpopulation and pressures for agrarian reform thus becomes the colonists' dilemma—that of a nonsustainable means of livelihood.

In rainforested regions, most deforested land is used for agricultural production: cash crops for export, pasture for cattle, and food for local markets and subsistence. The small, diverse agricultural systems that produce fruits, vegetables, grains, and small animals meet most of the local subsistence needs, but they provide relatively little input to the national economy. To the planner concerned with generating income to defray foreign debts, these small systems are all but invisible. Small home gardens are seldom found in development textbooks, and even more seldom on the agendas of development economists. Instead, the planner's drawing board is filled with schemes to transform the tropical landscape into fields of monocrops that are dependent on expensive inputs and determined by the rhythms of international markets.

This simplified scenario outlines the basic tension that exists in rural development in the tropics. Centralized planning promotes modern, monocultural agricultural systems and ignores the economic opportunities offered by the inherent diversity of rainforest ecosystems. But in destroying the diversity of the rainforests, these systems have proved to be, time and again, nonsustainable through time.

AGRICULTURAL DEVELOPMENT AND AGROECOSYSTEMS

Although it's hard to tell by looking at an industrial farm, agricultural systems are ecosystems; they are not exempt from the rules of Nature. Moreover, agricultural systems are ecological systems designed by humans to meet people's needs for sustenance and community over time. When human needs and ecological needs are not acknowledged in the design of an agricultural system, the system, in time, will fail. This is basically the story of modern agriculture in the tropics. Although many attempts have been made, government planners and those who implement their plans have consistently failed to find sustainable solutions to the complex problems of tropical agriculture—at great cost to the forest's fertility and human well-being.

Without their dense vegetation, the ancient soils in most rainforested regions become barren due to warm temperatures and abundant rain, conditions that leach the soil of nutrients. Tropical rainforest soils are, in fact, best suited for growing rainforest. When the complex arrangements of plants, roots, soil microbes, fungi, and decomposers are intact under the natural forest canopy, the soil is the living body that supports the lush forest diversity. But without its living components, cleared rainforest soil is vulnerable to the harsh sun and heavy rain.

Hence, the soils of forests that are cut for cropping retain their fertility only briefly. Cultivators must rotate their plots, allowing fields to lie fallow for long periods to regenerate. Therefore, the ratio of population to land must be low, for once the fertility is gone, another patch of forest must be felled and burned to release the nutrients necessary to grow more crops.

Increasing population pressures have made slash-and-burn farming obsolete; there simply is not enough forest to go around. Nevertheless, simple slash-and-burn or swidden agriculture does persist, and it is practiced primarily by peasants who have lost or lack access to more fertile land. The repetitive process of cutting, burning, and cropping until the fertility is exhausted has become a dismal cycle of deforestation and impoverishment.

Thus, nonsustainable agriculture is one of the central obstacles to protecting the rainforests. If the pressure on the rainforests is to be minimized, ways must be found to allow people to meet their needs while conserving the forests. There are two basic agricultural responses to this challenge.

First, there is the technical agroindustrial solution in the form of intensive monocrop agriculture. This is how agronomists, agricultural economists, and government planners respond to "severe limitations of soil resources." This approach, known as Green Revolution technology, makes use of specially adapted seed varieties, machinery, and chemical inputs like fertilizers (many of which are fossil-fuel based), insecticides, and herbicides. It is capital intensive—that is, a lot of cash is required to do research, to extend the technology to the farmers, and to extend them credit to buy the chemical inputs needed to grow crops in poor soils.

Although rational by scientific standards, this technical approach is as irrational as it is incomplete. Soil infertility, modern agriculture's primary focus, is only one obstacle. There are other ecological obstacles in the tropics, and many social and economic obstacles as well. Sustainable development is hampered by unclear land ownership, illiteracy, speculation-fueled increases in land prices, and the inaccessibility of credit and extension services. The result is a basic mismatch between ecological and human resources. Time and again, would-be development planners ignore these factors. Meanwhile, a tide of agriculturalists engulfs the forested tropical landscape and would-be development becomes debacle.

In the wake of development failures, an alternative approach to meeting rural needs becomes even more relevant. This approach derives from the many ecologically based agricultural systems that have been developed by the traditional cultures of the tropics. Many of these systems have been used or adapted by farmers who see the benefits of maintaining the inherent diversity and fertility of the land-scape—of working *with* tropical Nature rather than attempting to subdue and transform her. The greatest benefit of ecologically based agricultural systems—which is what we mean by *agroecosystems*—is that they are physically sustainable through time, and thus can pro-vide continued social benefits.

Agroecosystems still require a great deal of technical knowledge, but not the kind that is acquired in agricultural research stations. Practitioners must have an intimate knowledge of the diversity of plants in their system, and their cycles and interrelations with all as-pects of the environment, from the soil to the insects and birds that pollinate them. They must also know how plants can be varied in both space and time in order to maximize productivity, which is the objective of any good farmer. For this information to become ac-ceptable to planners, it must be encapsulated and, in a sense, legiti-mized by science.

Ecologists and biologists have made great strides in unraveling and describing the intricate and complex ecological processes of the trop-ical rainforests, including population dynamics, growth and regula-tion, productivity and diversity, nutrient-cycling mechanisms, and plant-animal interactions. Ecologists have recently begun to relate such information to the study of agroecosystems. And this has pro-duced the scientific field of agroecology, defined as the application of ecological concepts and principles to the design and management of sustainable agroecosystems.[1]

AGROECOLOGY: AN INTEGRATED APPROACH

In any agricultural system, ecological and environmental factors in-teract with social, economic, and political factors. The objective of agroecology is to meet the needs of both the ecosystem and the peo-ple. By integrating ecology and culture, agroecology has the poten-tial to resolve current development dilemmas with agricultural prac-tices better suited to the rainforests, and the people who live there.

Agroecology minimizes or eliminates dependence on the im-ported, often expensive, inputs of modern agriculture. It is also adaptable to the transportation, communication, and other infrastructural capabilities—or limitations—of the farmer. Freed from the need to rely on external elements, the farmer can integrate the conditions of tropical ecology into the agroecosystem, using all available ecological resources for the benefit of the farmer and the community. A fundamental lesson of agroecology is that human interactions with the agroecosystem need not interrupt naturally occurring processes and ecological integrity while meeting human needs. It's a win/win situation.

Because existing agroecosystems have endured the tests of time, they provide important lessons in sustainability. The first lesson is that sustainability can be achieved: agroecosystems are durable in the face of long-term ecological constraints and fluctuations, as well as an array of socioeconomic pressures. The second lesson is that modern industrial agriculture, almost exclusively concerned with maximizing production for short-term profits, is not sustainable. If long-term productivity is to be achieved, agricultural goals must shift toward the conditions required for sustainability: soil and water conservation, genetic diversity, and wise management. These ensure stable food supplies, a reasonable quality of rural life, and a safe and healthy environment.[2] In other words—and this is really a third lesson—agroecosystems accomplish what modern agricultural development has not: a balance between the goals of maximizing production and maximizing sustainable well-being.[3]

There are many other criteria by which the sustainability of an agroecosystem can be judged. Although they have long been ignored by development economists and planners, these criteria can provide directions for future planning efforts that aim at sustainability. The most important characteristics of a sustainable agroecosystem are:

- *a low dependence on external, purchased inputs,*
- *dependence primarily on locally available and renewable resources,*
- *benign or beneficial impacts on both the on- and off-farm environment,*

· *adaptation to and tolerance of local conditions, rather than*
   dependence on massive alteration or control of the environment,
· *a focus on the long-term maintenance of productive capacity,*
· *conservation of biological and cultural diversity,*
· *a foundation in the knowledge and culture of local inhabitants,*
· *the production of adequate domestic and exportable goods.*

None of these criteria function alone. Agroecosystem sustainability depends on the integration of all these elements at all levels of organization—from the crop plant or animal in the field, to the entire farm, to the region, and beyond.[4] The farming methods evolved by some native cultures fulfill all of these requirements and therefore have much to contribute to the development of ecologically sound and sustainable farming practices.[5] The following examples of traditional agroecosystems illustrate the wisdom of such farming practices.

The Wetland Agroecosystem is based upon a special adaptation to a dominant environmental factor that controls agricultural production: seasonal flooding. Most agricultural development projects in the tropics have attempted to eliminate or alter certain limiting conditions to fit the needs of imposed cropping systems. Such attempts usually involve high levels of energy or materials, such as fertilizers or structural materials. There are many well-known examples of massive irrigation, drainage, or desalinization projects that have attempted to alter existing ecological conditions. But when evaluated in terms of crop productivity and economic viability *even in the short term*, these projects have achieved only limited success and have contributed little to the needs of the local people.[6]

Waterlogging is common in low-lying areas of Mesoamerica where heavy rains fall, and soil erosion—a consistent outcome of large-scale water diversion projects—makes the drainage or irrigation of tropical farms particularly difficult. Local traditional farmers, however, have been quite successful in accommodating these factors in the design and management of sustainable agroecosystems.

Such agronomic skills date back to prehispanic uses of the Mesoamerican wetlands by the Mayan people of the Yucatan peninsula. This ancient and very organized civilization apparently developed several methods of farming that enabled them to cultivate wetlands.[7] Little is known about just how these lowlands were cultivated, but present-day traditional wetland systems of southeast Mexico may have derived, at least in part, from these relic Mayan systems.[8] In the state of Tabasco, a wetland agroecosystem, which was probably passed down from generation to generation, is managed by the descendants of indigenous populations.[9] There, maize is planted on higher ground around flood-prone areas in the wet season months of June to December. But as water levels drop during the dry season months of February and March, farmers follow the receding water line with another maize planting. Yields of four to five tons per hectare of dry grain are common, with some yields reaching ten. This is many times the average yield for mechanized production on lands that have been cleared and drained in the same region, and at a fraction of the labor and cost.[10]

Following the harvest, all crop and noncrop residues end up on the soil surface. This contributes to a key element in the system— soil fertility. During inundation, organic materials produced by the marsh plants or left by the previous cropping cycle are conserved and recycled under water. Nutrient minerals that enter the flooded fields are also captured, producing soils rich in organic matter, nitrogen, and other important plant nutrients. These soils reach a depth of 30 to 40 centimeters. The success of this system depends on taking advantage of this period of inundation, the critical phase for soil regeneration. A simple feature of Nature's design, seasonal flooding, provides a self-renewing opportunity for high productivity.

Multiple Crop Agroecosystems are more complicated than the simple flooded field system, but they can increase the sustainability of cropping systems on tropical soils cleared of forest.[11] In such systems, more than one crop is planted on the same piece of land during a given season, either simultaneously or in rotation. This increases production, uses resources more efficiently, and allows for more continuous productivity.

The maize, bean, and squash polyculture is one such traditional multiple-cropping system. There is evidence that the inhabitants of Central America have been intercropping maize and beans since prehispanic times. Today this practice continues to play an important role in increasing food production. In a series of studies done in Tabasco, Mexico, it was found that maize yields, intercropped with beans and squash, could be increased as much as 50 percent beyond the yields from planting maize alone.[12] The diversity of plants contributes to soil enrichment, therefore to yields. Thus, multiple cropping clearly reduces the dependence on fertilizers and creates a more stable basis for managing resources within the system.

In addition to enhancing soil fertility, interplanting can benefit the agroecosystem through the control of weeds and insect pests.[13] The thick broad squash leaves cast a dense shadow that blocks sunlight, making it difficult for weeds to grow. These leaves also release chemical by-products that have the potential to inhibit weed growth when washed by the rain into the soil. Herbivorous insects are also at a disadvantage in the intercrop system, and the presence of beneficial insects is promoted.[14] The interactive, intercropped systems are complex, yet they depend primarily upon natural processes to control pests and diseases on the farm. This natural and effective form of pest control is virtually ignored in modern agroindustrial systems.

Diverse Home Gardens are even more complex agroecosystems, and are of great value to tropical farmers. They are structurally diverse in a way that mimics the biodiversity and structure of the rainforest itself, with an overstory of trees and an understory of herbs, shrubs, small trees, and vines. Animals are often an integral part of the gardens as well. This diversity allows food to be harvested year-round, and yields a wide range of other products such as firewood, medicinal plants, spices, and ornamentals.

In one such home garden on the outskirts of Cañas, Guanacaste province, Costa Rica, a total of 71 plant species were found in an area of 1,200 square meters. The garden served as a source of food, firewood, medicine, and color and enjoyment for the household.

Some of the plants served more than one function, and most were distributed in the garden according to their uses. Trees were concentrated toward the back of the plot, which provided shade for the work area behind the house as well as a stabilizing border along the riverbank parallel to the back of the property. Annual food crops were concentrated toward the front of the garden in full sunlight, with ornamentals clustered in beds or containers around the house or along the pathway to the front of the property. Shaded animal pens housed two pigs, a goat, and a guinea pig. Several chickens, small dogs, and cats roamed the plot. Mango was the principal tree species, and maize, squash, beans, papaya, bananas, and yucca (cassava) were the main food crops. All family members engaged in the food-growing process, and in doing so, they shared an intimate appreciation for the natural workings of their environment.

Home gardens are extremely variable in size and design, and require an acute sensitivity to the specifics of the site. They can be organized to reflect a wide range of ecological and cultural considerations, including local variations in soil type, drainage patterns, cultural preferences, family size and age patterns, and the economic standing of the family. And they are adaptable to the changing needs of the family and the farm itself.[15] The ability of such gardens to change and develop as trees mature, markets change, and the socioeconomic status of the family changes—while also maintaining a sustainable basis for management and design—places them at the forefront of beneficial agricultural practices in tropical regions.

The traditional agroecosystems described here are in-place, tangible alternatives that offer a new set of standards and a new vision for tropical agriculture. A truly sustainable agriculture for the tropics cannot be developed solely through research conducted by people who are removed from traditional cultures. Tropical ecosystems are too complex. Therefore, developers and planners would do well to leave behind their cultural biases and work cooperatively with the remaining peoples of the rainforest. Such a cooperative effort could create a basis for a viable, sustainable way of life for all the peoples of the tropics.

FUTURE DIRECTIONS

The agroecological approach to tropical agriculture delves deeply into the complex factors that contribute to both cultural and agroecosystem sustainability. But the task of implementing agroecology at the policy level is equally complex. It requires people in both the developed and the developing worlds to extricate themselves from the destructive, short-term-profit development models that have been promoted so vigorously for the last 40 years. And it requires the acceptance of another system, one that respects the authority of cultures that are wise in the ways of agroecology to take the lead as "project planners." In other words, developing and implementing agroecological systems is a task commensurate with that of preserving the rainforests themselves. Both demand a shift in worldview.

Paradigm shifts have rarely, if ever, been made for expediency. But the stakes are higher than ever before. Developers have been slashing away at the tropical rainforests for decades, in the firm conviction that the industrial way of life could, and should, be implanted wherever it did not yet exist. Now the sustainability of industrial society itself, even under the conditions of temperate ecology, has become highly questionable. But the consequences of imposing the monocultural industrial mind-set upon the less developed tropical regions are beyond question: the drastic demise of both tropical ecosystems and cultures is now in progress.

The agroecological approach to farming in the tropics delivers a challenge to the cash-crop agro-export model that currently predominates in the region. Although agriculture for export—bananas, coffee, oranges, sugar cane—generates foreign income for debt-laden governments, it further deepens the long-term financial plight of tropical countries by eroding away Nature's capital, the soil and the forest. Moreover, the land tenure policies that support the agro-export model displace millions, many of whom take sharpened machetes to the rainforest. How can this be justified? People achieve more socially desirable and sustainable ways of producing food when they are allowed to meet their own needs. The only answer, again, is that it is difficult to make such a system shift.

Although the role of developed nations in encouraging such a system shift in the tropics is admittedly limited, concerned citizens in the United States can at least encourage a shift in the priorities of the development agencies from the agro-export model to the agroecosystem model. If we do not, the vicious cycle of deforestation and poverty will continue, and life on the planet will become increasingly imperiled. Agroecology offers a conceptual and practical alternative that underscores yet another lesson of the rainforest: that in Nature lie the wisest secrets we may ever discover about how to live healthily and sustainably with this Earth.

16

PROTECTED
AREAS
IN TROPICAL
RAINFORESTS

Five Lessons

JAMES D. NATIONS

•

In the tropical rainforest of Yasuní National Park, the sound of the future is the drone of a Super-Puma helicopter lifting off from the Daimi Uno oilwell site. Inside the helicopter are 12 exhausted oil-field workers, headed home after 22 days of exploratory drilling in Ecuador's Amazon jungle. Finally, the men are en route to Quito for a week of drinking, carousing, and rest. As the backwash of the helicopter fans across the rainforest canopy, the men look down on an ocean of green that stretches as far as they can see in all directions.

Eight miles into their flight toward the oil company's jungle headquarters at Waimo Base, the chopper pilots pass unknowingly over three small huts with palm thatch roofs. On the ground below, a pair of Waorani Indians, dressed in G-strings and balsa earplugs, aim three-meter blowguns at the helicopter's metal underbelly. Part of Ecuador's last uncontacted indigenous group, the Waorani pretend to knock the intruders from the sky with poisoned darts they normally reserve for monkeys. But the aircraft is gone in a blur, and the sound of the jungle once again becomes the whine of insect voices that passes for quiet in the Amazon.

Yasuní National Park, Ecuador's largest protected area and one of the largest rainforest parks in the world, covers one million hectares (10,000 square kilometers) of lowland tropical rainforest near the conjunction of Ecuador, Peru, and Colombia. The park is designed to protect part of the forest area that botanists call the most biologically diverse spot on the Earth's land surface.

It would have been enough for Nature to stop there. But Yasuní holds more than a wealth of plant and animal species. Beneath its thin red soils lie Ecuador's largest petroleum reserves. And in a nation dependent on oil exports for 70 percent of its income, oil is big business. The whir of the future has met the whine of the jungle, and the big money is betting on oil.

As I write this, smartly dressed engineers sit at their desks in Houston and Quito, sketching lines across maps of places they've never been. These lines are the roads their company will bulldoze across the face of the Amazon jungle during the fall of 1989. The mass of upturned soil and twisted trees the bulldozers push aside will become jungle roads used to construct an oil pipeline. The pipeline will transport its liquid cargo across the width of Ecuador, pumping it over the Andes to the coastal city of Esmeraldas. There, the oil will gush into the holds of giant tankers. A week later, the tankers will unload the oil at a refinery on the Texas coast. Transformed into gasoline and a hundred other products in a belch of stench and smoke, Yasuní's oil will filter its way through the veins of America's economy. You and I will pump it into our cars to drive to the Safeway to buy meat and vegetables packed in plastic that may also be made from the oil of Yasuní.

As we are pushing our shopping carts across the parking lot, a jaguar will be stalking a frightened capybara someplace in the Ecuadorean rainforest, and a dark-skinned Waorani child will be whimpering in her sleep, turning restlessly in her hammock.

Lesson one in the conservation of tropical rainforests: We are all involved in their destruction and their protection.

In our interconnected world of global markets, we are involved in rainforest destruction whether we like it or not. With our wooden picture frames, with the teakwood bowls we place on mahogany coffee tables, we destroy the tropical forest. With our gasoline, our food packaging, our boats and paneled offices, we eradicate the jungle. Living the lives of modern consumers, we eat the tropical forest.

While we work to change those habits and the institutions responsible for those destructive products, we must work hard to conserve the rainforests that remain. Unless we work deliberately and forcefully to preserve tropical rainforests, we will lose the little that remains. A large part of our work is to support national and international organizations that create and manage rainforest parks, to protest rip-and-burn business schemes that make a few families rich at the expense of biodiversity, and to watch what we eat and buy and burn.

Lesson two: In the struggle to protect tropical rainforests, the job must be done now or never. This day in Guatemala, as I write, the National Congress is in session to vote on the proposed creation of 35 new national parks and protected areas. If the yes votes carry, the parks the legislators declare will be the last large wilderness areas ever designated in Guatemala. More than half of the new park territory, 16,000 square kilometers, will focus on tropical forests.

Similar events have taken place in scores of nations around the tropical belt during the past two decades. National parks and wildlife reserves now protect more than 200,000 square kilometers of tropical rainforest throughout the world.[1] Some of these areas conserve undisturbed forest wilderness filled with tapirs, pacas, reptiles, monkeys, and a range of unknown plant species. Others are small pockets of rainforest remnants surrounded by human populations. Some are also home to indigenous families who have lived in the forest for centuries.

The sobering side of this news is that the decade of the 1980's, perhaps the first few years of the 1990's, will see the protection of the last rainforest areas on Earth. Rainforest regions not protected by the end of those years—not just by law, but in actuality—will never survive in their original state. In the name of progress, profits, and simple human needs, they will be transformed into less biologically diverse, less interesting, and probably less useful ecological systems. The majority of rainforest regions outside of parks and protected areas will be cleared and burned for a few more years of crops or cattle during your lifetime.

We are groping our way through humankind's final opportunity to protect, in their original condition, the forests that have been called "the richest, most exuberant expression of life on land."

So far, only 3 percent of the rainforest of Africa has come under protection, only 2 percent in Southeast Asia, and only 1 percent in South and Central America. Yet conservationists estimate that we must protect 10 to 20 percent of the world's remaining rainforests if we hope to conserve samples of all the world's rainforest habitats.[2]

The recent push for the declaration of new tropical forest parks has been advanced by two realizations. The first is the realization that tropical rainforests are vital to the future of the human species. They are vital as sources of direct, immediate benefit through watershed protection and as sources of timber, animals, and medicinal plants. They are also valuable as sources of future benefits such as new agricultural crops, natural insecticides, and medical discoveries.

The second realization is that these crucial ecosystems are being eradicated at alarming rates around the world. The benefits, both present and potential, that rainforests hold for humankind are evaporating in the smoke of agricultural fires and beneath the reservoirs of hydroelectric projects.

Taken together, these two realizations are prompting conservationists to redouble their efforts to create national parks and protected rainforest areas. They have learned that, in most rainforest regions, only those areas protected by law and by human beings on the ground are likely to survive intact past the turn of the century.

Lesson number three is a caveat: Not all of the protected rainforests will survive. As population growth, agricultural frontiers, and national development push up hillsides and into wilderness areas throughout the tropics, people are coming into conflict with national parks and protected areas that are critical to rainforest survival. Economic and political realities force rural families to exploit tropical forests and wildlife within and on the edges of parks and protected areas. Few pristine rainforest areas—parks or not—are likely to survive in places where people must struggle simply to provide their basic daily needs.[3]

But rainforest parks are destroyed by greed as well as need. As oil companies push roads through the Amazon, loggers file down the roads to wrench timber trees from the forest to sell on foreign markets. Following close behind the loggers come businessmen with visions of cattle ranches and oil palm plantations. Few of them are driven by need.

Even some of the colonists are in the forest for the money, knowing that access to land is their only hope for putting together a nest egg for the future. A section of one of Ecuador's protected rainforest areas is already being colonized by rural families seeking land to clear and sell. Most migrated into the area before park guards were hired or a park manager was on the spot. They followed oil roads into the Cuyabeno Wildlife Reserve and cleared and planted farm plots before the parks department was even aware they had arrived.

By national law, Ecuadorean colonists are allowed to settle on national forest lands and seek legal title to a 50-hectare plot (*finca*) from the Institute of Agrarian Reform and Colonization. Colonists' de facto occupation of the Cuyabeno reserve forced the Ecuadorean parks department to cede the cleared land to the families and move the reserve boundaries several kilometers to the east.

Although families were allowed to settle and seek title to only one finca at a time, censuses have revealed families in which husband, wife, and each child all hold 50-hectare plots. Even newborn babies are landowners.

In addition, half the families in some regions of the Ecuadorean rainforest begin clearing a second finca deeper in the forest while waiting for legal title to their first. When they receive title to the first finca, they sell it to speculators or other colonists and move on to their second plot to begin anew. Viewing the same process in the Brazilian Amazon, Marianne Schmink, a University of Florida anthropologist, called this pattern "the land rights industry."[4] An official with the Federation of Indigenous Communities of the Province of Napo, Ecuador (FCUNAE) called colonists who follow the practice "*negociantes de tierra*," or mini–land developers.

The threats to protected tropical forests do not come only from landless families, eager businessmen, and overzealous colonists. Corrupt and incompetent officials are also a threat. In Yasuní National Park, already threatened by oil development, the local head of the Institute of Agrarian Reform and Colonization has been deeding land and promoting colonization within the park along its eastern border with Peru. Called to task by Yasuní's only park guards (two of them for one million hectares), the official justified his action in the name of *Fronteras Vivas*, "living frontiers," to protect Ecuador from Peruvian invasions. Park officials in Quito roll their eyes when they hear the story and speak in soft asides of bribes and local corruption.

Lesson number four: In the face of population growth and expanding demands for land and tropical resources, working with tropical forest peoples—both indigenous communities and immigrant colonists—is the most important focus for rainforest conservation from this day forward.

Conservationists, biologists, and development planners have come to realize that the crucial need to conserve tropical rainforests must be balanced with the social and economic requirements of human beings. If families are forced to invade national parks or exploit forest reserves in order to stay alive, we can be certain that they will do so. Because of this realization, park planners will tell you that national parks and reserves must go beyond the goals of protecting species and preserving habitat; the objectives of conservation must take into account the needs of local people.[5] The goals of rainforest conservation must also be balanced with the broader interests of tropical nations at large. In the words of Jeffrey McNeely, of the International Union for the Conservation of Nature and Natural Resources,

"Protected areas must serve human society if they are to survive in a period of increasing demands on nature."[6]

Far from being a compromised position for conservation, this interdependence of protected areas and human needs can present the opportunity for new patterns of cooperation that benefit both resources and human families. But to ignore the needs of neighboring communities is to create a volatile future that can impoverish both parks and people. Mexican ecologist Arturo Gómez-Pompa states the concept simply: "We can no longer earmark an area as a 'Nature Reserve: Keep Out' and have it policed, while multitudes of starving peasants in the vicinity are looking for a suitable spot to plant next season's crop. This colonialist approach to conservation is doomed to failure."[7]

Or more bluntly, as one tropical park manager has stated it, "The people, the forest, and the wildlife, either thrive together in a balanced environment, or stagnate together in a wretched one."[8]

Thus, the crucial questions for rainforest parks have become: How can conservationists balance the need for wildlands with the needs of human communities? How can protected forest areas contribute more to human societies? What are the economic and social incentives to ensure the forest's survival? Where do we go from here?

One of the initial answers to these questions comes in the form of biosphere reserves, a type of conservation unit first promoted by the United Nations Educational, Scientific and Cultural Organization (UNESCO). In line with conservation's new way of viewing wildlands and human needs, biosphere reserves combine forest preservation with the needs of surrounding settlements.

Biosphere reserves usually have a series of zones, each with its own particular rules. At least one zone is always an unviolated core of natural vegetation that is permanently protected. This core area is surrounded by concentric rings of land used in increasingly intensive fashion. Moving outward from the protected center, first are buffer zones where local families gather medicinal plants and harvest wild resources. Scientists and tourists enter to collect specimens or take photographs. In the next ring out, local families may farm and collect wood. And in the outermost rings appear houses, hotels, and highways.

In UNESCO's biosphere reserves, indigenous peoples are encouraged to use the outer rings of the reserve as they have used the forest for centuries. Immigrant farm families living on the edges of the reserve are included in planning so they have an interest in the reserve's survival. The families serve as guardians for the buffer zones and for the protected inner core.

Almost 250 biosphere reserves exist in 65 countries, though only one-fourth of these protect tropical rainforest.[9] More biosphere reserves are proposed every year. The most crucial aspect of their success is that local people are included in their planning and development.

Creating and properly managing wildland areas is one of the key strategies for protecting tropical rainforests. When well staffed and well funded, protected areas give us the assurance that while we work with the citizens of tropical nations on the underlying problems that cause rainforest destruction, there will still be something left to defend when we finally have the chance to look up.

Meanwhile, on a local level, the basic strategy has to be to ensure that rural families are allowed to prosper by conserving natural resources instead of by destroying them. We need protected areas, but we also need intensive agriculture, fuelwood lots, and soil conservation that will allow us to set aside protected areas in the first place.

Lesson number five is a challenge: The most important step in rainforest conservation is not what happens inside the forest so much as outside, in the fields and in the lives of rural families and in the courtrooms and offices of decision makers in Indonesia, Brazil, Washington, and Tokyo. One new jungle road or one new tropical dam can have more impact than a generation of forest farmers.

In addition, we need more field research. We need to understand how problems in land ownership can prompt people to clear forest instead of conserving it. We need to identify the laws that work against sustainable use instead of for it. We must know more about the economics of land speculation and its role in forest destruction.

We must study traditional agricultural systems and learn how to transform them into new, sustainable systems of crop production on infertile tropical soils. We must find out more about the plants and animals that live in the tropical rainforest in the first place. And we must know how to make these species more valuable alive than dead.

There are countless lessons in the conservation of tropical rainforests, most of them still unlearned. Because the threats to tropical forests are dynamic, it follows that the lessons and strategies to counter these threats must also be dynamic. Every case is different; flexibility and adaptability should be our watchwords. Guidelines and experience are crucial, but there are few fixed rules in rainforest conservation.

Still, we can learn the most important lessons of rainforest conservation, and apply them, if we are willing to work with the citizens of tropical nations, and if our vision is of a world where destroying one of our fellow species is a violation of our own rights as living creatures. Our vision should be one of a world where human beings and the creatures we share the planet with can live together, dependent on one another and benefiting one another, as long as the Earth continues to turn. At its basis, that is the major lesson of the rainforest and of life itself.

PART FIVE

SAVING THE FOREST AND OURSELVES

•

"The greatest use of life is to spend it
for something that will outlast it."
WILLIAM JAMES

"Whatever you can do,
Or dream you can do,
Begin it.
Boldness has genius, power, and magic in it.
Begin it now."
GOETHE

•

17

ACTIVISM

You
Make
The Difference

RANDALL HAYES

•

Never doubt that a small group of thoughtful,
committed citizens can change the world;
indeed, it's the only thing that ever has.
MARGARET MEAD

•

~~~~~~

Veiled in the mysteries of ancient eras, the primeval rainforests seem to exist in a world apart, so remote that few temperate-zone dwellers have any appreciation of their value to our daily lives. Yet today and every day their disappearance is making our tax burdens heavier, the cost of living higher, the fascinating cultures of the world fewer, and the chances of survival on Earth slimmer.

The destruction of these forests results from the actions of the industrial societies of Europe, Japan, and the United States, which see the tropical rainforests only in terms of profit. As we have seen in previous chapters, many destructive projects in the tropics are financed by our tax dollars and investment capital. Corporations in which we own stock and from which we buy products are responsible for forest clearing. And our societies' basic patterns of consumption and wastefulness also contribute to the problem. Hence, we are largely responsible for tropical deforestation and the danger it poses to the biosphere, ourselves included.

In light of this responsibility, we also hold some of the keys to the rainforests' survival. Admittedly, the forces of destruction are powerful. To save the rainforests we must address the problems of war, hunger, overpopulation, and economic injustice, as well as global environmental degradation. But we can no longer claim ignorance. We have the knowledge, technology, and resources to set things right. The question remains whether we have the moral will.

If you feel that this destruction of the biosphere is fundamentally wrong and you feel moved to take responsibility, then it is time to join in the effort to save the rainforests. Step forward to grab people's attention. Win their support. Efforts to protect the rainforest can draw from Nature's design: ecosystems diverse in species are more vital and stable than those with only a few species. Likewise, a variety of approaches will make this campaign more vital and successful. Follow your own particular passion, use your own particular gifts, and you *will* make a difference.

Saving the rainforests is a multifaceted challenge incorporating everything from grassroots education to influencing domestic policy and international conventions. There is a great deal we can do. But, as Americans, we also must understand and respect the limits to our control and influence. It is neither diplomatic nor effective to tell Brazil and Malaysia to stop cutting down their forests when American markets contribute to the demand and when American forests have been cut so many times. But we can educate ourselves, our local merchants, and our own government about doing things differently so as to save the rainforests. It is time for us in the industrial North to focus on what we can do here at home, rather than "down there."

Whether you are an amateur activist, professional environmentalist, student, teacher, scientist, computer programmer, business person, parent, or any other kind of concerned citizen, you can play a vital role in the effort to save the rainforests. Every action you take brings us closer to stopping the destruction. Your example will motivate others. Action is the key. In the words of Henry Ford, "Those who believe they can do something and those who believe they can't are both right."

CHOOSING A COURSE OF ACTION

Previous chapters have explored the causes of tropical deforestation and strategies for stemming the tide of destruction. The following summary focuses on what you can do.

Some primary **causes** of rainforest destruction that you can influence—

- *development projects that destroy rainforests with funding from the U.S. Agency for International Development, the World Bank, InterAmerican Development Bank, and other lending institutions;*
- *dam building, road building, logging, mining, oil drilling, and other activities by U.S.–based corporations trading or operating in the tropics;*
- *U.S. consumer demand for tropical timber, for cheap beef served by fast-food chains, and for other rainforest products;*
- *power structures that feed upon inequities between peoples, regions, and countries.*

Current **strategies** to reduce these pressures on the forests—

- *campaigns to create popular support for rainforest protection;*
- *consumer intervention to halt the import of rainforest beef, timber, and other products;*
- *pressure on U.S. government policy and legislation, especially with regard to development aid;*
- *support for conservation organizations in tropical countries;*
- *efforts to reduce population growth;*
- *research to document the causes and extent of destruction, develop effective preservation practices, and develop ecologically based alternatives to meet people's needs.*

As a concerned individual, you can contribute in many ways. As you gather information, think about where your abilities, interests, and available time fit into the overall effort to save the rainforests. A natural way to spread the word, for example, is to follow current news through environmental newsletters, magazines, and the general media, and then communicate what you are learning to family, friends, and co-workers.

An important way to put your commitment into practice is to monitor your own consumption. Inquire about a product's origin before you buy it. Refuse to buy building materials and furniture made of teak, mahogany, and other tropical woods that are cut from the rainforests. Refrain from purchasing tropical wildlife such as parrots, macaws, snakes, and other animals. Much of the trade in these species is illegal. Encourage retailers to ask where products come from before they buy. Reducing the demand for these products is essential for reducing the destruction required to supply them.

A more direct way to learn about the rainforests is to visit them and see the situation for yourself. Trips to countries such as Belize and Costa Rica are less expensive than to the Amazon, Africa, or Southeast Asia. Visiting Central America will give you a first-hand understanding of the forces bearing down on the rainforests—and the very direct role of the United States. When you come back you can share what you have learned with your friends and family, empowered by having experienced the destruction and knowing beyond all doubt that change is imperative.

These are simple ways to incorporate your commitment into your lifestyle. But even greater change can come from coordinated actions. Working with others to save the rainforests can have a great impact on your community.

FORMING A GRASSROOTS RAINFOREST ACTION GROUP

Local organizations are the heart of the grassroots rainforest movement. They heighten community awareness through educational campaigns, consumer actions, and media events. And they concentrate the democratic will that pressures institutions to change.

As John Muir wrote in 1900:

*Any fool can destroy trees. They cannot defend themselves or run
away. And few destroyers of trees ever plant any; nor can planting
avail much towards restoring our grand aboriginal giants. . . .
Through all the eventful centuries since Christ's time—and long
before that—God has cared for these trees, saved them from
drought, disease, avalanches, and a thousand storms; but he cannot save them from sawmills and fools; this is left to the . . .
people!*

We need to sound the alarm, and citizen groups are society's best
whistle blowers. A small grassroots organization can start with family, friends, church, school, civic club, or any other group in your
community. The first step is to get excited; know that *you* can make a
difference. Then call a few friends and share your excitement; "*we*
can make even more of a difference." Set up a meeting or a party and
ask for ideas on how to take action. Manuals are available with information on small group activities and fundraising ideas. The following is a sample of the many ways both large and small groups can
help to preserve the rainforests.

Organize Letter-Writing Campaigns. At your first meeting you
can take immediate action by writing to corporations and government officials. Letter-writing campaigns are one of the truly effective
avenues of change. As Fundacion Natura, a leading conservation
group in Ecuador, commented about one successful campaign: "The
support letters and our action have made it possible to approach the
government authorities responsible for the integrity of this area to
propose a joint plan for its immediate protection." Corporations,
congressional representatives, international lending banks, and the
governments of tropical countries take the letters they receive seriously—each letter counts for several hundred citizens, or even thousands. So consider organizing monthly letter-writing parties. Letters
really do help.

Get the Word Out. There are many ways to get the word out and everyone's talents can be put to use in these campaigns. One way to get the word out is to distribute fliers, fact sheets, and newsletters—all of which need artists, writers, and other talented people to research, write, design, and publish them. Another way is to hold benefit concerts for the rainforests, where musicians and other performance artists can express their commitment and inspire others. At every opportunity, gather names for your mailing list so that you can keep an ever expanding number of interested people informed about your activities and current rainforest news.

The following categories provide more ideas for ways of getting the word out, always with the object of capturing the public's attention and support. As San Francisco's Scoop Nisker always says at the end of his radio news show, "Remember, if you don't like the news, go out and make some of your own."

Initiate Community Education Projects. Be creative. You could organize a conference for scientists, students, teachers, and the public. Education packets are available with which you could initiate special school programs such as teach-ins or class projects. You could give lectures and present slideshows to civic groups, garden clubs, church groups, schools, environmental groups, and peace groups. Faculty from university biology and forestry departments can help to present programs, talk to reporters, and provide information for research projects.

Establish Media Contacts and Create Media Events. As Norman Myers, a contributor to this book, says, "The publicity-generating power of citizen organizations is greater than we sometimes suppose. During the past two decades the great changes in American life—civil rights, the women's movement, environmentalism, consumer protection, among others—have all originated at the grassroots level. . . ."

Working with the media is essential for getting the word out and getting the point across, so it is worth the time and effort to cultivate media relations, no matter how small your group. Some effective approaches to working with the media include—

- *studying materials on media relations;*
- *establishing contacts with the local press and keeping them informed of rainforest issues;*
- *letting reporters in your community know of your interest in saving tropical forests;*
- *writing letters to the editor of your local newspaper;*
- *holding press conferences for rainforest events, such as visits by people from tropical countries and other visiting lecturers;*
- *inviting the media to panel discussions with prominent local leaders;*
- *inviting reporters to demonstrations, benefits, and other events;*
- *creating public service announcements for television and radio and asking local stations to broadcast them;*
- *listing your group's events in the calendar of your local paper.*

Organize Consumer Actions. Corporations responsible for rainforest destruction provide one of the primary pressure points upon which the rainforest movement can effectively focus. Corporations are very sensitive about maintaining a positive public image and do not like to have their undesirable activities publicized. But it is our "dollar votes" that ultimately determine whether a corporation continues its destructive practices. When we refuse to give those companies our business, they will have to change their ways. Burger King, for example, announced that it would stop importing rainforest beef after a nationwide boycott reduced its business by 12 percent. Actions you can take include—

- *researching rainforest products, identifying the corporations responsible for rainforest destruction, and developing educational materials;*
- *organizing demonstrations against the importation of tropical timber, rainforest beef, wildlife and other products;*
- *organizing boycotts when you need to increase the pressure (these may involve marches, rallies, human chains, and other forms of civil disobedience);*

- *helping to develop, publicize, and enforce a "code of conduct" for the timber industry, importers, and retailers;*
- *lobbying for effective import-labeling laws that would require, for example, a label stating where tropical timber was cut or rainforest beef was raised. This is important information for consumer campaigns;*
- *developing and popularizing alternatives to tropical timber products;*
- *adopting techniques from other campaigns such as the divestment strategy to fight apartheid in South Africa.*

Network with Other Rainforest Action Groups. Since the rainforest movement is decentralized, it is important to let others know what you are doing, share ideas, and coordinate actions. Networking creates a kind of synergy that gives the movement its momentum. By joining the Rainforest Action Network, the Rainforest Information Centre, and/or Econet, you can tap into the latest news and stay up-to-date on the current, most urgent, campaigns. This will allow your group to coordinate its activities most effectively.

EXERTING INFLUENCE AT THE NATIONAL AND INTERNATIONAL LEVELS

The rainforest issue involves more than ecology or environmental issues. It involves the fight for human rights, for stable democratic government, and for fair land distribution. To fight for these things, we need to know who controls "growth." Richard Grossman, former director of Environmentalists for Full Employment, has observed that "Rainforest is destroyed by those governments and multinationals who foster growth—growth at all levels. Growth First! is their creed."

To save rainforests we must understand how social—that is, economic and political—power is organized, how it exploits Nature, and how we can act on that information. Grossman points out that "jobs" and "growth" are slogans that serve as camouflage for the social forces that eliminate forests. Our acceptance of these slogans as sacred goals creates a serious problem if we don't ask questions such as:

Jobs making what? Destroying what? At what cost? Growth of what? Investment coming from whom? On whose terms? Under whose control? For whose benefit? Asking such questions brings us into the national and international arenas of the power brokers. In the United States at least, public officials are supposed to be accountable to the people, and they will respond if enough pressure is brought to bear on them. You can have influence at the national and international level in various ways.

Influence United States Policy. Small numbers of people with relatively small amounts of money can accomplish great things. The success of the international whaling campaign is just one example. Yet, the more massive the grassroots public appeal becomes, the more feasible it becomes for professional environmentalists to enter the halls of Congress, explain what the public wants, and request better help for getting the job done. These are things that you as an individual can do:

- *Study and support actions suggested by rainforest organizations and political lobbyists.*
- *Choose an issue to work for, such as—*
  funding for the United Nations Environmental Program's Man and the Biosphere Reserve Program;
  lobbying for foreign appropriations by the U.S. Congress for ecologically based food production, environmental protection abroad, and family planning;
  labeling laws and quotas for rainforest products, or products produced where rainforests formerly flourished;
  legislation requiring that U.S.–based corporations account for their actions overseas—for example, requiring environmental impact statements for activities planned in the tropics.
- *Pressure your congressional representatives to police the environmental role of the United States in the MDBs.*
- *Follow the news and the role of U.S. foreign policy in rainforested regions.*

- *Communicate directly with elected officials through letter-writing campaigns, telegrams, phone calls, and visits.*
- *Have information at your fingertips to give to decision makers.*

Influence the Banks. Find out who the lenders are and what they do. Intergovernmental lending institutions include the World Bank, InterAmerican Development Bank, Asian Development Bank, African Development Bank, and International Monetary Fund. The U.S. Agency for International Development is the main U.S. governmental agency funding foreign activities. The U.S. government also plays an important role in all of the above-mentioned lending institutions. Hence, your congressional representatives have a say in how these banks behave. In addition, many private banks help fund projects in rainforest regions and need to be pressured to change their policies, too. We can help by providing them with information on problems and proposals for improvements.

We also should support and publicize positive efforts, such as the reforestation of damaged watersheds, which the World Bank is funding. Publicizing positive actions by the MDBs, and also corporations, exerts more pressure on them not to go back on their promises and to take further positive steps.

We need to exert pressure for a Freedom of Information Act that applies to these banks. Such an act would allow taxpayers in donor countries and citizens in recipient countries access to bank planning documents. It is in large part the lack of access to this information that has contributed to one project failure after another, for local participation in the development process has been excluded.

Support Organizations in Tropical Countries. The reason to support organizations in tropical countries is to facilitate information flow and provide funds where they are most desperately needed—at the grassroots level. There are environmental groups in Latin America, Africa, and Southeast Asia that your organization could "twin up" with—that is, work with to help each other. You can raise money for your "twin," publicize it, write letters to support its issues, set up a tour to its country, and exchange visitors.

Even the smallest amount of money can do wonders to facilitate information flow and effectiveness. Money is needed for printing, postage, equipment, and travel. In the words of one Brazilian conservationist, "What we need right now is a decent manual typewriter—then we can think about a computer."

How Our Money Is Useful in the Tropics. If the Northern Hemisphere changed all the patterns of behavior that contribute to tropical deforestation, would that save the Amazon and other rainforested regions? The answer is no. Tropical countries would still destroy their rainforests, only a bit more slowly. But deforestation is not uncontrollable. Often a local government policy can also be turned around.

Therefore, we need to channel money, information, and other resources to tropical countries so that their citizens can work out solutions on their own terms. The concerned citizens in tropical rainforest areas urgently need our help. One way we can help them is to inform them about how American corporations and governmental agencies operate, and how our consumer culture degrades ecological systems and interferes with human welfare. People in Third World countries get inundated with the same advertising propaganda that we do, but they have little access to an ecological perspective on our culture or to the information necessary to fight its negative influences in their own countries. It is up to us to provide it.

Tropical countries also need more resources and assistance for the following—

- *environmental organizations that need office equipment, salaries, printing—the basics;*
- *literacy and family planning programs in rural areas;*
- *literature, faculty, research, and other resources for education at all levels;*
- *programs to meet people's needs in areas around parks, which will thereby take the pressure off protected forest areas;*
- *training and outfitting park personnel;*
- *supporting grassroots education campaigns.*

HOW TO CONVEY THE SCOPE
AND IMPORTANCE OF THE ISSUE

It is important to be both accurate and convincing in your presentation of the problem and its potential solutions. The following points may help you to communicate the scope of this issue:

- *Humans are killing life on Earth. We are impoverishing the future. But we can opt for a better future if we act.*
- *We are losing tropical rainforests at a rate of at least one acre every second; several species are becoming extinct every day.*
- *When our great grandparents were born, there were 16 million square kilometers of rainforest. There are now about 9 million square kilometers. The rate of deforestation is about 100,000 square kilometers per year, and a similar area suffers each year from such actions as selective harvesting of valuable hardwoods. At this rate, the rainforests will be gone by the middle of the next century.*
- *There are somewhere between 5 million and 50 million species on Earth; no one is quite sure. Of all the life on Earth, at least half of it, and possibly three-fourths, lives in the rainforests, but only about 500,000 tropical species have been described by science. The extinction of one half of life's diversity—and even the knowledge of it—will accompany the loss of the rainforests. Such a loss of species has not occurred since the age of the dinosaurs 65 million years ago.*
- *The indigenous inhabitants, the people who know the forest plants and animals best, are as endangered as the forests they live in.*
- *Losing a rainforest system is like letting an ancient library burn down before you read the books.*
- *Tropical rainforests are old growth forests, a nonrenewable resource.*
- *There are many global ecological and economic connections: birds that live in the tropics and control agricultural pests in the*

*United States will not return, the climate will change, many of
the genetic resources that sustain us will be eliminated.*
- *Ours is the last generation that has the opportunity to save the
Earth's remaining rainforests. It is up to us.*

These facts must be presented in a way that will engage others.
When you speak to friends or groups, try the following:

- *Be optimistic. There are countless alternatives to rainforest
destruction (this book is full of them).*
- *There are lots of avenues for action and, likewise, many
opportunities to develop new skills. Encourage people to apply
their own special interests toward saving the rainforests.*
- *Envision a society that is part of a sustainable ecosystem and
respects the vital role of tropical rainforests. Incorporate social
justice, sustainable economic systems, and ecological thinking
in your vision. Communicate this vision to others.*
- *Generalize, universalize, and personalize. For example,
generalize by talking about the problems of soil depletion and
watershed degradation caused by deforestation, then focus in on
the rainforests. Universalize by citing the impact of the
greenhouse effect on all of life on Earth, and then point out how
tropical deforestation contributes to this threat to the Earth's
climatic stability. Personalize by explaining how rainforest
destruction weakens the planet's life-support systems and reduces
our chances of survival.*

IT'S UP TO ALL OF US

Anyone can play a role in saving the world's rainforests. Individuals
and small groups working for the same goals can make a big difference. The "hamburger connection" boycott, for example, which focused on Burger King, was started by a few concerned individuals.
The boycott grew until it became a national campaign. And it
worked. Likewise, pressure from letter-writing and lobbying groups
forced the World Bank to set up an environmental department and
pushed legislation through the U.S. Congress to protect rainforests.

But we must not kid ourselves about how much must be done and how hard it will be to actually save the tropical rainforests. To achieve that goal, governments, corporations, and people must change. When people realize that much more is at stake than profits, that in fact what is at stake is survival, then we will gather the massive support that is needed. And when support is voiced on an unprecedented scale, then governments, corporations, and societies will have to respond.

Of course, the time is short. The rainforest destruction that is occurring right now is as menacing as the threat of nuclear weapons. Whether you are an American housewife or a Japanese businessman, your interests and those of your children are served by the protection of the tropical forests. It's time to ask ourselves a few questions and reach deep into our souls for the answers.

The forest is home to at least half of the Earth's biodiversity, and thousands of indigenous peoples. All have a right to live. Are we going to allow their extinction? Are we going to allow the Earth to be impoverished by our generation? Are we going to leave nothing for the future? Through our action or inaction now, we decide whether the future will share in the magnificent heritage of life on Earth.

If we care at all about life, we must save life's greatest expression, the rainforests. We have pressure points to put pressure on and we have the instinct to survive. This time of destruction will end when we demand it. John Seed, a prominent Australian environmentalist, has predicted that when we are dead and buried and our children's children ask them what the greatest accomplishment of the late twentieth century was, they will answer: "The rainforests were saved!"

Your hard work can also be a celebration, especially if you follow the late Edward Abbey's good advice for frazzled environmentalists.

> *Do not burn yourselves out. Be as I am—a reluctant enthusiast, a part-time crusader, a half-hearted fanatic. Save the other half of yourselves for pleasure and adventure. It is not enough to*

fight for the wilderness; it is equally important to enjoy it. While you can. While it's still alive.

So get out there and hunt and fish and mess around with your friends, ramble out yonder and explore the forests, climb the mountains, bag the peaks, run the rivers, breathe deep of that yet sweet and lucid air, sit quietly for a while and contemplate the precious stillness, that lovely, mysterious and awesome space.

Enjoy yourselves, keep your brain in your head and your head firmly attached to your body, the body active and alive, and I promise you one sweet victory over our enemies, over those desk-bound men with their hearts in a safe deposit box and their eyes hypnotized by desk calculators. I promise you this: you will outlast the bastards. You will live to piss on their graves.[1]

It is true that the rainforest crisis is one of the most important global ecological issues of our time and that the fate of the forests is up to each one of us, but this awareness need not be a burden. We can find cause for celebration in participating wholeheartedly in perhaps the greatest drama of all time, the battle for life on Earth. Let your love for the Earth be expressed as courage and rock-solid commitment. And then act—starting now!

18

COALITIONS
FOR THE
FOREST

JOHN P. MILTON

•

When faced with a prospect as enormous as the wholesale destruction of the tropical rainforests, concerned people must create coalitions—temporary alliances of different groups—in order to accumulate the political strength needed to meet the challenge. Fundamentally, coalitions are built by uniting people behind a common cause, and strengthening mutual communication and support; in fact, they operate very much the way an ecosystem operates: in a symbiotic fashion. As the Earth's greatest manifestation of symbiosis and cooperative behavior, the tropical rainforest provides an excellent model for the rainforest movement. In building coalitions we can emulate the processes of the rainforest and by so doing gather the vitality and momentum needed to stop their destruction.

My involvement in the rainforest movement has been inspired by my own experience in these forests. I began field work in the rainforests in the early 1960's, and in only 10 to 20 years I witnessed the complete annihilation of some of the world's most pristine ecosystems. During the 1970's, I coordinated a team of over 60 scientists that put together several hundred case studies of exactly what happens when development projects are implemented in tropical countries. Again and again the results were the same: devastating impacts on both the tropical environments and the peoples living in them.

The benefits of these projects went largely to a relatively few wealthy people living in the cities of those tropical countries, and to the developed nations. Under the misnomer of "development aid," investment dollars and machinery converted soils, forests, and minerals into "resources" that were exported out of those countries and into the rich nations of North America, Europe, and Japan—usually leaving behind a desolate, depleted tropical land. Through the misuse of their money and power, these rich nations have repeated similar ecologically catastrophic mistakes decade after decade; and it has now reached the point where the very fate of the Earth is threatened.

TIME TO ACT

I began engaging in the process of building coalitions for the tropical forests in the early 1980's. I was attending a gathering with Teddy Goldsmith, who puts out *The Ecologist* magazine in England, when we decided it was time to bring together all the environmental groups that had any existing or potential connection with tropical rainforest protection and try to pool our energies. We knew we must try to organize a coalition to yield people, ideas, and resources that could be brought to bear on stopping deforestation. And we knew that we must be very organized, for the interests that would block attempts to stop the destruction are powerful.

Threshold Center, an international center for environmental renewal with which I was associated, agreed to sponsor a series of "seed gatherings" to start the coalition-building process. In May 1985, representatives of over 20 environmental organizations met at Lost Hollow, a farm in the West Virginia hills, where we laid out our strategy. One of our first priorities at this catalytic meeting was to support the development of a coalition-building process in North America, Europe, and Japan. These areas are one root source of the problem because they both finance and consume the products of damaging tropical rainforest projects.

Threshold put its support behind the Rainforest Action Network in North America and similar coalition-building groups in Europe, Japan, Latin America, Australia, Southeast Asia, and the Pacific Region. Starting with remarkably small grants, those efforts have developed far beyond the expectations we had back in 1985. For example, the Rainforest Action Network (RAN) is now a major coordinating point for many coalition activities. It has helped to bring critical local-action issues to the attention of larger environmental organizations with lobbying capabilities, has informed national media, and has helped to raise funds for local rainforest protection groups and individuals. Moreover, RAN has been joined by literally dozens of other organizations in pressuring the institutions that are casting the tropics into an ecologically and socially disastrous development mold. But back in 1985 we knew that dealing with the powerful institutions of the temperate North was not enough. We had to extend our support to the tropics at the same time.

One tropical region that the Threshold coalition-building group felt was at a uniquely critical juncture was the Amazon Basin. As we have seen in previous chapters of this book, the greatest expanse of the world's existing undisturbed rainforest is in the Amazon Basin, particularly within Brazil. The Threshold group became involved in an effort to bring together Brazilian tropical forest peoples, Brazilian rubber tappers, and existing environmental groups, as well as Brazilian church groups with strong views on the environment, to form a Southern coalition to connect with the North. There were, and still are, several impediments to this process.

One of the problems has been the very poor information flow between environmental advocates in tropical countries and temperate zone countries. Any coalition-building process requires not only that we support each other, but that we gain access to the information, individuals, and resources necessary to support each other. Therefore, the first job is to improve communication systems. It is essential to get a flow of key individuals and groups going back and forth between tropical rainforest and temperate urban zones. So raising the money to do whatever is necessary to get the North/South flow going has been one of our highest priorities, whether it is a workable computer-modem system, a fund for small action-group telephone calls, or a crisis fund to provide travel money for key local tropical forest leadership to come to Washington to testify before Congress at points of critical timing.

Even within tropical regions, it is often very difficult for people to communicate and travel. In the case of the Amazon Basin, it isn't just Brazil; it's Peru, Colombia, Bolivia, Venezuela, Guyana, French Guiana, and Suriname—a vast area where tropical forest peoples have little opportunity to interconnect. When trying to form coalitions involving peoples who are very deeply rooted in their own bioregions and do not have a history of traveling from one part of the basin to another, it is very difficult to establish communications and get that coalition going. Therefore, our coalition-building strategy has also included providing support wherever possible to improve information flows within the tropical countries and the forest regions themselves.

The greatest obstacle to coalition-building is political opposition. Like the forest, the people trying to protect the forest historically have had little or no political voice, and therefore are subject to the same violence that is done to the forest. Attempts to build coalitions meet with coercion, arrests, and even murder. The repression of the Penan people in Malaysia for attempting to block the logging of their ancestral forest home is one instance of political brutality.

The coalitions to protect the forests of Amazonia have also suffered the violence of political opposition. There, UNI, the traditional peoples' alliance, joined forces with the rubber tappers' union. Although rubber tappers are not indigenous, they share a common interest with the indigenous people: to live in harmony with the tropical rainforests. As Aragoja, a rubber tapper, said at a public hearing in Sao Paulo:

I work with rubber trees in the Amazon. We live from tropical forests that others want to destroy. In my area, we have about 14 or 15 native products that we extract from the forests, besides all the other activities we have there. So I think the forests must be preserved. When developers think of felling trees, they always think of building roads, and the roads bring destruction under the mask called progress. Let us put this progress where the lands have already been deforested and let us leave those who want to live in the forest, who want to keep it as it is.

Encouraged by the example and support of UNI, the rubber tappers proposed a series of reserves that would allow them to continue their way of life in the forest. These "extractive reserves," similar to tribal reserves for the Indians, would preserve the rights of those people who live in harmony with the rainforest who are *not* Native Americans. The rubber tappers' union mobilized major public demonstrations in support of their rights and went straight to the Brazilian government to gain support, while also drawing support from international agencies. The coalition has resulted in the rubber tappers' union supporting indigenous peoples' tribal reserves, and in the traditional peoples' alliance supporting the rubber tappers' extractive reserves. But the more power a coalition gathers, the more opposition it meets.

A few days before Christmas in 1988 gunmen hired by cattle ranchers assassinated the head of the rubber tappers' union, Chico Mendes; it was the sixth attempt on his life. The decapitation of grassroots leadership in the rural tropics is commonplace, so the battle is far from won. But this murder received widespread coverage in the international media. Such coverage, unimaginable only a few years ago, ups the ante in the battle to save the rainforests.

AUSPICIOUS COINCIDENCE

The power of coalitions lies not only in the connections that exist at any given moment—who can be called, what resources can be mobilized, and so forth—but in the capacity to respond quickly to the opportunities and crises of the moment. A story about this book, the people behind it, and the synchronistic events that have linked individuals and organizations, offers an illustration of this.

In 1985 a group of young people traveled for five months in the Brazilian Amazon with the intention of gaining firsthand insight into the complexities of deforestation. During this trip, one of them,

Robert Heinzman, met an ecological anthropologist who impressed him very much—Dr. Darrell Posey.

After returning from the Amazon, Robert took the initiative and organized an international conference on rainforest destruction in Boulder, Colorado. He was joined in this effort by others, including Suzanne Head. Shortly after she began working with Robert, she met me and invited me to speak on coalition building at the conference, where many of the most active people in the rainforest movement convened. Out of that conference in 1987 came the idea for this book. And the conference also made important contributions to the growing coalition.

One such contribution was the Boulder Rainforest Action Group. The Boulder RAG is an effective group of dedicated grassroots activists who have joined forces with the national and international rainforest movement.

Another outgrowth emerged in January 1988, a year later. Members of the five-month Amazon expedition organized another conference in South Florida to address the rainforest situation in Latin America and the Caribbean. Among those attending the conference was Darrell Posey, accompanied by Kube-i and Paiak'an, two Kayapo Indian chiefs from the Amazon.

After the Kayapo spoke about how their lands were being threatened by the Brazilian government's plans to construct a series of dams, participants at the Florida conference were moved to act. Members of several environmental groups based in Washington, DC, agreed to host a visit by the Kayapo and Dr. Posey to key members of Congress, the World Bank, and the Treasury Department—points of power for approval of a $500 million World Bank loan to build the dams.

Much to the embarrassment of the Brazilian government, the well-spoken Kayapo made a considerable impact in Washington. As a result, the loan and the dam projects were called into question, and the pressure upon the Brazilian government to protect the forest and her people increased. This in turn led to further repressive measures: late in the summer of 1988, the Brazilians arrested and began prosecuting Dr. Posey and the Kayapo chiefs for "unlawful" meddling in Brazil's internal affairs *because* of this visit to the United States. The international coalition responded by organizing to support them. In the fall of 1988, Friends of the Earth, U.S., organized an international tour for Paiak'an to publicize his people's struggle and maintain the pressure on the Brazilian government to protect indigenous lands.

Had there not been some awareness, awareness increased over the years by the efforts of many, had there not been groups of informed people willing to creatively pursue opportunities to exert pressure for change—in short, had there been no coalition—there would have been few opportunities to continue the pressure for solutions. The mobilization of international concern creates an atmosphere of auspicious coincidence in which alternatives can emerge.

The power of coalitions lies in responsiveness, not in a structured and regulated plan of approach for solving the problem of rainforest destruction. Structured approaches can result from the efforts of coalitions, and are needed. But rainforest destruction is occurring too fast for slow-moving bureaucratic approaches to respond to emergencies. To meet emergencies, and to provide any basis for change, coalitions are needed. Their power arises from a shared intention and readiness to act in a timely manner—to see and to seize auspicious coincidence—as information and events unfold.

TURNING UP THE PRESSURE

In general, then, there are two basic types of coalitions for the rainforests: those located in the tropical countries and those in the temperate-zone countries. As these two kinds of coalitions grow and expand their influence, they need to emphasize a broader, more interconnected coalition process, a process exemplified by well-timed and coordinated actions, initiatives, and communications. Coalition builders are still learning how to support this broader coalition process. I am very encouraged by the work being done by the networks of traditional peoples that are forming in tropical countries; by the activist environmental groups that have developed rapidly in Malaysia, Indonesia, Thailand, India, and Brazil; and by the linkages that have occured between these and the various lobbying and environmental groups in North America, Europe, and Japan.

Strengthening these planetary linkages while supporting the growth of strong local and bioregional groups is going to be the ultimate key to reversing tropical rainforest destruction. Before long I hope to see a very strong and unified North/South, East/West rainforest coalition that spans temperate and tropical zones, to facilitate lobbying, local actions and initiatives, media coverage, and information flows of all kinds.

The only way tropical rainforests are going to be saved is by turning up the pressure on governments, banks, aid agencies, and international corporations. Therefore, I would like to suggest some new directions for coalition work. First, I would like to see more of our existing media, particularly television, utilized. On shows like "MacNeil/Lehrer," "20/20," "Nova," and the daily morning and evening news, there are all kinds of opportunities to build and improve the communications process through investigative reporting. When a "Nova" film is done, for instance, it often gets translated and distributed all over the world, which gives it a very powerful impact beyond what we see in the developed nations. If we are going to mobilize Congress to preserve the rainforests, we have to get current rainforest issues regularly into the evening and morning news. It's up to the coalitions to supply current information to the media and pressure them to take global forest issues to heart and report on them— not only through occasional specials on public or cable television, but also on the regular news programs of the major commercial networks. Special investigative news reports on the destructive implications of some of our public institutions' policies need particular emphasis.

Second, we need to intensify Gandhian nonviolent demonstrations. The World Bank, now soundly criticized for its destructive tropical forest policies, has begun to respond to the demonstrations held at its annual meetings over the last few years. But more demonstrations are needed—at the World Bank, and even more so at the

Asian Development Bank, the Inter-American Development Bank, the OAS, the United Nations Development Programme, and the U.S. State Department. Despite some high-sounding speeches and internal reorganization, these agencies continue to behave outrageously. So we must turn up the pressure for a transformation in their policies affecting the tropics; and the same principles apply to transforming the institutions responsible for temperate deforestation. At this point, all the world's forests are endangered.

We don't have much time. We are talking about an extremely short period during which most of the planet's tropical rainforests may vanish, given current trends. The rainforest is the greatest organ of this tremendous organic being we call Planet Earth, Gaia, the biosphere, or whatever your name for Mother Earth is. A very central organ of that life support system is threatened with imminent death. And nobody, including the scientists, knows what that means. In reality, we are conducting an extremely perilous experiment on this great organic being that is the Earth, and we have no idea what the full impacts of destroying the forests will be.

My view is that all of us who are concerned have to put ourselves on the line and protect what tropical forest remains. Our job is to be sure these forests remain for all the future generations of unborn plants, animals, and humans. In reality, the rainforest *is* us. That is the ultimate lesson of this planet and of the rainforest. If you look for the boundary between ourselves and what we call the external environment, it is not really there. The air we breathe is constantly passing in and passing out. Carbon dioxide/oxygen exchanges are part of the interconnectedness of all being. In the same way, the way we excrete, the way we eat, and the way we love are all part of our overall relationship with the Earth as a living system. There are in reality no solid boundaries between ourselves and the rest of the biosphere. On a deep level, we are all one interconnected entity; it's about time we behaved that way. One crucial step toward bringing people back into balance with the Earth is to transform those major development agencies, corporations, and governments that are financing the breakdown of that interconnectedness.

To make nonviolent demonstrations a more effective tool for corrective change, coalition activists must develop coherent strategies for change, strategies designed to have maximum impact with the least amount of effort. Demonstrations must be backed by detailed and accurate information on specific rainforest issues. We have to do our homework—scientifically, legislatively, and logistically—so that our demonstrations are carried out with precise timing at exactly the right place and with just the right amplitude. We must be balanced; we do not have time for either endless research or emotionally satisfying but ineffective actions.

Activists and lobbyists both must collaborate with the people who live in the areas affected, the tropical regions. Lobbying efforts in particular must be fully informed by and cooperatively organized with these people. In many ways, they are the ones who must guide us through the change process, for they are the ones who know the most about what is happening to tropical forests and indigenous peoples. This kind of collaboration is especially important since the development agencies have not been listening to those who live in the forests. When tropical forest shamans and leaders, such as the Kayapo chiefs, visit the United States, media campaigns could help to mobilize public opinion and provide accurate information to political leaders.

There is a third emphasis I would recommend to coalition organizers: focus pressure on key political figures who are not yet committed to tropical forest protection. We need to bring world forest issues right into the core of our presidential campaigns, make them part of the Democratic and Republican platforms—or Green platforms, for that matter. We need to start communicating with all the key congressional people on all the relevant appropriations and policy-making committees. This is basic intelligent lobbying, but it needs to be done more effectively.

ACKNOWLEDGING THE EARTH'S SACREDNESS

There is also a slightly different, but very important additional way to implement change. Most significant change in the world, looked at from a historical perspective, has been based on a fundamental shift in spiritual awareness and values. The destruction of the rainforests and their peoples ultimately reflects a spiritual malaise, the cure for which is therefore also spiritual.

We have reached the point, I believe, where the acknowledgement of the planet as one organic being is absolutely essential and inevitable. By ignoring this great interconnectedness, we have brought our species to the point where we now don't have any choice. We cannot afford to look at the Earth and all its nonhuman inhabitants as separate from ourselves, second-class citizens, or unworthy of consideration. As Chief Oren Lyons, a Native American, has stated, "The law of Nature is a spiritual law. It respects all life, for all life is equal. If we transgress it, the consequences will be dark and terrible." Therefore, I would propose three things.

First, we can encourage Jewish and Christian leadership in the United States and Europe to accept tropical rainforest issues as a major social responsibility. If mainstream spiritual leaders were to treat the loss of rainforests as a major stewardship issue, they could generate study groups and actions in churches and synagogues.

Second, meeting periodically to meditate on or pray for the protection and regeneration of the tropical forests and their peoples would be a direct step toward acknowledging the fundamental truth that the Earth is sacred. We must take personal responsibility for projecting the energies of love and compassion to heal the Earth. When we do that, we begin to feel our inseparability from the Earth internally, and our left-brained logic begins to follow our hearts. If we fail to do this, the same reductive, divisive ways of thinking will continue, and no deep healing of ourselves and the Earth will be possible.

Finally, I would like to propose the dedication of one hour at the peak time of the Spring and Fall equinoxes for the people of the world to pray, meditate, or visualize in their own ways, for the preservation and renewal of the world's forests and their people. This "Moment for the World's Forests" could be promoted through the rainforest coalition and be followed by meetings to plan actions that will help to bring harmony back to our relationship with the Earth.

The rainforests don't ask very much from us—just a little CO_2 and a little excrement now and again—but they give a lot. The least we can do to give something back is to set aside two days a year when we stop our activity for one hour and join together for the healing and renewal of these forests. From that inner movement of our hearts, outer changes will follow. Full, deep commitment to expressing our love for the Earth can actually begin to heal the wounds of the Earth and to restore the magnificent tropical rainforests. It's quite possible that nothing less will do it.

19

A

NEW LEAF

MORRIS BERMAN ,

•

Earth and all you behold:
tho' it appears without, it is within.
WILLIAM BLAKE

•

~~~~~~

The idea of trees existing within the psyche is perhaps a curious one. When we review the statistics of rainforest destruction—amply reported in this volume—we are fully aware that the process being described is "out there." We are witnesses, more likely distant observers, of these events: that since 1945, half of the world's rainforests have been cut down; that at the present rate of destruction, they will be even more dramatically reduced by the year 2000; that the resulting "greenhouse effect" could heat the globe to the point that the polar ice caps might melt, inundating the world's coastal cities. This is, ostensibly, the stuff of science fiction; even the year 2000 itself, a mere decade away, seems remote, "out there," the end of the millennium.

I suspect the year 2000 will come and go, like any other year; I also fear that many or even most of the predictions being made by ecologists regarding the destruction of the tropical rainforests, and the disastrous consequences of that event, may come to pass. Whether we can avoid that at this point is unclear, but I want to suggest that hope may come from unexpected quarters, namely the human psyche. I wish to propose a rather strange notion—that trees actually exist within our psyches; that their destruction is, as a result, starting to drive us crazy; and that the pain of this insanity is pushing the human race toward a quantum leap in consciousness, one absolutely necessary for the continuation of life—all life—on this planet.

Prior to the 16th century, there was no need to state Blake's notion of the unity of the Outside and the Inside so openly. That the universe was the macrocosm, and the human being the microcosm, and that there was a perfect correspondence between the two, was the cognitive mainstream, the dominant worldview or perceptual framework for virtually everyone on the planet. In this framework, the Earth itself was seen as a living thing, and consciousness itself, from our point of view, was "magical." Trees played an important part in this. The worship of trees was central to the religious life of European peoples from earliest times. The oak was sacred to the Druids, and in Rome, the sacred fig tree of Romulus was worshipped down to the days of the empire. The fig tree has also been an esoteric Christian symbol, and legend has it that the Bodhi tree, under which the Buddha attained enlightenment, was a fig tree as well (*Ficus religiosa*). It is also the case that the cabala, a system of Jewish number mysticism, is based upon a "tree of life."

In general, the concept that the life of a human being is bound up with the life of a tree is a very common one, and is popular in many parts of the world. Trees, for example, typically occur for millions of people as dream symbols. In sources as diverse as the *Edda* of Icelandic mythology, and the famous Dead Sea Scrolls of Qumran, a dream about a felled tree was a portent that a death had occurred, or was about to. In Greek mythology, trees are the incarnation of certain gods (the laurel for Apollo, the olive for Athena), and various tales tell of heroes and heroines being changed into trees. The ancient Chinese believed that certain trees had magical powers. The willow, they held, could ward off evil influences; the peach tree could confer longevity. In Nordic mythology, the world itself is a tree, known as Yggdrasil, and it connects all parts of the universe. One of its roots stretches down to the Fountain of Wisdom. The

Norse god Odin agreed to lose an eye in order to drink from this, and in so doing, became the patron of seers and poets.

On an unconscious level, we have probably never accepted abstract scientific notions of trees as objects (collections of atoms) or the Earth as an inanimate object or indifferent planet. The American philosopher William James once recounted an incident that occurred at the conclusion of a (very technical) lecture he gave on the origins of the Earth. A little old lady in the audience came up to him and fixed him with her eyes, eyes that nevertheless contained a twinkle in them. "That was very interesting, Mr. James," she told him, "but I happen to know that the Earth sits on the back of a large turtle." Not wishing to offend her, James asked, as politely as he could, what was supporting the turtle. "You're a very clever man, Mr. James; I expected you'd ask that. But I have an answer for you. The turtle is supported by *another* large turtle." When James began to ask her what was it that was supporting *that* turtle, the little old lady replied—and by now she was actually cackling—"It's no use Mr. James—*it's turtles all the way down!*"

Ordinarily, for me, this would be no more than an amusing anecdote, except for the context in which I read it: a Native American newspaper, which printed it under a headline that was an old Indian saying: "When the turtle dies, the world collapses." It may not be *literally* true that the world is sitting on the back of a turtle—or a tree, for that matter—but it is *materially* true, and there are no two ways about it. Ancient magic and modern ecology, it turns out, have a lot in common, for both assume the existence of an interconnected web of life. On the premodern analogy of macrocosm and microcosm, if the Earth's crust was its skin, and the rivers its veins, then the forests were its hair, its protective fur. And in actual fact, for millions of years trees did protect the Earth, sheltering more than 75 percent of its dry land. (Today they cover less than one-third of it, with desert area dangerously increasing every year.) In a similar fashion, some ecologists have referred to the rainforests as the "lungs of the Earth" because of their ability to absorb carbon dioxide, produce oxygen, possibly regulate many atmospheric balances, and thus allow the planet to "breathe" and not overheat. All of this embodies the notion of a correspondence between trees and human life. In both cases, we are talking about vital organs. How long do you think you could live without your lungs? Pluck out a vital organ such as this, from the human being or from the Earth, and a chain reaction follows almost immediately. All of these things—turtles, trees, oceans and rivers, animal species—live or die together; the industrial-age model of replaceable or interchangeable parts just does not apply here, and this is something that, remote or not, we are not going to be able to hide from.

The same set of rules applies to the human psyche, which "contains" the Earth and permeates—and is permeated by—things such as turtles and rainforests. As the cultural anthropologist Gregory Bateson once pointed out, it all really is, in a sense, alive. To kill Lake Erie, or cut down the Amazonian rainforest, on the (post-1600 A.D.) model that it's all "out there" is to court disaster, because it is *not* all "out there." Mind pervades everything we do. It is significant, for example, that the destruction of the rainforest is concomitantly wiping out a plant known as the rosy periwinkle, which contains materials effective in fighting a number of cancers, particularly leukemia. (Tribal healers have known of its medicinal properties for generations.) Now if one can recognize that the motives for destroying the rainforests are heavily economic, and that the growth of the world's GNP by leaps and bounds is like the spread of a cancer, then the fact that this malignant mindset (translated into behavior) is killing off a plant that combats leukemia is no accident. It is all of a piece: psychological states have material consequences, and vice versa. In fact, the U.S. National Cancer Institute has identified more than 2,000 rainforest plants with the potential to fight cancer; the cancerous behavior of the industrial-age psyche may well render many of them extinct by the next century. The Transamazon Highway is an example of the cancer of the spirit, even while it destroys cancer-fighting plants.

The coincidence between psyche and concrete activity is not to be overlooked. It is just this (antimagical, antiecological) consciousness that enables the destruction of the rainforest to proceed apace, for if it is all just inert "stuff," then there is nothing to be lost in exploiting it. The resulting wasteland, however, is psychological as well as material, and was predicted as early as the third century A.D. in a magical text known as the *Asclepius*, part of the so-called Hermetic corpus. Hermes, or Mercury, the messenger of the gods, tells his student Asclepius that a time will come when the gods will leave the Earth. "Do you weep at this, Asclepius?" asks Hermes.

> *There is worse to come. . . . In that hour, weary of life, men will no longer regard the world as a worthy object of their admiration and reverence. . . . This All will be in danger of perishing; men will esteem it a burden; and thenceforward they will despise and no longer cherish this whole of the universe, incomparable work of God, glorious construction, good creation made up of an infinite diversity of focus. . . . For darkness will be preferred to light; it will be thought better to die than to live; none will raise his eyes towards heaven. . . .*
>
> *The gods will separate themselves from men. . . . Only evil angels will remain. . . . Then the earth will lose its equilibrium, the sea will no longer be navigable, the heavens will no longer be full of stars. . . . The fruits of the earth will moulder, the soil will be no longer fertile, the air itself will grow thick with sadness. Such will be the old age of the world. . . .*

Clearly, Hermes' prediction, that "the Earth will lose its equilibrium," is virtually upon us. What to do about it? We can lobby our congressman; we can join the Sierra Club; we can disrupt the board meetings of banks that are subsidizing the destruction of the rainforests—all that is valuable, probably necessary. There is, however, a deeper challenge here, one that must go hand in hand with all this, and that is the possibility of precipitating a shift in consciousness, one that will enable us, like Blake or Bateson, to recognize that trees really do exist in our psyches, and that mental health can only be maintained by the set of attitudes inherent in such a shift. Significantly, Hermes doesn't stop his story with this tale of destruction; he predicts a stage beyond it, in which all these trends will be reversed: "That is what the rebirth of the world will be: a renewal of all good things, a holy and awesome restoration of Nature herself, imposed by the will of God in the course of time." In fact, for many people in the so-called First World today, such a rebirth is already apparent, already underway. James Lovelock's Gaia hypothesis, that the Earth really *is* a living entity, has captured the imagination of millions; and we are, in the late 20th century, finally witnessing a challenge to an exploitative mindset that has been dominant since the close of the 16th century. There is a change in the air, and it is something like this: modern science, and scientific consciousness, makes for an excellent tool, but for a very poor worldview. Only the sacred—a reverence for trees—can serve as a worldview; everything else is ancillary. This change of mind, or psyche, has a large following today, and this means, perhaps, that destruction is not a foregone conclusion. Rather, a race is on, as we approach the third millennium, to get our consciousness back in balance, just as we seek to restore equilibrium to the Earth. And should we make it, should we reverse the trend of the last four hundred years, it will not (I do not think) be "imposed by the will of God," but rather emerge out of the psyche itself. For the psyche knows that the destruction of the planet is the destruction of the psyche as well, and it is not going to give up without a fight. It is the psyche's job to resist madness, and in that very powerful force lies reason to hope. The rainforest thus emerges as a symbol, a reminder that human health and planetary health are identical, and also within our grasp. "My life is your life," the tree is saying to us; "this is not a metaphor." Reenchanting the world, and reenchanting ourselves, are part of the same process.

NOTES

INTRODUCTION: VISIONS OF THE RAINFOREST

1. Food and Agriculture Organization and United Nations Environment Program, *Tropical Forest Resources* (Rome: FAO, 1982); Norman Myers, *Conversion of Tropical Moist Forests* (Washington, DC: National Academy of Sciences, 1980); see also J. M. Melillo, et al., "A Comparison of Recent Estimates of Disturbance in Tropical Forests," *Environmental Conservation* 12:1 (1985), pp. 37–40.

2. I borrow the idea for this list from: Marius Jacobs, *The Tropical Rain Forest: A First Encounter* (New York: Springer-Verlag, 1988). This global view of the rainforests is a good primer on the basics of rainforest (or rain forest) ecology, and very much in the tradition of an earlier classic: P. W. Richards, *The Tropical Rain Forest: An Ecological Study* (Cambridge: At the University Press, 1952).

CHAPTER 1: TROPICAL FORESTS AND LIFE ON EARTH

1. Marius Jacobs, *The Tropical Rain Forest: A First Encounter* (New York: Springer-Verlag, 1988).

2. T. L. Erwin, "The Tropical Forest Canopy: The Heart of Biotic Diversity," in E. O. Wilson, ed., *Biodiversity* (Washington, DC: National Academy Press, 1988), pp. 123–29.

3. N. Applezweig, "Steroid Drugs from Botanical Sources: Future Prospects," in E. Campos-Lopez, ed., *Renewable Resources, A Systematic Approach* (New York: Academic Press, 1980), pp. 369–78.

4. B. Bolin et al., eds., *The Greenhouse Effect, Climatic Change, and Ecosystems* (New York: John Wiley and Sons, 1986).

5. James E. Lovelock, *The Ages of Gaia: A Biography of Our Living Earth* (Oxford: At the University Press, 1988).

6. Norman Myers, *The Primary Source: Tropical Forests and Our Future* (New York: W. W. Norton, 1984).

CHAPTER 2: TROPICAL BIOLOGY: A SCIENCE ON THE SIDELINES

1. The Automated Web for Canopy Exploration was made possible with funds from a Rolex Award for Enterprise, the Institute of Current World Affairs, and the Heinz Foundation.

2. Donald R. Perry, "The Canopy of the Tropical Rain Forest," *Scientific American* 251:5 (1984), pp. 138–47; Eric Eckholm, "Secrets of the Rain Forest," *The New York Times Sunday Magazine* (January 17, 1988), pp. 21–28.

3. P. W. Richards, *The Tropical Rain Forest: An Ecological Study* (Cambridge: At the University Press, 1952).

4. Nalini M. Nadkarni, "Canopy Roots: Convergent Evolution in Rain Forest Nutrient Cycles," *Science* 214 (1981), pp. 1023–24.

5. Donald R. Perry, *Life Above the Jungle Floor* (New York: Simon & Schuster, 1986).

6. Terry Erwin, "*Agra*, Arboreal Beetles of Neotropical Forests: *Agra Platyscolis* Group Systematics (Carabidae)," *Systematic Entomology* 7:2 (1982), pp. 185–210.

7. Robert May, "How Many Species Are There on Earth?" *Science* 241 (1988), pp. 1441–49.

8. Donald R. Perry, *Primate Temple: An Arboreal Theory of Human Evolution* (Boston: Little, Brown & Co., 1990).

9. Donald R. Perry, "The Feet of Birds," Report to the Institute of Current World Affairs, DRP3 (1986).

CHAPTER 3: FIVE HUNDRED YEARS OF
TROPICAL FOREST EXPLOITATION

1. This tale will be told at greater length and with full documentation in the author's forthcoming book, *The American Role in the Environmental History of the Third World*.

2. David Watts, *The West Indies: Patterns of Development, Culture and Environmental Change Since 1492* (Cambridge: At the University Press, 1987), chaps 1–5.

3. Narda Dobson, *A History of Belize* (Trinidad and Jamaica: Longman Caribbean, 1973), p. 55.

4. See several chapters in Richard P. Tucker and J. F. Richards, eds., *Global Deforestation and the Nineteenth-Century World Economy* (Durham, NC: Duke University Press, 1983).

5. Warren Dean, "Deforestation in Southeastern Brazil," in Tucker and Richards, op. cit.

6. Frederick Upham Adams, *Conquest of the Tropics* (Garden City, NY, 1914), p. 252.

7. Roger Burbach and Patricia Flynn, *Agribusiness in the Americas* (New York: Monthly Review Press, 1980). For an important recent study of the environmental implications of multinational corporations, see Charles Pearson, *Down to Business: Multinational Corporations, the Environment, and Development* (Washington, DC: World Resources Institute, 1985).

8. For the little-known story of Japanese forestry, see Conrad Totman, *The Origins of Japan's Modern Forests* (Honolulu: University of Hawaii Press, 1985).

9. Gerardo Budowski, "The Opening of New Areas and Landscape Planning in Tropical Countries," Address at the XII Congress of the International Federation of Landscape Architects (Sept. 8, 1970).

10. Jan Laarman, "Export of Tropical Hardwoods in the Twentieth Century," in Richard P. Tucker and J. F. Richards, eds., *Global Deforestation in the Twentieth Century* (Durham, NC: Duke University Press, 1988).

11. Evelyne Hong, *Natives of Sarawak: Survival in Borneo's Vanishing Forests* (Penang: Institut Masyarakat Malaysia, 1987).

12. The most insightful survey of the Chipko movement is Vandana Shiva and J. Bandyopadhyay, "The Evolution, Structure and Impact of the Chipko Movement," *Mountain Research and Development* 6 (May 1986), p. 2.

CHAPTER 4: RAINFORESTED REGIONS OF LATIN AMERICA

1. A. Gentry, "Tree Species Richness of Upper Amazonian Forests," *Proc. Natl. Acad. U.S.A.* 85 (1988), pp. 156–59.

2. Scott A. Mori, B. M. Boom, and G. T. Prance, "Distribution Patterns and Conservation of Eastern Brazilian Coastal Forest Tree Species," *Brittania* 33 (1981), pp. 233–45.

3. G. T. Prance, ed., *Biological Diversification in the Tropics* (New York: Columbia University Press, 1982), p. 714; T. C. Whitmore and G. T. Prance, eds., *Biogeography and Quarternary History in Tropical America. Oxford Monographs on Biogeography* 3 (Oxford: Clarendon Press, 1987); J. Haffer, "Speciation in Amazonian Forest Birds," *Science* 165 (1969), pp. 131–37; K. S. Brown, Jr., "Geographical Patterns of Evolution in Neotropical Lepidoptera. Systematics and Derivation of Known and New Heliconiini (Nymphalidae: Nymphalinae)," *Jour. Ent. B* 44 (1976), pp. 201–42; C. Schubart, "Climatic Changes During the Last Glacial Maximum in Northern South America and the Caribbean: A Review," *Interciencia* 13 (1988), pp. 128–37.

4. William Denevan, ed., *The Native Population of the Americas in 1492* (Madison: University of Wisconsin Press, 1976).

5. W. Balée, "Análise Preliminar de Inventário Florestal e a Etnobotânico Ka'apor (Maranhão)," *Bol. Mus. Paraense Emílio Goeldi* 2:2 (1986), pp. 141–67, and "A Etnobotânica Quantitativa dos Indios Tembe (Rio Gurupi, Pará)," *Bol. Mus. Par. Emílio Goeldi, Sér. Bot.* 3:1 (1987), pp. 29–50; B. M. Boom, "Useful Plants of the Panare Indians of the Venezuelan Guayana," *Adv. Econ. Bot.* 8 (in press), and "Ethnobotany of the Chácobo Indians, Beni, Bolivia," *Advances in Economic Botany* 5 (New York Botanical Garden, 1987); and G. T. Prance et al., "Quantitative Ethnobotany and the Case for Conservation in Amazonia," *Conservation Biology* 1 (1987), pp. 296–310.

6. J. O. Browder, "The Social Costs of Rain Forest Destruction: A Critique and Economic Analysis of the 'Hamburger Debate,'" *Interciencia* 13 (1988), pp. 115–20; S. B. Hecht, "Environment, Development and Politics: Capital Accumulation and the Livestock Sector in Eastern Amazônia," *World Development* 13 (1985), pp. 663–84; D. R. Shane, *Hoofprints on the Forest: Cattle Ranching and the Destruction of Latin America's Tropical Forests* (Philadelphia: Institute for the Study of Human Values, 1986).

7. P. M. Fearnside, "Jari at Age 19: Lessons for Brazil's Silviculture Plans at Carajás," *Interciencia* 13 (1988), pp. 12–24.

8. J. P. Malingreau and C. J. Tucker, "Large-Scale Deforestation in the Southeastern Amazon Basin of Brasil," *Ambio* 17 (1988), pp. 49–55.

CHAPTER 5: ASIA'S FORESTS, ASIA'S CULTURES

1. R. N. Tagore, *Tapovan* (Hindi) (Tikamgarh, India: Gandhi Bhavan).

2. R. S. Troup, *Silvicultural Systems 1928* (Oxford: At the University Press, 1928).

3. J. A. Bethel, "Sometimes the Word is 'Weed,'" *Forest Management* (June 1984), pp. 17–22.

4. W. Schlich, *Schlich's Manual of Forestry* (London: Bradbury, Agnew and Co., 1910), p. 1.

5. Heri Achmadi, "Raging Fires Wiping Out Tropical Forest," *Business Times*, Malaysia (Nov. 6, 1987); "Wound in the World," *Asia Week* (July 13, 1984); and SKEPHI (The NGO Network of Indonesia), *Berita Hutan* (Sept.–Oct. 1987).

6. J. P. Lanly, *Tropical Forest Resources* (Rome: FAO, 1982), p. 60.

7. A. Alcala, quoted in Catherine Caufield, *In the Rainforest* (London: Picador, 1986), p. 162.

8. UNESCO, *Tropical Forest Ecosystems* (Paris: UNESCO, 1978), p. 487.

9. Ibid., p. 459.

10. FAO, *Forest Resources of Tropical Asia* (Rome: FAO, 1981), p. 191.

11. T. Sriburi, "Forest Resource Crisis in Thailand," *Forest Resource Crisis in the Third World* (Penang: Sahabat Alam Malaysia [SAM], 1987).

12. K. K. Peng, "A Third World Perspective of the Forest Resource Crisis," *Forest Resource Crisis in the Third World* (Penang: SAM, 1987).

13. Vandana Shiva and Jayanto Bandyopadhyay, *Ecological Audit of Eucalyptus Cultivation* (Dehra Dun: Research Foundation for Science and Ecology, 1987).

14. "Eucalyptus Planting Sparks Fiery Protest," *The Nation*, Thailand (June 14, 1988).

15. H. Ngau et al., "Malaysian Timber Exploitation for Whom," *Forest Resources Crisis in the Third World* (Penang: SAM, 1987), p. 42.

16. Vandana Shiva and J. Bandyopadhyay, "The Evolution, Structure, and Impact of the Chipko Movement," *Mountain Research & Development* 6:2 (1986), pp. 133–42.

CHAPTER 6: NO CONDITION PERMANENT:
THE RAINFORESTS OF AFRICA

1. World Resources Institute and International Institute for Environment and Development, *World Resources 1987* (New York: Basic Books, 1987), p. 272.

2. Catherine Caufield, *In the Rainforest* (New York: Alfred A. Knopf, 1985), p. 82.

3. World Resources Institute, op. cit. p. 284.

4. Norman Myers, *The Primary Source: Tropical Forests and Our Future* (New York: W. W. Norton, 1984), pp. 46 & 55.

5. Jean-Paul Lanly and UNEP, *Tropical Forest Resources*, FAO Forestry Paper No. 30 (Rome: FAO, 1982), p. 82.

6. Population Reference Bureau, *1987 World Population Data Sheet* (Washington, DC: Population Reference Bureau, 1987).

7. Paul Harrison, *The Greening of Africa* (New York: Viking/Penguin, 1987), pp. 60–61, 331–32.

8. FAO Forestry Dept., "Changes in Shifting Cultivation in Africa," *Unasylva* 37:150 (1984/5), pp. 40–50.

9. Francois Nectoux and Nigel Dudley, *A Hard Wood Story: Europe's Involvement in the Tropical Timber Trade* (United Kingdom/London: Gwayne/Friends of the Earth, 1987), p. 5.

10. World Resources Institute, op. cit., p. 284.

11. Nectoux and Dudley, op. cit., p. 83.

12. Ibid., pp. 11–16.

13. Ibid., p. 47.

14. Franz Schmithusen, *Forest Legislation in Selected African Countries*, FAO Forestry Paper No. 65 (Rome: FAO, 1986), pp. 1–2.

15. World Resources Institute, op. cit.

16. Jason Clay, "Parks and People," *Cultural Survival Quarterly* 9:1 (Feb. 1985), pp. 2–5.

CHAPTER 7: EXTINCTION: LIFE IN PERIL

1. Paul R. Ehrlich and Anne H. Ehrlich, *Extinction: the Causes and Consequences of the Disappearance of Species (New York: Random House, 1981); Lester R. Brown et al., State of the World 1988* (New York: W. W. Norton, 1988).

2. Council on Environmental Quality and U.S. State Dept., *The Global 2000 Report to the President* (Washington, DC: U.S. Government Printing Office, 1980); World Resources Institute and International Institute for Environment and Development, *World Resources, 1987* (New York: Basic Books, 1987).

3. Ehrlich and Ehrlich, op. cit.

4.. P. M. Vitousek, P. R. Ehrlich, A. H. Ehrlich, and P. A. Matson, "Human Appropriation of the Products of Photosynthesis," *Bioscience* 36:6 (1986), pp. 368–73.

5. David Ehrenfeld, *The Arrogance of Humanism* (New York: Oxford University Press, 1987).

6. Brown et al., op. cit.

CHAPTER 8: INDIGENOUS PEOPLES:
THE MINER'S CANARY FOR THE TWENTIETH CENTURY

1. For a detailed overview of the situation of indigenous peoples, see Julian Burger, *Report from the Frontier: The State of the World's Indigenous Peoples* (London: Cultural Survival/Zed Press, 1987). For regular, in-depth reporting on indigenous peoples, see *Cultural Survival Quarterly* and the International Work Group for Indigenous Affairs (IWGIA) *Newsletter*. For a catalog listing of titles published by groups working with indigenous peoples, write Cultural Survival, 11 Divinity Avenue, Cambridge, MA 02138.

2. See "Deforestation: The Human Costs," *Cultural Survival Quarterly* 6:2 (1982).

3. See "Militarization and Indigenous Peoples: Part I—The Americas and the Pacific," and "Part III—Africa, Asia and the Middle East," *Cultural Survival Quarterly* 11:3, 4 (1987).

4. See Anthropology Resource Center et al., *Native Resource Control and the Multinational Corporate Challenge: Aboriginal Rights in the International Perspective* (Boston: ARC, 1982).

5. See William M. Denevan, ed., *The Native Population in the Americas in 1492* (Madison: University of Wisconsin Press, 1976).

6. See "Poisons and Peripheral People: Hazardous Substances in the Third World," a 1981–82, three-part series published in the *Cultural Survival Newsletter* on the impact of the export of pesticides, medicinal drugs, and industrial and mining hazards on indigenous peoples in the Third World.

7. See The Institute of Social Analysis (INSAN), *Logging Against the Natives of Sarawak* (Selangor, Malaysia: INSAN, 1989); Evelyne Hong, *Natives of Sarawak: Survival in Borneo's Vanishing Forests* (Pulau Pinang, Malaysia: Institute Masyarakat, 1987).

8. See note 3 and "Relocation and Resettlement—Part I and II," *Cultural Survival Quarterly* 12:3, 4 (1988).

9. See Jason W. Clay and Bonnie Holocomb, *Politics and the Ethiopian Famine 1984–1985* (Cambridge, MA: Cultural Survival, 1986); Jason W. Clay, Sandra Steingraber and Peter Niggli, *The Spoils of Famine: Ethiopian Famine Policy and Peasant Agriculture* (Cambridge: Cultural Survival, 1988).

10. See "Brazil," *Cultural Survival Quarterly* 13:1 (1989), a discussion of the consequences of Brazilian policies on the country's Indians and rainforests.

11. See, for example, Jason W. Clay, *Indigenous Peoples and Tropical Forests: Models of Land Use and Management from Latin America* (Cambridge: Cultural Survival, 1988).

12. Each of the examples mentioned below that describe the attempts of an indigenous group to protect their way of life and their environment is discussed in more detail in *Cultural Survival Quarterly*.

CHAPTER 9: MULTILATERAL DEVELOPMENT BANKS
AND TROPICAL DEFORESTATION

1. M. Nelson, *The Development of Tropical Lands: Policy Issues in Latin America* (Washington, DC: Johns Hopkins University Press, 1973).

2. Susanna Hecht et al., "The Economics of Cattle Ranching in Eastern Amazonia," Graduate School of Planning, University of California at Los Angeles (1988), unpublished paper.

3. See World Bank, *Indonesia: The Transmigration Program in Perspective* (Washington, DC: World Bank, 1988).

4. See, for example, U.S. Congress, "Environmental Impact of Multi-

lateral Development Bank Projects," Hearings before the Subcommittee on Banking, Finance and Urban Affairs, U.S. House of Representatives, June 28 and 29, 1983. See also, for example, U.S. Congress, "International Concerns for Environmental Implications of Multilateral Development Bank Projects," Hearing before a subcommittee of the Committee on Appropriations, U.S. Senate, May 1, 1986. Washington, DC.

5. U.S. Congress, Foreign Appropriations Act for Fiscal Year 1986, Section 540, enacted in Continuing Appropriations Act for 1986, House Joint Resolution 465, approved December 19, 1985. See also, U.S. Congress, Foreign Appropriations Act for Fiscal Year 1987, Section 539, enacted in Continuing Appropriations Act for 1987, House Joint Resolution 738, Public Law 99-591, approved October 30, 1986. Washington, DC.

6. One recent study interpreting remote sensing data estimates that deforestation is proceeding in the Brazilian Amazon on a scale much greater than previously thought. The study, conducted by the Brazilian space agency and forestry ministry, concluded that a conservative estimate of the area of annual tropical forest burning in the Brazilian Amazon region was 200,000 square kilometers, of which 80,000 square kilometers came from newly or recently converted pristine forest. A. Setzer, "Relatorio de Actividades do Projeto IBDF-INPE 'WEQE'—Ano 1987" (Brasilia: Instituto de Pesquisas Espaciales, 1988).

7. H. Geller, End-Use Conservation: Options for Developing Countries, World Bank Energy Department Paper no. 32 (Washington, DC: World Bank, 1986).

8. For a description of the genesis of the extractive reserves concept, see S. Schwartzman, "Extractive Reserves: the Rubber Tappers' Strategy for Sustainable Use of the Amazon Rain Forest," in J. Browder, ed., Fragile Lands of Latin America (Boulder: Westview Press, 1989).

CHAPTER 10: TAKING POPULATION SERIOUSLY:

POWER AND FERTILITY

1. This chapter is excerpted from "The Missing Piece in the Population Puzzle: Power and Fertility," Food First Development Report #4 (Summer 1988). Available from The Institute for Food and Development Policy, 145 Ninth St., San Francisco, CA 94103.

2. Frances Moore Lappé and Joseph Collins with Cary Fowler, Food First: Beyond the Myth of Scarcity (New York: Ballantine, 1977); Frances Moore Lappé and Joseph Collins, World Hunger: Twelve Myths (New York and San Francisco: Grove Press/Food First Books, 1986).

3. Per capita cropland data from Francis Urban and Thomas Vollrath,

"Patterns and Trends in World Agricultural Land Use," *Foreign Agricultural Economic Report, no. 198* (Washington, DC: U.S. Dept. of Agriculture, Economic Research Service, 1984), table 2; Life expectancy from World Bank, *World Development Report 1985*, (New York: Oxford University Press, 1985), table 1, p. 174.

4. At least half of that lies completely idle. See "The IMF and the Impoverishment of Brazil," *Instituto Brasileiro de Analises Socias e Economicas (IBASE)* (Rio de Janeiro, September 8, 1985), p. 18. See also, Mac Margolis, "Land Disputes Trigger Wave of Violence in Brazil," *Washington Post* (August 29, 1985).

5. For more on the forces behind rainforest destruction in Indonesia, see K. Kartawinata and A. P. Vayda, "Forest Conversion in East Kalimantan, Indonesia: The Activities and Impact of Timber Companies, Shifting Cultivators, Migrant Pepper-Farmers and Others," in F. DiCastri et al., eds., *Ecology in Practice* (Paris: UNESCO).

6. Val Plumwood and Richard Routley, "World Rainforest Destruction—The Social Factors," *The Ecologist* 12:1 (1982), p. 14.

7. Perdita Huston, *Message from the Village* (New York: The Epoch B Foundation, 1978), p. 119, cited in Hartmann, *Reproductive Rights and Wrongs*, p. 48.

8. Susan George, *Fate Worse than Debt* (New York: Grove Press/Food First Books, 1988).

9. World Bank, *World Development Report 1987*, table 27. We've included Cuba in this list of 74 low and lower-middle income countries because it was so classified for the first period of our time series. Only in recent years has the World Bank reclassified Cuba as a "nonreporting nonmember economy." Countries of a million or fewer in population are excluded from the bank's statistics.

10. According to the Indian Census, the population growth rate of Kerala averaged 1.8 percent annually between 1971 and 1981 (*Census of India*, Kerala State, Part 2A, Statements 3 and 8, pp. 28 and 32). Interview with Dr. K. C. Zachariah at the World Bank, Population and Human Resources Division, April 1986.

11. Robert J. Lapham and W. Parker Mauldin, "Contraceptive Prevalence: The Influence of Organized Family Planning Programs," *Studies in Family Planning* 16 (May–June 1985), pp. 177–237.

12. A. V. Jose, "Poverty and Inequality: The Case of Kerala," in Azizur Rahman Khan and Eddy Lee, eds., *Poverty in Rural Asia* (Bangkok: International Labour Organization, Asian Employment Programme, 1983), p. 108.

13. *World Development Forum* 6 (Feb. 29, 1988), p. 1, quoting the New Delhi Family Planning Foundation. The infant mortality rate in India is 100; in Kerala it is 30.

14. This may well explain the rise in female infanticide in China since the 1979 change in policy. See "The Threat of Population Growth," *World Press Review* (Aug. 1987), p. 59.

15. Ratcliffe, "China's Population Policies." See also news release from the Population Reference Bureau (Apr. 28, 1988).

16. The fertility rise may also be a consequence of the Chinese government's 1980 decision to relax its stringent policy governing age at marriage, and its recent relaxation in enforcement of the one-child policy.

17. See, for instance, Lappé and Collins, *Food First* and *World Hunger: Twelve Myths.*

18. Frances Moore Lappé, Rachel Schurman, and Kevin Danaher, *Betraying the National Interest* (New York and San Francisco: Grove Press/ Food First Books, 1988).

CHAPTER 11: CENTRAL AMERICA:
POLITICAL ECOLOGY AND U.S. FOREIGN POLICY

1. For the best statistical overview of environmental conditions in Central America, see H. Jeffrey Leonard, *Natural Resources and Economic Development in Central America* (Washington, DC: International Institute for Environment and Development, 1987).

2. Cahn, Robert, ed., *An Environmental Agenda for the Future, by Leaders of America's Foremost Environmental Organizations* (Washington, DC: Agenda Press, 1985).

3. Kevin Danaher et al., *Help or Hindrance? United States Economic Aid in Central America* (San Francisco: Institute for Food and Development Policy, 1987), p. 15.

4. Walter LaFeber, *Inevitable Revolutions: The United States in Central America* (New York: W.W. Norton and Company, 1984). Also Walter LaFeber, "The Alliances in Retrospect," in Andrew Maguire and Janet Welsh Brown, eds., *Bordering on Trouble: Resources and Politics in Latin America* (World Resources Institute, 1986).

5. Leonard, op. cit., p. 99. Also Robert Williams, *Export Agriculture and the Crisis in Central America* (Durham, NC: University of North Carolina Press, 1986), p. 113.

6. Williams, op. cit., pp. 129–51.

7. For a clear articulation of this ideology and policy, see Henry Kissinger et al., *Report of the National Bipartisan Commission on Central America*

(Washington, DC: U.S. Government Printing Office, 1984). For an analysis, see *Changing Course: Blueprint for Peace in Central America and the Caribbean* (Washington, DC: Institute for Policy Studies, 1984).

8. Lawrence Mosher, "At Sea in the Caribbean," in Maguire and Brown, op. cit.

9. Most information in this chapter on El Salvador comes from Daniel Faber and Bill Hall, *El Salvador: Ecology of Conflict*, Green Paper Number Four (San Francisco; Environmental Project on Central America [EPOCA], 1989). Also see Jenny Pearce, *Promised Land: Peasant Rebellion in Chalatenango El Salvador* (London: Latin America Bureau, 1986).

10. Arms Control and Foreign Policy Caucus of the U.S. Congress, "Bankrolling Failure: U.S. Policy in El Salvador and the Urgent Need for Reform (Washington, DC: U.S. Congress, November 1987), p. 24; and "Environment and Natural Resources: A Strategy for Central America" (U.S. Agency for International Development, March 1989).

11. Robert A. Rice and Joshua Karliner, *Militarization: The Environmental Impact*, EPOCA Green Paper Number Three (San Francisco: EPOCA, 1986). See also *Environment Under Fire: Ecology and Politics in Central America*, a video documentary by EPOCA and Moving Images (San Francisco, 1988).

12. Gustavo Adolfo Ruiz, *The Environmental Impacts of the Contra War*, a paper presented at the First Central American Environmental Action Conference (Managua, 1987).

13. World Wildlife Fund country report: *Nicaragua* (Washington, DC: WWF, 1987).

14. Peter Rosset and John Vandermeer, eds., *Nicaragua: Unfinished Revolution* (New York: Grove Press, 1986).

15. John B. Oakes, "Greening Central America," *New York Times* (Apr. 22, 1988).

CHAPTER 12: THE CONSUMER CONNECTION:
PSYCHOLOGY AND POLITICS

1. Jennifer Stoffel, "What's New In Shopping Malls?," *New York Times* (Aug. 7, 1988), p. F11.

2. Ellen Graham, "The Pleasure Dome," *Wall Street Journal* (May 13, 1988), pp. 5R–6R.

3. Ibid.

4. Stoffel, op. cit.

5. "Planet of the Year: Endangered Earth," *Time* (Jan. 2, 1989), p. 65.

6. Matthew L. Wald, "Fighting the Greenhouse Effect," *New York Times* (Aug. 28, 1988), sec. 3, p. 8.

7. Anne H. and Paul R. Ehrlich, "Population, Plenty, and Poverty," *National Geographic* 174: 6 (Dec. 1988), p. 938.

8. Priscilla Turner, "Can We Prevent Suicide by Garbage?," *LIFE* 11:14 (Dec. 1988), pp. 158–60.

9. John Langone, "A Stinking Mess," *Time* (Jan. 2, 1989), p. 47.

10. Rainforest Action Network, "Tropical Timber Fact Sheet" (Apr. 13, 1988).

11. U.S. Bureau of the Census, *Statistical Abstract of the United States 1988*, 108th edition (Washington, DC: U.S. Department of Commerce, 1987), p. 807.

12. John Robbins, *Diet for a New America* (Walpole, NH: Stillpoint Publishing, 1987), p. 135.

13. Ibid., p. 126.

14. Ibid., pp. 227–40.

15. U.S. Bureau of the Census, op. cit., p. 622.

16. H. Jeffrey Leonard, *Natural Resources and Economic Development in Central America* (Washington, DC: International Institute for Environment and Development, 1987), pp. 87–89.

17. Robbins, pp. 350–63.

18. Luigi Zoja, *Drugs, Addiction, and Initiation* (Boston: Sigo Press, 1989).

19. Stephan Bodian, "Addiction to Perfection: An Interview with Marion Woodman," *Yoga Journal* no. 83 (Nov.–Dec. 1988), pp. 52–54.

20. Marion Woodman, *The Pregnant Virgin: A Process of Psychological Transformation* (Toronto: Inner City Books, 1985), p. 16.

21. Stanislav Grof, "Spirituality, Alcoholism, and Drug Abuse: Transpersonal Aspects of Addiction," *ReVision* 10:2 (Fall, 1987), p. 3. See also Anne Wilson Schaef, *When Society Becomes an Addict* (New York: Harper & Row, 1987).

22. For information on products and manufacturers, write to the Council on Economic Priorities, 30 Irving Place, New York, NY 10003. They publish *Shopping for a Better World: A Quick and Easy Guide to Socially Responsible Supermarket Shopping, Rating America's Corporate Conscience*, and a full list showing which company makes each product.

23. See Bill Devall and George Sessions, *Deep Ecology: Living as if Nature Mattered* (Salt Lake City: Gibbs M. Smith, 1985); and Bill Devall, *Simple in Means, Rich in Ends: Practicing Deep Ecology* (Salt Lake City: Gibbs-Smith, 1988).

CHAPTER 13: THE DEVELOPMENT OF

TROPICAL RAINFOREST ECONOMICS

1. See Stephen G. Bunker, *Underdeveloping the Amazon* (Urbana: University of Illinois Press, 1985); Richard B. Norgaard, "Socioecosystem and Ecosystem Coevolution in the Amazon," *Journal of Environmental Economics and Management* 8 (1981), pp. 238–54; and Michael Redclift, *Sustainable Development: Exploring the Contradictions* (London: Methuen, 1987).

2. New and traditional conceptions of the nature of Western science are described by Marjorie Grene, "Perception, Interpretation, and the Sciences: Towards a New Philosophy of Science," in David J. Depew and Bruce H. Weber, eds., *Evolution at a Crossroads: The New Biology and the New Philosophy of Science.* (Cambridge: M.I.T. Press, 1985).

3. Herman E. Daly, "The Economic Thought of Frederick Soddy," *History of Political Economy* 12:4 (1980), pp. 469–88.

4. Susanna Hecht, Richard B. Norgaard, and Giorgio Possio, "The Political Economy of Cattle Ranching in the Amazon," *Interciencia* (Sept.–Oct. 1988).

5. For example, see Donald N. McCloskey, *The Rhetoric of Economics* (Madison: University of Wisconsin Press, 1985); and Ezra J. Mishan, *Economic Myths and the Mythology of Economics* (Atlantic Heights, NJ: Humanities Press International, 1986).

CHAPTER 14: WHY SUPERNATURAL EELS MATTER

1. Ernest C. Migliazza, "Yanomama Grammar and Intelligibility" (Ph.D. dissertation, University of Indiana, 1972).

2. William J. Smole, *The Yanoama Indians: A Cultural Geography* (Austin: University of Texas Press, 1976); and Raymond Hames, "Game Depletion and Hunting Zone Rotation among the Ye'kwana and Yanomamo of Amazonas, Venezuela," in *Working Papers on South American Indians*, vol. 2 (Bennington: Bennington College, 1980).

3. Kenneth I. Taylor, "Sanuma Fauna: Prohibitions and Classifications," *Monograph No. 18* (Caracas: Fundacion La Salle, 1974), p. 93.

4. Emilio Fuentes, "Los Yanomami y las Plantas Silvestres," *Antropolica* 54 (Caracas: Fundacion La Salle, 1980), pp. 3–138; Jaques Lizot, "Les Yanomami Centraux," Cahiers de L'Homme, n.s. XXII (Paris: Ecole des Hautes Etudes en Sciences Sociales, 1984).

5. Darrell A. Posey, "Indigenous Knowledge and Development: An Ideo-

logical Bridge to the Future," *Ciencia e Cultura* 35:7 (1983), pp. 874–94; Darrell A. Posey, "Indigenous Management of Tropical Forest Ecosystems: The Case of the Kayapo Indians of the Brazilian Amazon," *Agroforestry Systems* 3 (1985), pp. 139–58; Darrell A. Posey et al., "Ethnoecology as Applied Anthropology in Amazonian Development," *Human Organization* 43:2 (1984), pp. 95–107.

6. Posey, 1985, op. cit.

7. Kenneth I. Taylor, "Knowledge and Praxis in Sanuma Food Prohibitions," in Kenneth M. Kensinger and Waud H. Kracke, eds., *Food Taboos in Lowland South America. Working Papers on South American Indians,* vol. 3 (Bennington: Bennington College, 1981), pp. 25–54. Cf. Daniel R. Gross, "Protein Capture and Cultural Development in the Amazon Basin," *American Anthropologist* 77:3 (1975), pp. 526–49.

8. Posey, 1985, op. cit. pp. 180–81.

CHAPTER 15: AGROECOLOGY: RESHAPING AGRICULTURAL DEVELOPMENT

1. Stephen R. Gliessman, "The Ecological Element in Farm Management," *Proceedings of a Conference on Sustainability of California Agriculture* (Davis: University of California, 1986).

2. P. A. Allen and D. Van Dusen, eds., *Global Perspectives in Agroecology and Sustainable Agriculture* (Santa Cruz: University of California, 1988). See also Wes Jackson et al., eds, *Meeting the Expectations of the Land* (Berkeley: North Point Press, 1984).

3. G. Conway, "Agroecosystem Analysis," *Agricultural Administration* 20 (1985), pp. 31–55.

4. R. D. Hart, "Agroecosystem Determinants," in R. Lowrance et al., eds., *Agricultural Ecosystems* (New York: Wiley, 1984), pp. 105–20.

5. Miguel A. Altieri, *Agroecology; The Scientific Basis of Alternative Agriculture* (Boulder: Westview Press, 1987); see also G. C. Wilken, *Good Farmers: Traditional Agricultural Resource Management in Mexico and Central America* (Berkeley: University of California Press, 1988).

6. D. Barkin, *Desarrollo Regional y Reorganizacion Campesina: La Chontalpa como Reflejo del Problema Agopecuario Mexicano* (Mexico City: Editorial Nueva Imagen, 1978).

7. J. P. Darch, *Drained Field Agriculture in Central and South America* (London: BAR International Series 189, 1983); see also A. Gomez-Pompa and J. J. Jimenez-Osornio, "Some Reflections on Intensive Traditional Agriculture," paper presented at the meetings of the Society of Economic Anthropology, Riverside, University of California, April 3–4, 1987.

8. A. Gomez-Pompa, "On Maya Silviculture," *Mexican Studies* 3 (1987), pp. 1–17.

9. A. Orozco-Segovia and S. R. Gliessman, "The Marceno in Flood-Prone Regions of Tabasco, Mexico," in J. Gonzalez et al., eds., *Pasado y Presente en los Sistemas Agricolas en Mexico* (Mexico: SEP, 1988).

10. M. F. Amador and S. R. Gliessman, "Response of Three Species (Corn, Beans, and Squash) in Polyculture in the Chontalpa, Tabasco, Mexico," in S. R. Gliessman, ed., *Research Approaches in Agroecology* (New York: Ecological Studies Series, Springer, 1988).

11. Ibid.

12. Ibid.

13. S. R. Gliessman, "Allelopathic Interactions in Crop-Weed Mixtures: Applications for Weed Management," *Journal of Chemical Ecology* 9 (1983), pp. 991–99.

14. D. K. Letourneau, "Associational Resistance in Squash Monocultures and Polycultures in Tropical Mexico," *Environmental Entomology* 15 (1986), pp. 285–95.

15. A. Gonzales Jacome, "Home Gardens in Central Mexico," in I. S. Farrington, ed., *Prehistoric Intensive Agriculture in the Tropics* (Oxford: BAR International Series 232, 1985).

CHAPTER 16: PROTECTED AREAS IN TROPICAL RAINFORESTS:

FIVE LESSONS

1. Thomas E. Lovejoy, "The Science of Amazon Conservation," *The Environmentalist* 3:5 (1983), pp. 57–61; Norman Myers, *The Sinking Ark: A New Look at the Problem of Disappearing Species* (New York: Pergamon Press, 1979), p. 222.

2. Meyers, op. cit.

3. Edward C. Wolf, "Challenges and Priorities in Conserving Biological Diversity," *Interciencia* 10:5 (1985), pp. 236–42.

4. Marianne Schmink, "The Rationality of Tropical Forest Destruction," in Julio C. Figueroa et al., eds., *Management of the Forests of Tropical America: Prospects and Technologies* (Río Piedras, Puerto Rico: Institute of Tropical Forestry, U.S. Department of Agriculture Forest Service, 1987).

5. Jeffrey A. McNeely and Kenton R. Miller, eds., *National Parks, Conservation and Development: The Role of Protected Areas in Sustaining Society* (Washington, DC: Smithsonian Institution Press, 1984).

6. Ibid., p. 4.

7. Thomas Holzinger, "Preserving the Ecology in Tropical Areas," *R&D Mexico* 2:11 (Mexico: CONACYT, 1982), p. 29.

8. McNeely, op. cit., p. 183.

9. William P. Gregg, Jr., and Betsy Ann McGean, "Biosphere Reserves: Their History and Their Promise," *Orion Nature Quarterly* 4:3 (1985), pp. 41–51.

CHAPTER 17: ACTIVISM: YOU MAKE THE DIFFERENCE

1. Edward Abbey, *Hayduke Lives! A Sequel to the Monkey Wrench Gang* (New York: Little, Brown & Co., 1989).

THE AUTHORS

J. BANDYOPADHYAY *is a leading expert on natural resource management.* He has pioneered studies on the ecological impact of forestry projects and mining projects, and on the ecological roots of the intensification of drought and desertification. *His books include* India's Environment: Crisis and Responses *and* The Ecological Audit of Eucalyptus Cultivation. *Currently Dr. Bandyopadhyay is a senior faculty member in the Mountain Environment Division of the International Centre for Integrated Mountain Development in Kathmandu, Nepal.*

MORRIS BERMAN *is a free-lance writer and lecturer living in Seattle. He is the author of* The Reenchantment of the World *and* Coming to Our Senses. *Dr. Berman has taught at several universities in the United States and Canada and has lectured widely in Europe and North America on themes of personal and cultural change.*

JASON W. CLAY, *an anthropologist, is director of research at Cultural Survival, a nonprofit human rights organization that works with tribal people and ethnic minorities throughout the world. He is founder and editor of* Cultural Survival Quarterly *and the monograph series,* Cultural Survival Reports. *Dr. Clay has written three books, including* Indigenous Peoples and Tropical Forests: Models of Land Use and Management from Latin America, *and many articles on the urgent problems confronting indigenous peoples in the modern world.*

ANNE H. EHRLICH *is a senior research associate in the Department of Biological Sciences at Stanford University, where she con-*

ducts research on reproductive strategies of butterflies and resource partitioning among coral reef fishes. Dr. Ehrlich was a consultant to the Global 2000 Report to the President *and a commissioner for the* Greater War Risks Study (GLAWARS). *Since 1985, she has chaired the national Committee on Environmental Impacts of Warfare of the Sierra Club.*

PAUL R. EHRLICH *is Bing Professor of Population Studies at Stanford University. His research interests have included the population biology of butterflies, reef fishes, birds, mites, and some other organisms. He is author or co-author of over 20 books and hundreds of articles. Together, the Ehrlichs have conducted field studies in every continent (including Antarctica), and have been in tropical forests in a dozen countries around the world. They have co-authored over a half-dozen books, including* Extinction *and* EARTH.

JULIAN GERSTIN *is a writer/editor, musician, and paralegal who lives in Berkeley, California. His involvement in rainforest issues resulted from many years of performing the traditional musics of Ghana, Brazil, and Cuba. He has traveled in West Africa and Central America.*

STEPHEN GLIESSMAN *directs the Agroecology Program and teaches environmental studies at the University of California, Santa Cruz. He occupies the Heller Endowed Chair of Agroecology at UCSC and has been a Kellogg Fellow. Dr. Gliessman lived for nine years in Latin America, where he farmed coffee and vegetables, ran a nursery, and taught and conducted research in tropical agriculture. His most recent book is* Research Approaches in Agroecology.

ROBERT GRANTHAM *is a graduate in Environmental Biology from the University of Colorado and a founding member of the Boulder Rainforest Action Group. Born in Vancouver, British Columbia, he has traveled in Europe, lived in Asia, and spent time in the rainforests of Australia, Indonesia, Puerto Rico, Hawaii, and*

*coastal British Columbia. Mr. Grantham plans to return to B.C.
to promote environmental education and the grassroots movement to
protect the remaining forests of that province and the world.*

RANDALL HAYES *is an action-oriented conservationist and the
director of the Rainforest Action Network, or RAN. He coproduced
the award-winning film,* The Four Corners, a National Sacrifice
Area? *From working with Native Americans during the filming, Mr.
Hayes learned about the plight of native people in tropical rainforests.
Now he is a leader in the effort to halt the destruction of tropical
rainforests worldwide and in the fight for the rights of indigenous
rainforest-dwellers.*

SUZANNE HEAD *became an environmental activist after studying and teaching Buddhism and warriorship principles for 14 years.
She is a writer and editor with a focus on deep ecology issues and
the information officer at the Rainforest Action Network.*

ROBERT HEINZMAN *holds a masters degree in environmental
studies from the Yale School of Forestry and Environmental Studies.
He has conducted research in the Brazilian Amazon and in northern
Guatemala, and has participated in grassroots education efforts in
the United States on issues of tropical deforestation. Mr. Heinzman
is also co-director of the Kuja Sni Research Group, a nonprofit
environmental organization dedicated to holistic solutions for ecological problems.*

JOSHUA KARLINER *is cofounder of the San Francisco–based
Environmental Project on Central America (EPOCA), a project of
Earth Island Institute. EPOCA works for peace, justice, and the
environment in Central America. Mr. Karliner received his B.A. in
Latin American Studies at Santa Cruz and has surfed his way
throughout Latin America. He is currently researching the environmental situation in the Philippines.*

FRANCES MOORE LAPPÉ *is the author of* Diet for a Small Planet *and cofounder of Food First/Institute for Food and Development Policy in San Francisco. Her most recent co-authored works include* World Hunger: Twelve Myths *and* Betraying the National Interest. *Ballantine Books recently released her latest book,* Rediscovering America's Values.

JOHN P. MILTON *is a tropical ecologist, environmental consultant, and activist. After working with governments and international conservation organizations, he turned to grassroots organizing. His many publications include* Ecological Principles for Economic Development *and* The Careless Technology: Ecology and International Development. *Mr. Milton now conducts NatureQuest programs, which help people rediscover Nature's power to regenerate our commitment to the Earth.*

NORMAN MYERS *is an international consultant in environment and development, with a focus on resource relationships between the developed and developing worlds. Dr. Myers has worked as a consultant for the Rockefeller Brothers Fund, U.S. National Academy of Sciences, the World Bank, the Smithsonian Institution, and many other organizations. His works include* The Sinking Ark, The Primary Source, *and* The Gaia Atlas of Planet Management.

JAMES D. NATIONS *is an ecological anthropologist who lived with the Lacandon Maya in once-forested Chiapas, Mexico while doing research for his doctoral dissertation. He lives with his family in Guatemala as a Fulbright Scholar, assisting in the development and implementation of park planning. As director of the Center for Human Ecology based in Austin, Texas, Dr. Nations has conducted research throughout Latin America. He is the author of a high school text on tropical forests and coeditor of the book* Social Dynamics of Deforestation in Latin America and Its Solutions.